JOHN KEATS:
THE LIVING YEAR

The Old Mill House, Bedhampton.

JOHN KEATS:

THE LIVING YEAR

21 September 1818 to 21 September 1819

by

ROBERT GITTINGS

BARNES & NOBLE, INC.

PUBLISHERS · BOOKSELLERS · SINCE 1873

First published 1954
Reprinted 1954, 1960, 1962, 1968

Published in the United States by
Barnes & Noble
New York 10003

Printed in Great Britain

To
H. G. C. M. and A. D. J.

Gaudes carminibus; carmina possumus
donare et pretium dicere muneri.

There is a great deal of reality about all that Keats writes: and there must be many allusions to particular Circumstances, in his poems: which would add to their beauty & Interest, if properly understood—To arrest some few of these circumstances, & bring them to view in connexion with the poetic notice of them, is one of the objects of this collection.

RICHARD WOODHOUSE, in his MS. Commonplace Book of Keats's poems.

CONTENTS

ILLUSTRATIONS

The pages from Keats's copy of the *Literary Pocket Book*
for 1819, and the page from Keats's copy of Burton's
The Anatomy of Melancholy are reproduced by kind permission of the Committee of the Hampstead Public
Libraries.

FOREWORD

ANY new book about Keats must require a foreword. The word "new" itself, applied to a subject which has attracted so much varied scholarship, must be explained. Yet the mass of work which already exists may itself supply a reason why a new book can be written. Every generation (including Keats's own) has provided its special picture of the poet. His chameleon personality has lived on after his death in the changing colours with which critics and biographers have painted him. We now see him in a kaleidoscope of past impressions, sometimes revealing but often blurring the vividness of his life and work.

A new story, such as this, has then a justification, but also carries a warning; it too may only reflect a personal taste and an opinion of the moment. No honest biographer can claim to have avoided this; but at least to insure against it, I have tried to see that not only the story told here but the evidence supporting it is genuine and new. For the framework one must always be indebted to the great biographies of the past, but for the crucial point in nearly every episode, I hope to show the evidence of a new or of an unobserved fact.

For this reason I have avoided a full biography from birth to death, and for another reason too. When all is said and done, the poems are the thing. Nearly all the greatest poetry of Keats was written in the 365 days of a single year. In this book, a prologue and an epilogue tell what happened before and after; the main chapters re-tell the story of that year. Each chapter has to do with the writing of 100 or more lines of Keats's poetry. For the general reader, exact references to these lines are given at the end of each chapter. Those who have already made Keats their study may turn, for confirmation of various points in the story, to the notes and appendices numbered in the text and printed at the end of the book.

ACKNOWLEDGMENTS

EVERY modern writer, as I have suggested, must record a debt to the great senior Keats editors of our time, and to the fruits of their exhaustive work. Three of their printed books are the basis of this, as they must be of all new studies of Keats. They are *The Letters of John Keats*, edited by Maurice Buxton Forman; *The Keats Circle. Letters and Papers, 1816–1878*, edited by Hyder Edward Rollins; and *Keats' Poetical Works*, edited by H. W. Garrod. This present volume's debt to the first two may be measured by the numerous references to them in its notes, and by the insignificant minority of occasions on which I have been unable to agree with them. With Dr. Garrod's exact scholarship in collating the texts of Keats's poems, I have not ventured to suggest any disagreement; I have also to thank him for his friendly and helpful comments on my dating of some poems.

For the inspiration of their books, and for the even greater inspiration of their remarks, I am greatly indebted to three other living writers. These are Miss Dorothy Hewlett, whose *A Life of John Keats* is likely to remain for a long time the most readable general work on the poet; Dr. J. R. MacGillivray, whose *John Keats: A Bibliography and Reference, 1816–1946*, not only sums up with impeccable scholarship all printed work on Keats, but adds to it his own most admirable and salutary foreword on the vicissitudes of the critical attitude; and lastly Mr. Edmund Blunden, whose books on this subject are like good conversation, and whose conversation is like a good book.

My other debts fall into two or three general categories. Of the official representatives and staffs of public bodies, I must specially thank J. H. Preston, Assistant Curator, Keats House, and the Committee of the Hampstead Public Libraries. Others who have assisted me in this field are the County Archivist, Middlesex County Record Office; W. H. Ives, Keeper of Military Records, Commonwealth Relations Office; E. A.

Willats, Reference Librarian, Central Public Library, Islington; the War Office Library; the Holborn Borough Council; H. K. G. Bearman, County Librarian, West Sussex; Miss A. L. Reeve, Assistant Archivist, West Sussex; the Librarian, the Guildhall Library; Dr. L. D. Ettlinger, Warburg Institute; A. Taylor Milne, Secretary and Librarian, the Institute of Historical Research; and Strathearn Gordon, Librarian of the House of Commons.

For help on specialised and local subjects I am most grateful to Colonel A. H. Burne, D.S.O., the historian of the Royal Artillery Mess; Major V. C. D. Hodson, for his similar work on military records of the East India Company; Captain and Mrs. B. R. Willett, whose detailed local research has identified beyond doubt the Old Mill House, Bedhampton, as the house where Keats wrote the major part of *The Eve of St. Agnes*, and where, incidentally, he spent his last night in England; Gerald Brodribb, for his work on Hastings and its literary associations, and for a photograph of *The New England Bank Inn*, Bo Peep; W. K. Lowther-Clarke, D.D., for his work on the history of Chichester Cathedral, and to the Dean and Chapter of the Cathedral for permission to reproduce a photograph; A. H. Peat, for his work on the heraldry of Sussex churches, and for access to family records; Wilson R. Harrison, M.Sc., Ph.D., for his expert advice on handwriting and his work on photographic prints of manuscripts.

Among those who have given me access to property and to documents, I owe very special thanks to the Right Honourable the Earl of Bessborough, P.C., G.C.M.G., whose kindness has enabled me to pay frequent and fruitful visits to the unique Chapel of Lewis Way at Stansted, details of which are reproduced in the illustration opposite page 87 of this book; to H. C. Brooke-Taylor, who has generously placed family letters at my disposal, and has allowed me to reproduce the correspondence with John Taylor printed in Appendix D; and to E. J. Barnes, the present owner of the house in which Keats stayed in Chichester.

Among those who have placed their knowledge and research at my disposal I particularly thank George Morey, Ph.D., Mrs. J. R. H. Moorman, and Miss Joanna Richardson. The book has received invaluable comments from Robert Butman,

Christopher Fry, and George Mallaby, C.M.G., and has benefited from the attentions of Miss Phyllis M. C. Drayson, Miss Joan P. Kettle and Miss Ena Sheen, while the index owes much to Miss Hana Bartošová. Finally, I must thank for their forbearance my colleagues of the School Broadcasting Department, B.B.C., and my wife who has lived with the progress of this book.

AUTHOR'S NOTE

THROUGH the kindness of Professor H. E. Rollins I have received, during the final proof stages of this book, a copy of his "Keats's Misdated Letters", *Harvard Library Bulletin*, Vol. VII, No. 2. This has been particularly helpful in confirming some of the redating of certain letters, at which I had already arrived, and more especially in assigning, for the first time, correct dates to some passages in Keats's long journal letters to his brother George, thus enabling me to make the narrative more accurate.

R. G.

PROLOGUE:

HYPERION TO *HYPERION*

I

ON Monday, 14th of September, 1818, James Augustus Hessey, of Taylor & Hessey, booksellers and publishers, held a party in the firm's headquarters, 93 Fleet Street.[1] It was a small gathering of relatives, connections of the business, and authors. The senior partner of the firm, John Taylor, a scholarly man who had identified the author of *The Letters of Junius*, was not present, but the firm's legal, literary, and financial adviser, Richard Woodhouse, was there. This slightly-built, red-haired lawyer of the Temple combined an acute brain with a generous and enthusiastic nature. For poetry in particular he had a passion which sometimes kept him, and others, up until the early hours of the morning, reading and reciting; his ambition was to recognize and assist contemporary genius in this kind. With him, and like him natives of Bath, were Hessey's brothers-in-law, Bob and Fred Falkner. The cheerful intimacy of this family and business circle was nearly marred by one of the authors present, John Percival, Fellow of Wadham, and a Nottinghamshire man like Taylor. He was unwell, probably in love, and certainly morose; but no gathering could long be dull when completed by the two major authors of the firm, William Hazlitt and John Keats.

Utterly unlike, except in their recognition of each other's genius, they had at this precise moment one thing in common. Both had been attacked, savagely and grossly, in the August number of *Blackwood's Edinburgh Magazine*. This periodical, which had just received the powerful backing of Byron's publisher, John Murray, had a line of personal invective quite its own. Hazlitt, whose complexion was certainly dark, but who kept in health by his own spectacular style of playing fives and racquets, was stigmatized as pimpled, and subjected to unsavoury remarks on his morals and habits. He was extremely angry, and had just decided to sue *Blackwood's*, which he did so successfully that his opponents not only settled out of court, but Murray, a respectable figure, hastily withdrew his capital from the magazine. Hazlitt was Taylor & Hessey's latest author. The firm had published his *Lectures on the English Poets* that summer, and Hessey was now negotiating the rights —always a ticklish matter with Hazlitt—for his *Lectures on the English Comic Writers*, which were to be delivered in November.

John Keats had a slightly longer connection with the firm, in spite of being at this time not yet twenty-three years old. On his 21st birthday, this orphan son of a groom and a livery-man's daughter had announced to his guardian, Richard Abbey, a City tea-broker, that he intended to make a pro-fession of poetry. As several hundred pounds of the money administered for him by Abbey had already been spent in qualifying Keats as a doctor, the business man was horrified. He had written off John, together with his younger brothers George and Tom, as thoroughly untrustworthy, and had concentrated the full weight of his guardianship on their schoolgirl sister Fanny, who now became virtually a prisoner in his home at Walthamstow. Keats's first book of poems had fulfilled his ex-guardian's prophecy and come to no good, in spite of the admiration and encouragement of Leigh Hunt and others, but it at least brought him to the notice of Taylor & Hessey, and of their adviser, Woodhouse.

In April, 1817, the firm had contracted for Keats's next book, a long poetic romance entitled *Endymion*, which they published exactly a year later. Keats had spent the year writing this poem while he roamed about, living on capital and publisher's advances, and staying in the Isle of Wight, Margate, Canterbury, Hastings, Oxford, and Box Hill. He and his brothers, also now striking out on their own, had taken up lodgings at No. 1 Well Walk, Hampstead, in cramped but comfortable little rooms kept by Bentley, the postman. Mrs. Bentley's kindness to her young lodgers was thought by them to outweigh the small space and the noise of the ginger-haired Bentley children, but in these confined quarters Tom, the youngest brother, fell ill. He spent the winter and spring, 1817–18, at Teignmouth in Devonshire, accompanied first by

George Keats and then by John. John was at Teignmouth when *Endymion* appeared, and there he wrote his first long poem for a new volume, *Isabella, or The Pot of Basil*. That spring, George Keats celebrated his coming-of-age as dramatically as John. He collected his capital from Abbey, and emigrated in June, intending to buy settlement land in Illinois from another Taylor & Hessey author, Morris Birkbeck. With him he took a sixteen-year-old bride, Georgiana Wylie. Keats left Tom at Hampstead in the care of Mrs. Bentley, saw George and Georgiana off at Liverpool, and proceeded himself on a walking-tour of the Lake District and the West of Scotland with a lively Scottish neighbour from Hampstead, Charles Brown.

He returned to Hampstead from this strenuous tour in the middle of August; he came back early for his own health, but he would have been obliged to return, anyhow, for his brother's. Tom's illness, consumption, had taken a sudden turn for the worse. This, and *Blackwood's* review of *Endymion*, had greeted his homecoming. Yet at Hessey's party, his first public appearance since his return, he was in good spirits. Tom seemed to have improved; at any rate, he was well enough for Keats to stay the night with Hessey, and not break up the party for the journey of three miles back through Camden Town to Hampstead. As for the review, Keats seemed not to care about it. A so-called criticism, in which his qualifications as a doctor were the subject of heavy-handed insult, was in a style beneath contempt. Yet he alarmed at least one of his companions, Woodhouse, who was eagerly looking forward to Keats's promised new epic, *Hyperion*. Far from announcing that he had started the new work, Keats launched into one of the hypothetical harangues of which he was so fond—what he and his friends called his "rhodomontades". There was now, so Woodhouse understood him to say, nothing original left to be written in poetry; all its riches and beauties had been sufficiently explored, so he himself would write no more. When the party broke up, Woodhouse left disquieted, and continued to ponder this unsettling statement during the leisure of a month's holiday at Bath. Hessey was more philosophic about his guest for the night, and took a hopeful and refreshingly objective view of Keats.

He is studying closely, recovering his Latin, going to learn
Greek, and seems altogether more rational than usual—
but he is such a man of fits and starts he is not much to be
depended on. Still he thinks of nothing but poetry as his
being's end and aim, and sometime or other he will, I
doubt not, do something valuable.

"Sometime or other"—a week after this meeting, on Monday,
September 21st, 1818, Keats plunged into the most amazingly
creative year that any English poet has achieved. Two great
unfinished poems on the same theme, *Hyperion* and *The Fall of
Hyperion*, mark the opening and the close of this period, to the
very same day of the year. In this exact year, Keats wrote,
with numerous other works, practically every poem that
places him among the major poets of the world. Hessey's
cautious prophecy dramatically came true; how and why it
did is the matter with which this present book deals.

II

All that has been written about Keats has so far thrown up
three main explanations for this remarkable year. None is
satisfactory, though each may share a part of the truth. It is
said that he wrote with the desperate energy of one already
diseased, already attacked by the consumption which carried
off his brother; that he met at this time a Hampstead neighbour,
Fanny Brawne, to whom he soon became engaged, and that
most of his work in this year is connected with his love for her;
thirdly, that he was working out in this year some coherent
scheme of poetry and philosophy, of which his works are the
signs and symbols.[2]

The first two of these reasons have been vastly exaggerated;
the third has been over-rationalized. Keats was in robust
health during most of the coming year; his occasional ill-
nesses have been shown, on medical evidence, to have little
connection with the form of disease which finally attacked
him.[3] The legend that he early became engaged to Fanny
Brawne—on Christmas Day, 1818, to be precise—is firmly
embedded in the Keats tradition, and has been repeated by
writer after writer; yet it is only guesswork. On the contrary,

all the evidence, including that of Fanny Brawne herself, points to their engagement being long delayed, and not taking place until well into 1819.[4] As for his having any consistent scheme of thought and philosophy, Hessey's note on him as "a man of fits and starts" is supported by other friends. Gifted as he was, Keats was only twenty-two, and his life was a series of rapidly-changing states of mind rather than any rational scheme; indeed, it is with surprise that Hessey notes how unusually rational he was on this one occasion.

Hessey, a close, cool-headed, yet not unsympathetic observer, gives most of the clues we should follow to reach, for perhaps the first time, some real idea of what went on in this year. His first sentence is a major key—"He is studying". Study, for Keats, meant reading for the purpose of helping his own poetry. He read with an intensity that can hardly be imagined. His Hampstead neighbour, C. W. Dilke, noticed with what intensity Keats followed any train of thought;[5] he went through every word of a book, annotating, underlining, and marking nearly every page from cover to cover, absorbing every phrase, cadence, and intonation of the author. What might be a pastime with other men was a passion with him, not a passive exercise but an active pursuit, not a skipper's treat but a systematic task. His life, his letters, his words, thoughts, and his poems themselves take on the character of whatever book he is studying.

A concrete instance will make this clear. During the coming year, Keats read continually in *The Anatomy of Melancholy*, that great seventeenth-century compendium by Robert Burton; his close attention to Burton can be followed month by month, sometimes even day by day, in the words of his own poems and letters. Keats wrote in February, March, and April, 1819, a long journal-letter to his brother George in America,[6] from which these are three extracts, one from each month, dated as they were written. They deal with three characteristic sides of Keats—pleasure, philosophy, and poetry.

1. (*Friday, February* 19*th*, 1819: *on wine and food.*) Other wines of a heavy and spirituous nature transform a Man to a Silenus; . . . I said this same Claret is the only palate-passion I have I forgot game—I must plead guilty to the

breast of a Partridge, the back of a hare, the backbone of a grouse, the wing and side of a Pheasant and a Woodcock *passim*.

2. (*Friday, March* 19*th*, 1819: *on hearing a friend's father is dying.*) This is the world—thus we cannot expect to give way many hours to pleasure—Circumstances are like Clouds continually gathering and bursting—While we are laughing the seed of some trouble is put into the wide arable land of events.

3. (*Wednesday, April* 21*st*, 1819. *La Belle Dame Sans Merci.*)

> O what can ail thee Knight at arms
> Alone and palely loitering?
> The sedge has withered from the Lake
> And no birds sing!

Here, also in sequence, are three extracts from Volume One of Keats's copy of Burton.[7]

1. Yet these are brave men; Silenus ebrius was no braver . . . a dyet drink in the morning, cock-broth, China-broth, at dinner, plumb-broth, a chicken, a rabbet, rib of a rack of mutton, wing of a capon, the merry-thought of a hen, &c. (*pages* 105 *and* 108).

2. Even in the midst of all our mirth, jollity, and laughter, is sorrow and grief; or, if there be true happiness amongst us, 'tis but for a time: a fair morning turns to a lowring afternoon (*page* 159).

3. As Bellerophon in Homer

> That wandered in the woods sad all alone,
> Forsaking mens society, making great moan
> they delight in floods and waters . . . (*page* 280).

Keats catches the exact cadence of his reading; his list of game, for instance, could be added to Burton's and accepted easily as that author's. It is also noteworthy that here and elsewhere—for this is only in one of his many letters—his ideas follow the order of subjects suggested by a particular book; noteworthy, too, that he is always much affected by poetry quoted by another author. His reading marched in step with his life and work, became a part of it, a day-by-day influence. Keats had read deeply already, especially in the major poets, but he came even to them much later in life than many young men, and retained the freshness of discovery in his reading. Spenser obsessed him at the age of eighteen, Wordsworth at twenty, and Shakespeare, latest and most powerful, at twenty-one. Milton and Leigh Hunt, both less happy influences on Keats, made tremendous inroads into his style while the mood for them was on. His changes of enthusiasm were instant and noticeable; when he switched from Spenser to Wordsworth, he was rebuked for it in verse by a friend. If we read Keats's poetry with this in mind, much of its source at once will become clear. It seldom lies in the half-echoed chime of some earlier memory, but in the obsessive beat of the book of the moment.

"Such a man of fits and starts"—that note, in fact, is Hessey's second clue. Keats himself admitted it and justified it. A poet of his nature was like the chameleon, taking the colour of everything he touched. He had no identity save that which he received from immediate outside impressions—of books through his reading, of people, places, and events. This was Keats's poetic creed; he may have rationalized his own nature in making it, but it is nevertheless true of him. He is different from any other poet because of his extraordinary sensitivity to the impression of the moment; if we are to understand his poetry we must regard it not as a lumber-room and store-house of what was past in his life, but as a sensitive plate, reproducing what was present, an almost instantaneous development. His works form a poetic diary of his daily life. This was realized by Woodhouse, the most clear-sighted of his close friends. Woodhouse returned from his summer holiday to write Keats an anxious letter about his friend's renunciation of poetry at Hessey's. He received the famous reply which embodied Keats's theory of the "chameleon poet". With this in mind, the lawyer at once began an annotated manuscript book of all the poems of Keats he could lay hands on. Against one of the earliest poems to be copied, he made this profoundly true note:[8]

> There is a great degree of reality about all that Keats writes: and there must be many allusions to particular Circumstances, in his poems: which would add to their beauty & Interest, if properly understood.—To arrest

some few of these circumstances, & bring them to view in connexion with the poetic notice of them, is one of the objects of this collection.

That too is the principal object of this present book.

1

CHARMIAN AND POOR TOM

"BUT above all the other symptomes of lovers"—as Keats was to read exactly a year later (September 21st, 1819) in Burton's *Anatomy of Melancholy*[1]—"this is not lightly to be over passed, that of what condition soever, if once they be in love, they turn (to their ability) rimers, ballet-makers and poets." Keats's ability as a poet was already considerable; with him, even the slightest breath of love was likely to produce great results. "Love poured her Beauty into my warm veins" he had just written, translating Ronsard. In fact, it started him on *Hyperion*.

It was not as simple as that, for Keats in love was not a simple character. To look at he seemed to be one of those fortunately attractive people for whom all personal matters are likely to be plain sailing. Gay, lively, with a splendid sense of humour and great energy, he was a person who would be noticed at once by men and women. The attraction he had for all sorts of people seemed almost like a spell. His very short stature passed almost unnoticed owing to the beautiful proportion of his body and his strong broad shoulders. His curly reddish-gold hair was only less striking than his eyes, whose magical expression and keen look was remarked upon by a dozen of his friends. To read a book, particularly Shakespeare, with him was a pleasure only rivalled by going for a walk with him in the country; he seemed, in Fanny Brawne's words, "formed for every thing good".

Yet, as if to prove his own dictum that very few eyes can judge a man from his outward appearance, he had within him what he himself called a horrid morbidity of temperament. This, by some freak of family circumstances or of later experience, was concentrated almost entirely in his feelings towards women. He was completely conscious of this; two months earlier he had bared his heart to a friend. "I am certain I have not a right feeling towards Women. . . . When I am among Women I have evil thoughts, malice spleen—I cannot speak or be silent—I am full of Suspicions and therefore listen to nothing—I am in a hurry to be gone——" Keats put this down to the ideals which he had held in boyhood being consistently shattered since that time. We may fill in this picture by remembering that he had actually nursed his dying mother when he was at the age of puberty; that the morbidly reverential picture of womanhood that this experience implanted was early set against the coarse realities of the wards of an early nineteenth-century hospital. There was this double streak of sentiment and coarseness in Keats himself. He was after all a young man of the Regency period. Manners were rough, and humour crude. He attended parties where bawdy toasts were given, and a sexual joke enjoyed. He and his brothers in their private family language spoke of women with a mixture of idealism and worldliness, and they hid nothing from each other. "With respect to women," Keats wrote to Tom just before his return from Scotland, "I think I shall be able to conquer my passions hereafter better than I have yet done."

In point of fact, it was just at this time that he became most vulnerable. The reason is partly that until now he had been protected by the intense family feeling that existed between the three brothers. The admiration of George and Tom had helped to mature him as a poet; like Wordsworth, with his "fireside divan" of adoring wife, sister, and sister-in-law, he needed their support; the most delightful side of their family intimacy is shown in the letters he himself wrote to brighten the dull restricted life of their schoolgirl sister. On the other hand, the charmed circle of the brothers softened his fibre and restricted his powers of resistance to the outside world, as he himself realised when distance and death had broken it. He shared too much of his life with them for his own health of mind, or, as it proved, of body. This sharing of emotion, too, held back his experience of love. In a sense, the three young men had their love-affairs in common. One of Keats's earliest sonnets is addressed to Georgiana Wylie, whom George married. The Keats boys flirted with sets of sisters—the Mathew girls, originally friends of George, the Jeffrey sisters whom they met at Teignmouth, and with the Reynolds girls, sisters of John Hamilton Reynolds, the brilliant young writer.

George emigrated, Tom fell ill; John plunged into love and poetry. On the evening of September 20th-21st, 1818, he tells Charles Wentworth Dilke the second half of this step only:[2]

> I wish I could say Tom was any better . . . although I intended to have given some time to study alone I am obliged to write, and plunge into abstract images to ease myself of his countenance his voice and feebleness—

Reynolds, younger than Dilke, but more of a man of the world, and in love himself, was allowed to hear more:[3]

> I never was in love—yet the voice and the shape of a Woman has haunted me these two days—at such a time when the relief, the feverous relief of Poetry seems a much less crime—This morning Poetry has conquered—I have relapsed into those abstractions which are my only life— I feel escaped from a new strange and threatening sorrow— and I am thankful for it.—There is an awful warmth about my heart like a load of Immortality.
>
> Poor Tom—that woman—and Poetry were ringing changes in my senses.

Still he did not name the woman, though her influence on the new poem begins to be clear. Three weeks later Keats wrote to his brother George,[4] to whom he always felt he could tell everything. It was at Reynolds's own house that he met the woman; she was a cousin of the Reynolds sisters, called Jane Cox; the ladies were malicious about her, and no wonder.

> She is not a Cleopatra, but she is at least a Charmian. She has a rich eastern look; she has fine eyes and fine manners. When she comes into a room she makes an impression the same as the Beauty of a Leopardess. . . . You will by this time think I am in love with her; so before I go any further I will tell you I am not—she kept me awake one Night as a tune of Mozart's might do——

This was clearly the same beauty whose voice and shape haunted him three weeks earlier; her voice particularly—

> I speak of the thing as a passtime and an amuzement
> than which I can feel none deeper than a conversation
> with an imperial woman the very 'yes' and 'no' of whose
> Lips is to me a Banquet. . . . She walks across a room in
> such a manner that a man is drawn towards her with a
> magnetic Power. . . . As a man in the world I love the
> rich talk of a Charmian. . . .

And that, with some scornful asides about the Miss
Reynoldses, "on the look out"—Keats never fully forgave
a mean spirit in them or anyone else—was Miss Jane Cox.
He had plunged in and out of love, and into the start of his
poem; the cause is apparent in the blank verse lines he began
to write. Twenty lines of the new strong vein, which Keats
was to work deeper and deeper this year, have barely passed
when there enters the figure of Thea, the "Goddess of the
infant world". She gives at once a sensation of magnificence,
of size and power, and her face suggests not the creature of
Greek mythology she is supposed to be, but of another civilisa-
tion altogether

> When sages looked to Egypt for their lore.

Keats, like the artist Joseph Severn and many of his young
friends, was influenced by the Egyptian acquisitions of the
British Museum, which had been described that year in a new
catalogue.[5] Yet at this particular moment it is more probable
that he had a woman in mind, and not an exhibit or a catalogue. This is why his goddess looks not Greek but Egyptian.
The impression of dignity and grace, "an imperial woman",
the Egyptian face, "at least a Charmian", the "deep organ
tone" and "large utterance" of Thea, "the tune of Mozart's"
and "the rich talk of a Charmian" all combine in the same
picture. So too do the words of the poem and the phrases of
his letters. Thea's feeling about her heart

> as if just there,
> Though an immortal, she felt cruel pain:

is Keats's "There is an awful warmth about my heart like a
load of Immortality."

Meanwhile, as if to test him, the poem met with discouragement in its first week. The abuse of the *Blackwood* review was known to Keats; he may also have seen a review in the *British Critic* of June, which, by anticipating the methods of *Blackwood's* and extending them *ad absurdum*, provided almost a parody of that magazine. Such cheap and violent sneers could safely be ignored; the critics had overplayed their hand. But about September 27th[6] the *Quarterly Review*, delayed since April, came into circulation, and with it Croker's review of *Endymion*. This was a different matter. In spite of heavy humour, wilful pretence of misunderstanding, and political prejudice of the 'Tory' school of literature, this was a genuine attempt at criticism, written in terms which the average reader of the day would appreciate; it was therefore all the more damaging to the book's chances with the reading public. Many would echo Croker's plea for a poetic style based on "a complete couplet inclosing a complete idea", and there was a deadly half-truth in his examples of Keats, at his weakest, searching for, and often deplorably finding, a rhyme at any cost. The review was supposedly based on Keats's own self-criticism in his preface to *Endymion;* it must have struck deeply into the poet's confidence for that reason alone. Yet the final answer to the Byronic sneer that Keats was "snuffed out by an article" is the fact that he continued to write *Hyperion*. He had his reward. On October 3rd he read in the *Morning Chronicle* a long, reasoned, critical but generous defence of *Endymion* against the *Quarterly*. The watchful Hessey, who did not know that Keats was seeing the *Chronicle*, at once sent the cutting to him at Well Walk.

By that time, Keats had progressed with the "large utterance" of Thea, and the speeches between her and Saturn, which form what may be called the introduction to *Hyperion,* since it is only when they cease that Hyperion himself appears. Whenever a poem of his turned to dialogue, Keats himself instinctively turned to Shakespeare; at this very moment he was re-reading *King Lear*.[7] In Act III, scene 4, of his folio edition he underlined the words "poore Tom" and added pathetically beside them, "Sunday evening, Oct. 4 1818". There could be no more tragic example of the way in which, after the expulsion of Charmian from his mind, poetry and

poor Tom were still ringing changes in it. This part of *Hyperion*
is full of echoes of the play.[8] Keats must have actually written
with the folio beside him, for as he opened the volume, his
eye would have fallen on the blank page, at the end of *Hamlet*
and before the beginning of *King Lear*, where, eight months
before, he had written

> On sitting down to read King Lear once again
>
> O Golden-tongued Romance, with serene Lute!
>   Fair plumed Syren, Queen of far-away!
>   Leave melodizing on this wintry day
> Shut up thine olden Pages, and be mute.
> Adieu! for, once again, the fierce dispute,
>   Betwixt Damnation and impassion'd clay
>   Must I burn through; once more humbly assay
> The bitter-sweet of this Shakesperean fruit.
>
> Chief Poet! and ye Clouds of Albion,
>   Begetters of our deep eternal theme!
> When through the old oak forest I am gone,
>   Let me not wander in a barren dream:
> But, when I am consumed in the fire,
> Give me new Phoenix wings to fly at my desire.

Thea's line about the new terror of Jove's lightning, which

> Scorches and burns our once serene domain

echoes this; but, more than that, Keats's mind hovered over
the haunting and completely Keatsian line

> When through the old oak forest I am gone

to make of it three or four of the finest lines in the whole range
of his poetry, the image of the oaks:

> As when, upon a tranced summer night,
> Those green-rob'd senators of mighty woods,
> Tall oaks, branch-charmed by the earnest stars,
> Dream, and so dream all night without a stir . . .

The first week of October, during which Keats was reading *King Lear* and writing these lines, also heralded the reappearance of his most picturesque friend, Benjamin Robert Haydon. Haydon was a windmill-tilter, an outsize example, even in the history of English art, of a man obstinately spending a whole life doing the thing for which he was least suited. With his sight permanently impaired by an illness in childhood, he set his eyes and brain to the most exacting task he could possibly have contrived for them. He wished to be a historical painter in the grand manner of the high Renaissance. Oblivious of the fact that people now lived not in Elizabethan or Jacobean mansions but in neat Georgian or Regency houses, he crammed his large studio with huge unsaleable areas of paint. This was his monumental weakness. Haydon's strength and attraction lay in his buoyant enthusiasm. He inspired his pupils, and in later years won great victories for the popular appreciation of art by his rousing lectures to working-class audiences. He lives for us, when his less attractive features of boasting and spongeing are forgotten, for two things. One is his vindication of the Elgin Marbles, in the teeth of the experts, as genuine examples of classical art. The other is his immortal party in his studio, which still stands at the corner of Lisson Grove and Rossmore Road. Wordsworth and Keats were there, and Lamb, immortally drunk, insulted a Civil Servant. Haydon, an avid sharer of high experience of every sort, wrote it all down in his diary with a fire which never for one moment glimmers from his vast dull canvases.

This summer, recurrent eye-trouble had interrupted his work on one of these, *Christ's Entry into Jerusalem*, where Keats himself appears in a very reasonable likeness as a spectator in the crowd. Like Taylor, Dilke, and other of Keats's friends, he was staying with relatives in the country and had missed the homecoming from the Scottish tour. Early in the first week in October he returned, anxious to hear all, and heralded by a letter in which he mildly reproved Keats for not having written to him from Scotland.

Haydon was one of those people whose personality exacts promises which are then regretted, while Keats was always apt to promise more than he could do. Yet he had faithfully kept one promise to his brother Tom. He had written to Tom, from the moment he left Lancaster to the day the tour was cut short at Inverness, a series of seven long journal letters, forming, as he had promised they would, a complete account of the Scottish tour. Tom had passed them on to Reynolds, who had returned them. All seven, which Tom had numbered, or intended to number in order, were now back with Keats at Well Walk. Tom's illness was beginning to make it impossible for Keats to leave him for more than a few hours at a time,[9] and the walk to Lisson Grove took a good half-hour. He would have no time to stay and chat, while Haydon was too exuberant a personality to invite over to Hampstead with Tom in his present state.

In this dilemma, Keats decided to select some of the letters and drop them at the studio for Haydon to read. With his sensitive flair for judging the taste of each one of his many friends, Keats chose for the flamboyant Haydon two letters, Numbers 4 and 7, which described the ascent and the view from the tops of mountains, the first the view of Ailsa Crag,[10] and the second the actual ascent of Ben Nevis.[11] Each contained a sonnet on the subject, which Haydon would appreciate as the recipient of one of Keats's earliest and best poems in this form. As Keats glanced at these two letters before slipping over the Finchley Road and back, he read again his own account of the ascent through the lower mist to the summit of Ben Nevis, and recalled the "eagle skies" of the sonnet on Ailsa Crag. These sensations, revived in him, helped to create the lines in which, for the rest of *Hyperion* Book I, he takes leave of Saturn and Thea,

> Through aged boughs that yielded like the mist
> Which eagles cleave upmounting from their nest.

He also, as he might have known, took leave of the two letters; for Haydon never gave them back.[12]

(*Hyperion* Book I, 1–157)

2

A NATIVITY ODE AND
THE SCOTCH LETTERS

THE Scotch letters that remained—Numbers 1, 2, 3, 5 and 6—play such an important part in Keats's subsequent work that it is worth spending some time on them; but first there is the progress of the first book of *Hyperion* to consider. In spite of the nagging worry of Tom's illness, things were looking up. Keats read in the *Morning Chronicle* of October 8th another defence of *Endymion*, shorter but accompanied by numerous quotations. To save Hessey the trouble of sending him the cutting, Keats wrote to him at once,[1] in terms which show what a firm and sensible view he had taken of the attacks:

> Praise or blame has but a momentary effect on the man whose love of beauty in the abstract makes him a severe critic on his own Works. My own domestic criticism has given me pain without comparison beyond what Black-wood or the Quarterly could possibly inflict. . . . I have written independently *without Judgment.*—I may write independently, & *with Judgment*, hereafter. . . . In Endymion, I leaped headlong into the Sea, and thereby have become better acquainted with the Soundings, the quicksands, & the rocks, than if I had stayed upon the green shore, and piped a silly pipe, and took tea & comfortable advice.

So on with *Hyperion*, "with Judgment", but perhaps this time with too much judgment, or, as he was to think later, with too much conscious art.[2]

It is often assumed that *Hyperion* is based closely in language and construction on Milton's *Paradise Lost*; but that is not true of the poem as a whole. It is true that the section he was now writing, describing the palace of Hyperion, is very like Milton indeed. So is Hyperion's entrance—

He enter'd, but he enter'd full of wrath;
His flaming robes stream'd out beyond his heels,
And gave a roar, as if of earthly fire,
That scar'd away the meek ethereal Hours
And made their dove-wings tremble. On he flared . . .

It may well have been the Miltonism of this passage that made
him give up writing *Hyperion* a year later; for it is here, at line
217 of this first version, that he stuck fast in his attempt at a
second version. The "Miltonic inversions", as he called them,
of this part of the poem made Keats finally despair of finding
an individual voice for the whole work.

Certainly these inversions, noun and adjective reversed in
the Latin manner, lie thick on the ground—*omens drear, palace
bright, metal sick, rest divine, fragrance soft, Phantoms pale, nadir
deep, remnants huge, marble swart, plumes immense, porches wide,
radiance faint*—and so on.[3] In spite of the splendour of some
of the images, the style is almost a parody. Yet it does not
sound as though Keats had been reading *Paradise Lost* itself,
in spite of his copy of Milton's epic being underlined and annotated more heavily than his other reading-books. The Miltonic
inversions of this part of the poem have a second-hand air,
as if they had passed through the mouths of other poets.
Much can be traced to two poems written in Keats's own time,
one an original poem and the other a translation—Wordsworth's *The Excursion* and Cary's *The Vision of Dante*. The
Dante, in Taylor & Hessey's edition, had been with Keats
on his Scottish tour; he had quoted from it as recently as his
letter to Dilke, when he began *Hyperion*. As for *The Excursion*,
Keats never wavered in his admiration of Wordsworth's
philosophic poem. Both Cary and Wordsworth used a modified
Miltonic manner, with its turns and inversions; it is noteworthy that Keats, speaking elsewhere of "the sad embroidery
of the Excursion", uses thus Milton's own words from *Lycidas*
to describe it.[4]

Yet it is clear that Keats was reading some Milton at this
time; it cannot all be put down to the poetic ventriloquy of
Cary and Wordsworth.[5] His phrase in the letter to Hessey,
about piping a silly pipe, hints that this reading is to be found
not so much in the masterpieces of Milton's age, but in his

younger and more pastoral poems, such as the *Ode on the Morning of Christ's Nativity*. There is a strong proof of this in another letter written by Keats just at this moment.

On October 14th the first letter arrived from his brother George in America. There was any amount of domestic detail to enjoy, from a cricket-match in which George had played at Philadelphia to the all-important news that Georgiana was expecting a baby next spring. Keats sat down to reply on the evening of October 14th,[6] while Tom slept and the full moon poured its light in at the window. His news was as sad as theirs was hopeful; but soon his pen was away, with the freedom he always felt with George, speaking even more confidently of his poetry—"I think I shall be among the English Poets after my death"—and telling the story of his attraction towards Jane Cox, now safely over. Then Keats launched into politics and political morality, and it is in this context that Milton appears three times, twice named and once by inference, as a type of devotion to his country's good. George was advised to infuse some such spirit into America; Keats brimmed over with this idea into a poetic prophecy of George's child as the first American poet:

> 'Tis 'the witching time of night'
> Orbed is the Moon and bright
> And the stars they glisten, glisten
> Seeming with bright eyes to listen
> For what listen they?
> For a song and for a charm
> See they glisten in alarm
> And the Moon is waxing warm
> To hear what I shall say.
> Moon keep wide thy golden ears
> Harken Stars, and hearken Spheres
> Hearken thou eternal Sky
> I sing an infant's lullaby,
> A pretty Lullaby!
> Listen, Listen, listen, listen
> Glisten, glisten, glisten, glisten
> And hear my lullaby?
> Though the Rushes that will make
> Its cradle still are in the lake:
> Though the linnen that will be

Its swathe is on the cotton tree;
Though the wollen that will keep
It warm is on the silly sheep;
Listen Stars light, listen, listen,
Glisten, Glisten, glisten, glisten
And hear my lullaby!
Child! I see thee! Child I've found thee
Midst of the quiet all around thee!
Child I see thee! Child I spy thee
And thy mother sweet is nigh thee!—
Child I know thee! Child no more
But a Poet *ever*more
See, See the Lyre, the Lyre
In a flame of fire
Upon the little cradle's top
Flaring, flaring, flaring
Past the eyesight's bearing—
Awake it from its sleep
And see if it can keep
Its eyes upon the blaze.
Amaze, Amaze!
It stares, it stares, it stares
It dares what no one dares
It lifts its little hand into the flame
Unharm'd, and on the strings
Paddles a little tune and sings
With dumb endeavour sweetly!
Bard art thou completely!
Little Child
O' the western wild
Bard art thou completely!
Sweetly with dumb endeavour—
A Poet now or never!
Little Child
O' the western wild
A Poet now or never!

It is this unexpected nativity ode to the

Little Child
O' the western wild

that brings us face to face with the resemblance between what
Keats is writing and a particular poem of Milton's—the *Ode*

on the Morning of Christ's Nativity. Quite apart from the echo
of its opening

> It was the Winter wilde,
> While the Heav'n-born childe

there are clear parallels. Keats's stars watch for a miraculous
infant, just as Milton's do:

> The Stars with deep amaze
> Stand fixt in stedfast gaze,
>   Bending one way their pretious influence,
> And will not take their flight,
> For all the morning light,
>   Or Lucifer that often warn'd them thence;
> But in their glimmering orbs did glow,
> Untill their Lord himself bespake, and bid them go.

In feeling and expression, the two nativity odes are one.

It is clear too that Keats wrote his nativity ode at the same
time as he was in the midst of the flaming imageries of the
palace of Hyperion. Its 'flaring, flaring, flaring' with Hyperion's
"On he flared", the repetitions of 'blaze' and 'amaze', all
form the same verbal picture. The little ode is a small spark
thrown off by the much greater conflagration of the epic, and
this part of the epic has a connection with the much greater
ode of Milton.

To find what poem Keats was reading while he composed
does not, of course, explain the process of composition, nor
suggest that there is any the less of an original miracle in that
process. Rather the reverse; it shows how material can be
transmuted, and how the ultimate moment of transmutation
always escapes analysis. It is in what a poet first writes and
then cancels or rejects that we see how he transcends his source.
So it is here. It is not only that the whole background atmosphere and skyscape of Milton's Ode and this part of *Hyperion*
are the same, the heavenly bodies, ready to move by a divine
agency, waiting for the regular approach of the dawn. The
details of particular lines, as Keats first wrote them, reveal
their source. To take the famous half-line, which presses as if
upon a nerve—

But horrors portioned to a giant nerve
Oft made Hyperion ache.

This was at one time written, as a whole line,

Oft pressed his curly chin upon his breast

while five lines later in the sky-scenery of the palace is the line

And all its curtains of Aurorian clouds

The last stanza but one of Milton's Ode begins

So when the Sun in bed,
Curtained with cloudy red,
Pillows his chin upon an orient wave

Again, Hyperion at first jarred his golden region, not "from
the basements deep" but "from the deep foundations", while in
Milton's Ode the Creator "cast the dark foundations deep".
Then again, originally, at about line 273 of *Hyperion*, there was
a line

Glow'd through and still about the sable shroud

recalling the Ode's description of the Egyptian god Osiris:[7]

Naught but profoundest Hell can be his shroud,
In vain with Timbrel'd Anthems dark
The sable-stoled sorcerors bear his worshipt Ark.

Nor are the resemblances merely verbal. As well as the
atmosphere of expectant waiting before dawn, there is the
whole theme of the defeat and dispersal of the conquered older
gods and spirits of former worship. Keats's "prophesyings of
the midnight lamp" recall Milton's

the pale-ey'd priest from the prophetic cell
and
The Lars, and Lemures moan with midnight plaint

The strange picture of the marshy spirits and the terrifying
serpent image in *Hyperion* has distinct kinship with

> Th' old Dragon underground

and

> Typhon huge ending in snaky twine,

Milton's spirits are defeated by the infant Christ, and Keats's by the "infant Thunderer, rebel Jove".

However much the Ode affected Keats's poem—and it seems clear its influence was considerable—it is certain that Keats himself was growing weary and finding composition difficult. Perhaps that is why this passage always left a bad taste in his mouth, like the savour of brass in Hyperion's. The strain of steady composition and the equally steady deterioration of Tom's health, side by side, must have been intolerable. Yet he could not stop writing, even if he had wished, in case Tom should guess himself a burden. Somehow the strain must break. On October 15th, he left Tom for a few hours to visit George's mother-in-law, Mrs. Wylie, and to give her George's letter. Not finding her in, he handed it to one of her sons, Henry, whom he met in the street. On the evening of the 16th, he snatched an evening with Dilke and Charles Brown, now both returned to London, and living in the two parts of the semi-detached house they had built at Hampstead, Wentworth Place. Keats's mind was both too agitated and too preoccupied for him to contemplate going on with the long poem.

Prose might be the solution. A few days before, John Hamilton Reynolds had returned from the West Country where he had reviewed *Endymion* in a local paper. He had discussed with Keats a new project, which he referred to as "the Tale". Reynolds's mention[8] makes it sure that this was another of those tales from Boccaccio, like *Isabella*, which they had proposed to make into a joint book, and which he was now encouraging Keats to write and publish alone; but Keats never even began this prose tale, in spite of announcing twice to George that he would. However, the story of the next few days is connected with some prose which he had already written.

On October 21st, 1818, Keats, worried and conscious that he was not getting on very fast with his letter to George, wrote[9]

> For want of something better I shall proceed to give you some extracts from my Scotch Letters—Yet now I think

on it why not send you the letters themselves—I have
three of them at present. I believe Haydon has two which
I will get in time.

This parcel of letters, as Keats called it, was despatched before
October 31st, when he wrote as a postscript on a separate
sheet "This day is my Birth day". The three letters were in
Keats's hands during the last ten days of October, 1818; after
that time he never saw them again. It is important to be clear
exactly which three letters he sent, and which two—for the
letters like the little nigger boys seemed liable to vanish—
remained with him after the end of this month.

Which three were they, out of the seven he had written to
Tom from the North? It would seem that they were the first
three he wrote, Numbers 1, 2 and 3,[10] since these have been
recovered from American sources only, and this can be proved
by elimination. Haydon had numbers 4 and 7. Number 6
Keats had somehow mislaid; he said so when he eventually
copied it for George eleven months later.[11] This left only
Number 5, which he had to keep back deliberately.[12] It
opened with a string of bawdy puns by Brown and contained
Keats's own mildly dirty poem, *The Gadfly*. Keats did not wish
this to be read by his sixteen-year-old sister-in-law, for whose
benefit he even changed the word "breeches" into the less
suggestive "trowsers" when he came to copy out Letter 6. It
can only have been Letters 1, 2 and 3 which he re-read and
sent across the Atlantic in these last ten days of October, 1818.
What was contained in these letters would be strongly associated with these ten days, and thereafter vanish from anything
but his unconscious memory. This indeed proves to be the
case. The first hundred lines of the second book of *Hyperion* are
full of direct quotations from these three letters,[13] as he looked
over them before sending them to America. Such quotations
never occur again; but there is another poem, also written in
this week of October, which quotes directly from these letters.
This poem is connected with a startling and so far unexplored
chapter in Keats's life.

(*Hyperion* Book I, 158-end: Book II, 1–100)

3

BRIGHT STAR AND THE
BEAUTIFUL MRS. JONES

IT has never before been certain when the first version of
Keats's sonnet, *Bright Star*, was written. This is partly because
the famous final version, which he copied out on his voyage to
Italy in 1820, was for a long time thought to be the original
composition, a miraculous dying spark of inspiration in the
face of disease and despair. As this version was copied by
Fanny Brawne into Keats's pocket Dante, where it can still
be seen, the poem has become associated in everyone's mind
with Keats's fiancée. Yet there is an earlier version of the
sonnet, which exists only in Charles Brown's handwriting,
while the year which it is dated, 1819, only shows the year in
which Brown copied it.

> Bright star! would I were stedfast as thou art!
> Not in lone splendour hung amid the night;
> Not watching, with eternal lids apart,
> Like Nature's devout sleepless Eremite,
> The morning waters at their priestlike task
> Of pure ablution round earth's human shores;
> Or, gazing on the new soft fallen mask
> Of snow upon the mountains and the moors:—
>
> No;—yet still stedfast, still unchangeable,
> Cheek-pillow'd on my Love's white ripening breast,
> To touch, for ever, its warm sink and swell,
> Awake, for ever, in a sweet unrest;
> To hear, to feel her tender-taken breath,
> Half-passionless, and so swoon on to death.

This first version was composed as early as the last week in
October, 1818, when Keats was finishing the first book of
Hyperion, before he had met Fanny Brawne,[1] and at a time

when his changeable and excitable nature was occupied with quite another lady.

Since this is at least four months earlier than anyone[2] has ever suggested the sonnet was written, it is worth looking at some proofs of this from Keats's own reading before going further. The main proof lies in the first of the three Scotch letters, which he was looking at for the last time in these final ten days of October. Letter one has hardly begun[3] before Keats launches into this description of the view over Lake Windermere, or Winander mere—

> There are many disfigurements to this Lake—not in the way of land or water. No; the two views we have had of it are of the most noble tenderness—they can never fade away—they make one forget the divisions of life; age, youth, poverty and riches; and refine one's sensual vision into a sort of north star which can never cease to be open lidded and stedfast over the wonders of the great Power.

It can only be while he had this passage actually before his eyes that he wrote the first eight lines of the sonnet; the likeness is so close that there can be no question of memory. It is also clear how close this likeness is to the last eight lines of *Hyperion* Book I, themselves to all intents and purposes a blank verse octave of a sonnet on the same theme:

> Hyperion arose, and on the stars
> Lifted his curved lids and kept them wide
> Until it ceas'd; and still he kept them wide:
> And still they were the same bright, patient stars.
> Then with a slow incline of his broad breast,
> Like to a diver in the pearly seas,
> Forward he stoop'd over the airy shore,
> And plung'd all noiseless into the deep night.

This evidence alone seems to show that Keats wrote the octave of the sonnet *Bright Star* between Books I and II of *Hyperion*, at the end of October, 1818.

Another set of evidence also ties the sestet of the sonnet to this time—quite apart from the word "passionless", which Keats used, then cancelled, a little earlier in *Hyperion*. This is the play of *Troilus and Cressida*, which he was reading at the time, turning once more to Shakespeare for the dialogue at the end of *Hyperion* Book I. The likenesses between what he was writing in *Hyperion* and this play[4] are enough to send us again to Keats's folio Shakespeare, and to the longest continuous passage which he underlined in *Troilus and Cressida*, the scene between Troilus and Pandarus in Act III, scene 2:

> *Pan.* Have you seene my Cousin?
> *Troy.* No Pandarus: I stalke about her doore
> Like a strange soule upon the Stigian bankes
> Staying for waftage. O be thou my Charon,
> And give me swift transportance to those fields,
> Where I may wallow in the Lilly beds
> Propos'd for the deserver. O gentle Pandarus,
> From Cupids shoulder plucke his painted wings,
> And flye with me to Cressid.
> *Pan.* Walke here ith' Orchard, Ile bring her straight.
>> *Exit Pandarus.*
>
> *Troy.* I am giddy; expectation whirles me round,
> Th' imaginary relish is so sweete,
> That it inchants my sence: what will it be
> When that the watry pallats taste indeede
> Loves thrice reputed Nectar? Deathe I feare me
>   woon*
> ~~Sounding~~ distruction, or some ioy too fine,
> Too subtile, potent, and too sharpe in sweetnesse,
> For the capacitie of my ruder powers;
> I feare it much, and I doe feare besides,
> That I shall loose distinction in my ioyes,
> As doth a battaile, when they charge on heapes
> The enemy flying.
>> *Enter Pandarus.*
>
> *Pan.* Shee's making her ready, sheele come straight; you must be witty now, she does so blush, & fetches her winde so short, as if she were fraide with a sprite: Ile fetch her; it is the prettiest villaine, she fetches her breath so short as a new tane Sparrow.
>> *The correction is in Keats's handwriting.

There is no doubt how much the sestet of the sonnet is like this passage, in emotion and expression, and, especially when we look at the last couplet, even in particular words. The parallel words "swoon" and "death" are made even more distinct by the alteration of the former in the Folio being actually in Keats's own hand, while the last sentence of Pandarus's last speech, "she fetches her breath so short as a new tane Sparrow", is beautifully echoed by the "tender-taken breath", a phrase itself so Shakespearean, in the sonnet. It seems positive, from his reading alone, that Keats wrote the whole sonnet while he had the three Scotch letters in his hand and was reading *Troilus and Cressida*—that is, at the end of October, 1818.

Yet reading alone is inadequate to explain the depth and passionate feeling of *Bright Star*, more human and breathing perhaps in this early version than in its finally accepted form. It crystallizes an experience and an emotion which at this very time occupied the whole of Keats's being.

The story is told in the continuation of his letter to George. For some reason, he was for a time enjoying greater freedom from his duty of nursing Tom. Henry and Charles Wylie, George's brothers-in-law, called at Well Walk on Sunday, October 18th; possibly they may have been alarmed by the strain imposed on Keats, and made some arrangement by which he could get some respite from the atmosphere of the sick-room. Again Haslam, a friend whose continual kindness at this time Keats mentions, may have stepped in and undertaken some of the nursing. At all events, the next week saw Keats visiting Town more than at any time since Tom's illness had worsened. This freedom brought, on Monday the 19th, an unpleasant shock. Abbey, the tea-broker, Keats's former guardian and still the guardian of Fanny Keats, came out with the prohibition that Fanny must only visit her dying brother once more before the Christmas holidays.[5] This was not because of the danger of infection, but because at her last visit she had "been to other places besides Well Walk". It is ironic that Abbey did the right thing—for Fanny lived to a ripe old age—for what seems to us the wrong reason; but it did not seem wrong to him. The only two places Keats could have taken his sister to in Hampstead were Dilke's and Leigh Hunt's. Dilke's wife was away ill, so Fanny's visit would have been technically unchaperoned, while Hunt's was just the reputation to appal Abbey.

On Thursday, October 22nd, though, Keats had what was obviously a day of great pleasure. It began well with a letter from the understanding Woodhouse, now returned to his chambers in the Temple. He urged Keats not to take any notice of the reviews, and not to follow his own theory, expressed when they had last met at Hessey's party, that he should stop writing. Keats visited Town, dined with Mrs. Wylie, and went on to Hessey's, perhaps hoping to meet Woodhouse; there he enjoyed the even more stimulating experience of another meeting with Hazlitt, who was trying to get an advance on his next book.[6] They walked together to Covent Garden, where Hazlitt was going to play racquets. His dark companion with the slack loping stride must have provided a relief of the spirit for Keats, who always admired him; it is also possible that the meeting provided him with the most beautiful word in the sonnet—"Eremite".[7] From Hessey Keats received the good news that *Endymion*, stimulated by newspaper controversy, had, in publisher's phrase, "begun to move". Friday saw him back at Hampstead visiting Hunt, where he had a less cheering meeting with another publisher, Ollier, who had lost heavily on his first book. At the week-end he was again in Town. He re-opened his letter to George, in a state of great excitement, to chronicle an adventure.

Since I wrote thus far I have met with that same Lady again, whom I saw at Hastings and whom I met when we were going to the English Opera. It was in a Street which goes from Bedford Row to Lamb's Conduit Street— I passed her and turned back—she seemed glad of it; glad to see me and not offended at my passing her before. We walked on towards Islington where we called on a friend of her's who keeps a Boarding School. She has always been an enigma to me—she has been in a Room with you and with Reynolds and wishes we should be acquainted without any of our common acquaintance knowing it. As we went along, some times through shabby, sometimes through decent Street(s) I had my guessing at work, not knowing what it would be and prepared to meet any surprise—First it ended at this House at Islington: on parting from this I pressed to attend her home. She consented, and then again my thoughts were at work what it might lead to, tho' now they had received a sort of genteel hint from the Boarding School. Our walk ended in 34 Gloucester Street, Queen Square—not exactly so for we went up stairs into her sitting room—a very tasty sort of place with Books, Pictures a bronze statue of Buonaparte, Music, aeolian Harp; a Parrot, a Linnet—a Case of choice Lique(u)rs &c. &c. &c. She behaved in the kindest manner—made me take home a Grouse for Tom's dinner—Asked for my address for the purpose of sending more game—As I had warmed with her before and kissed her—I though(t) it would be living backwards not to do so again—she had a better taste: she perceived how much a thing of course it was and shrunk from it—not in a prudish way but in as I say a good taste. She contrived to disappoint me in a way which made me feel more pleasure than a simple Kiss could do—She said I should please her much more if I would only press her hand and go away. Whether she was in a different disposition when I saw her before—or whether I have in fancy wrong'd her I cannot tell. I expect to pass some pleasant hours with her now and then: in which I feel I shall be of service to her in matters of knowledge and taste: if I can I will. I have no libidinous thought about her—she and your George are the only women à peu près de mon age whom I would be content to know for their mind and friendship alone.

One has to pause here, as Keats did in writing his letter, not only to take breath in his rapid and vivid narrative, but to take another look at this human and delightful picture of something that has happened to every young man at one time or another, caught for eternity by Keats's genius and gusto for life. It is also time to ask who the lady was.

Keats kept the secret she exacted—that they should be acquainted without any of their common acquaintance knowing it. He kept it so well that he never once revealed her name, even in these full and frank letters which he continued to write to George. In fact, 135 years have passed before a chance business letter from Hessey to Taylor, unobserved till now, has identified a lady well-known to the circle of Keats's publishers, who was in the habit of staying or living at Hastings.[8] Her name was Mrs. Isabella Jones.

She always seemed, Keats said, an enigma to him; but she emerges from her long obscurity as a very decided and lively character, one who may well have had her reasons for appearing at times enigmatic. She was still young—"à peu près de mon age", as Keats says—and she was certainly beautiful; she was specially remembered nearly twenty years later by Reynolds,[9] an expert in such matters, as "beautiful Mrs. Jones", and she sat this winter for her portrait by A. E. Chalon, which appeared in the Royal Academy exhibition of 1819.[10] She was in the habit of spending her summers in or near Hastings with an elderly, irascible, and apparently rich Irishman named Mr. Donal O'Callaghan;[11] there is no mention of any Mr. Jones. She wintered in London, and was very hospitable. She prided herself on giving parties where one could meet pretty women and sensible men, and where the sensible men could show their good sense by looking at the pretty women. Her case of liqueurs, which Keats noticed, contained some of the choicest Scotch whisky, and wherever she went she seems to have been able to command expensive and well-furnished lodgings.[12] She had a lively, not to say a biting wit, and she wrote an excellent style. Her literary tastes were those fashionable in her day; she read novels of the Gothic "horror" type—the counterpart of the modern thriller—popularised by Mrs. Ann Radcliffe, and was interested in the poetry of Barry Cornwall. She was a particular intimate of Taylor, and seems to have shared in the gatherings of the brilliant coterie the publisher assembled when he edited the *London Magazine* in the early 1820s—Hood, Clare, Lamb, Cary, and Reynolds. It is noteworthy that she seems already to have read the comparatively unknown *Endymion*, since she spoke of it six months later as a favourite book of hers.

Keats had first met her while he was still writing *Endymion*; he visited Hastings, after a stay at Canterbury, at the end of May or the beginning of June, 1817.[13] The second meeting, which he mentions, had been exactly a year later, when he and George, probably as a last bachelor party before the latter's marriage, had gone to see Charles Mathews "pop-gun it at the pit" in an entertainment at the Lyceum Theatre in the Strand.[14] Now they met for the third time. It was a pure coincidence, but a strange one. Isabella Jones lived up to the striking and

beautiful design with which she sealed her letters—the sun
setting behind a range of hills with the motto "Je reviendrai".
Together they walked up Theobald's Road, before bearing
left towards the Angel at Islington. The friend on whom she
called was almost certainly a Mrs. Green of Duncan Terrace
near the Angel; about five months after this visit, Richard
Woodhouse received the following letter from this address:[15]

> Mrs Colonel Green's Compliments to Mr Woodhouse and
> feels exceedingly obliged to M^r W—— for the perusal of
> *Endymion* and the other trifle—There are a great number
> of beauties in the *former* which speaks highly for the
> authors growing Genius—A Stranger perhaps might fancy
> him too *wild* in some of his passages but M^{rs} G knowing
> the Author at a time when the *Fire* of his imagination
> appeared agitated with a *Thirst* for *fame*—can easily
> excuse him *for the—sudden bursts* of *enthusiasm* which
> *pervades* his *affectionate Constitution*. Should M^{rs} G—— ever
> see the Author she certainly must rally him—for a great
> *Mistake*—committed in the Book of trifles and which *by
> this time he must* be *a very great* Judge. M^{rs} G begs to be
> kindly remembered to him and should at all times be
> happy to see both Mr Woodhouse and the Author of
> Endymion—

This Mrs. Green was the wife of Lieutenant-Colonel Thomas
Green of the 6th Regiment of Native Infantry, Madras
Presidency, who had been invalided out of the Indian Army
after over twenty-five years of service.[16] From her letter it
seems clear that her acquaintance with Keats[17] was a slight
one, since she had only just received *Endymion* at Woodhouse's
hands at the end of March, 1819, nearly a year after publication. What is striking is that her description of her meeting
with Keats—"at a time when the *Fire* of his imagination
appeared agitated with a *Thirst* for *fame*"—might be, allowing
for its mixed metaphor,[18] a description of his own feelings as
he goes on to display them at this very time.

Keats returned the same way back towards Holborn, in the
same excited state, and with, as he so expressively put it, his
"guessing at work", as well it might be, about the beautiful
and enigmatic companion at his side. They repassed Lamb's
Conduit Street, and turned into one of the smaller parallel

roads, Gloucester Street, now known as Old Gloucester Street.
The houses here are a neat Regency row, occupied at that
time mainly by small tradesmen and business men, some of
whom let as lodgings the large and well-lit rooms on the first
and second floors. Time and change have not dealt kindly with
this part of Holborn; No. 34 itself has disappeared, but neighbouring houses have survived a door or so away, and it is
evident that these Gloucester Street houses were more or less
uniform in character. We can therefore get a very good idea
of the rooms which Keats visited when Isabella Jones invited
him upstairs. All the houses on this side of Gloucester Street
have one thing in common, which is noticeable directly one
enters, and that is the marked square panelling of the hall and
all the rooms on the entrance and first floors. We can easily
visualize Keats in one of the large light front rooms, with its
square panels, parrot's cage, and all the other "tasty" furnish-
ings. It was this setting, imaginatively heightened, which was
still vivid in his mind as he went on post-haste with his letter
to George.

> I shall in a short time write you as far as I know how I
> intend to pass my Life—I cannot think of those things
> now Tom is so unwell and weak. Notwithstand(ing)
> your Happiness and your recommendation I hope I shall
> never marry. Though the most beautiful Creature were
> waiting for me at the end of a Journey or a Walk; though
> the carpet were of Silk, the Curtains of the morning
> Clouds; the chairs and Sofa stuffed with Cygnet's down;
> the food Manna, the Wine beyond Claret, the Window
> opening on Winander mere, I should not feel—or rather
> my Happiness would not be so fine, as my Solitude is
> sublime. Then instead of what I have described, there is a
> Sublimity to welcome me home. The roaring of the wind
> is my wife and the Stars through the window pane are
> my Children. The mighty abstract Idea I have of Beauty
> in all things stifles the more divided and minute domestic
> happiness—an amiable wife and sweet Children I con-
> template as a part of that Beauty—but I must have a
> thousand of those beautiful particles to fill up my heart.
> I feel more and more every day, as my imagination
> strengthens, that I do not live in this world alone but in a
> thousand worlds. No sooner am I alone than shapes of

epic greatness are stationed around me, and serve my Spirit the office which is equivalent to a King's body guard—then 'Tragedy with sceptr'd pall, comes sweeping by." According to my state of mind I am with Achilles shouting in the Trenches, or with Theocritus in the Vales of Sicily. Or I throw my whole being into Triolus, and repeating those lines, 'I wander, like a lost Soul upon the stygian Banks staying for waftage", I melt into the air with a voluptuousness so delicate that I am content to be alone. These things combined with the opinion I have of the generallity of women—who appear to me as children to whom I would rather give a Sugar Plum than my time, form a barrier against Matrimony which I rejoice in.

This splendid passage has been quoted again and again for its philosophy and its meaning; perhaps that is why everyone has neglected the plain clue in its words—that here is the occasion with which the *Bright Star* sonnet must be associated, the time when the passage from Letter One to Tom and the scene from *Troilus and Cressida* were present together in Keats's mind. The references to the two are obvious, especially when the Troilus quotation is coupled with the strange expression "Cygnet's down" (instead of, say, swansdown); for this also is a phrase underlined by Keats in his Folio, from Act I, scene 1—

to whose soft seizure
     The Cignets Downe is harsh

To clinch this certainty, "Winander mere" from Letter One is seconded by something else, which chimes with another of the letters to Tom, Letter 3. In that letter, Keats had copied his lyric *Meg Merrilies*, with its description of old Meg staring at the moon, the hills, and the trees, so that

     Alone with her great family
     She lived as she did please.

This is the same thought and practically the same expression as "the roaring of the wind is my wife and the Stars through the window pane are my Children." This is the time when the first three Scotch letters and the play of *Troilus and Cressida* were vividly present in Keats's mind. It is the time when he composed the first version of *Bright Star*, and it is also the time, during the week-end of October 24th-25th, when he was so deeply stirred by his meeting with Isabella Jones.

There is yet another confirmation. Either on Monday, October 26th, or Tuesday the 27th, Keats wrote his famous reply[19] to the letter he had received a few days earlier from Woodhouse. This is the reply of which Woodhouse noted[20] "believe in the truth of every syllable of Keats's letter, taken as a descrip^n of himself & his own Ideas & feel^{gs}." These ideas and feelings repeat, to a remarkable degree, the philosophy of the letter to George, and were obviously written at more or less the same time:

My dear Woodhouse,
Your Letter gave me a great satisfaction; more on account of its friendliness, than any relish of that matter in it which is accounted so acceptable in the 'genus irritabile'. The best answer I can give you is in a clerk-like manner to make some observations on two principle points, which seem to point like indices into the midst of the whole pro and con, about genius, and views and atchievements and ambition and coetera. 1$^{st.}$ As to the poetical Character itself (I mean that sort of which, if I am any thing, I am a Member; that sort distinguished from the wordsworthian or egotistical sublime; which is a thing per se and stands alone) it is not itself—it has no self—it is every thing and nothing—It has no character—it enjoys light and shade; it lives in gusto, be it foul or fair, high or low, rich or poor, mean or elevated—It has as much delight in conceiving an Iago as an Imogen. What shocks the virtuous philosopher, delights the camelion Poet. It does no harm from its relish of the dark side of things any more than from its taste for the bright one; because they both end in speculation. A Poet is the most unpoetical of any thing in existence; because he has no Identity—he is continually infor(ming) and filling some other Body—The Sun, the Moon, the Sea and Men and Women who are creatures of impulse are poetical and have about them an unchangeable attribute—the poet has none; no identity—he is certainly the most unpoetical of all God's Creatures. If then he has no self, and if I am a Poet, where is the Wonder that I should say I would write no more? Might I not at that very instant have been cogitating on the characters of Saturn and Ops? . . .

Quite apart from the often-quoted philosophy of this passage, it contains another series of parallels with the composition of *Bright Star*. In the first 200 words, Keats uses the expression "relish" twice in just the sense that Shakespeare made Troilus use it in the marked speech. Saturn and Ops he had just reached in Book II of *Hyperion*, where he wrote "Of Ops the queen all clouded round from sight"; while most evident of all is his use of the word "unchangeable" both in this letter and in *Bright Star*. In the letter, Keats says that the poet cannot be unchangeable like other human beings; in the sonnet, by contrast, he wishes at least in love to be "unchangeable", to be for once like other people.

These intense feelings, both on love and on poetry, had been brought to the surface by his meeting with Isabella Jones, "when", to quote Mrs. Colonel Green, "the *Fire* of his imagination appeared agitated with a *Thirst* for *fame*". This was the dominant theme of everything he uttered at this moment. His determination to outbid the critics of *Endymion* and be a major poet burst out from the restraint under which he had kept it in the past month. To Woodhouse he wrote "I will assay to reach to as high a summit in Poetry as the nerve bestowed upon me will suffer", and to George he spoke of "the yearning Passion I have for the beautiful, connected and made one with the ambition of my intellect". Ambition—"I am ambitious of doing the world some good"—or Fame became with Keats at this moment a passion which marched hand-in-hand with his conception of poetry. "The faint conception I have of Poems to come brings the blood frequently into my forehead", he wrote.

More than one of these "poems to come" was to be inspired by Isabella Jones. That *Bright Star* in its first form was inspired by her seems inescapable. How much it can also be regarded as addressed *to* her is another matter. It may be simply the poetic expression of the tumultuous feelings on Love, Fame, and Poetry, a theme to which Keats returns frequently in the next few months, and which this chance yet apparently destined meeting had so strangely released.

(*Bright Star* sonnet: 1st version)

4

THE MOURNFUL HOUSE
AND FANNY BRAWNE

As with us mortal men, the laden heart
Is persecuted more, and fever'd more,
When it is nighing to the mournful house . . .

KEATS came back from exhilaration to sad reality at No. 1 Well Walk. These opening lines of the next section of *Hyperion* hold a mirror to the month of November. It is the month of this year of Keats's poetic life about which we know least; Tom, after a slight improvement, was daily worse.[1] As the end came nearer and nearer, Keats can hardly have left his side. He was alone; other company would have agitated the dying Tom. There is no evidence that his sister Fanny made the one grudgingly-allowed visit to her brother's bedside. Keats was not seen in public. He did not attend a single one of Hazlitt's Lectures on the English Comic Writers, which began this month. He dared not write to George, for fear Tom should guess the letter was about him. We do not hear of his reading anything. Life, with deadly insistence, was marking time for him.

Yet the poem went on. It is true that Keats, in the middle of next month, speaks of his pen as having grown "too goutty for verse", and as late as New Year's Eve he said that *Hyperion* was "scarce began".[2] Keats set standards of speed and size for his compositions which are often misleading. He had worked on parts of *Endymion* at the rate of 50 lines a day, and he was later to refer to *The Eve of St. Agnes* (378 lines, composed in about a fortnight) as "a little poem". In what he considered light poems or minor verse, he could reel off a hundred to two hundred lines in an evening. The average of ten lines a day, needed to complete the second book of *Hyperion* by the end of November, must have seemed to him painfully slow, the poem itself hardly under way at all.

The progress of the poem itself is painful. The four main speeches—of Saturn, Oceanus, Clymene, and Enceladus—hang fire. They never flame up into live individual verse. They are the finest kind of "made" poetry, but only once perhaps do they achieve a moment of vision. They have nothing of the clash and awful glitter of the parallel second book of *Paradise Lost*, the grand debate in Hell. It is perhaps misleading even to make this comparison. The echoes of Keats's reading of *Troilus and Cressida* had not yet faded; the debate is unlike Milton's from the start. It resembles the discussions of the play, shifting from the Greek to the Trojan camp and back again, but without Shakespeare's sinewy line.

The one flash of lightning, in fact, in the last hundred lines of Book II, seems to have come from some re-reading or re-sorting of the remaining Scotch letters, Nos. 5 and 6, which from now on play such a part in many of Keats's poems. Perhaps Keats read them again in a conscious attempt to recapture the mood of the beginning of the book, and to restore a fallen grandeur to his hero; in this he partly succeeded:

> In pale and silver silence they remain'd,
> Till suddenly a splendour, like the morn,
> Pervaded all the beetling gloomy steeps,
> All the sad spaces of oblivion,
> And every gulf,' and every chasm old,
> And every height, and every sullen depth,
> Voiceless, or hoarse with loud tormented streams:
> And all the everlasting cataracts,
> And all the headlong torrents far and near,
> Mantled before in darkness and huge shade,
> Now saw the light and made it terrible.
> It was Hyperion:—a granite peak
> His bright feet touch'd, and there he stay'd to view
> The misery his brilliance had betray'd
> To the most hateful seeing of itself.
> Golden his hair of short Numidian curl,
> Regal his shape majestic . . .

Yet even in this echoed brilliance the tone is one of misery. Little can have happened to Keats in this month to lift his despair. The one incident which we can date securely, to the second week of November, was a charming one, and would have been gratifying if he had been in the mood. Forwarded through Taylor & Hessey, a gift of £25 and a complimentary sonnet arrived for him from an unknown admirer in Teignmouth. The name of the donor, "Mr. P. Fenbank", did not strike Keats as genuine; he spoke of the gift as an anonymous one, though he wrote a reply to the Post Office address which accompanied the present. Like him, we can do no more than guess who sent it. A strong case has been made out for Woodhouse, but this would assume that the lawyer was capable of a clever bluff on Taylor and Hessey, or all three were in the conspiracy together.[3] There was also the enigmatic, generous and well-read lady of his recent meeting; but perhaps *Star of high promise*, the opening words of the sonnet, is too obvious to be a reply to his own *Bright Star*. The most likely guess would be a genuine resident in Teignmouth, Miss Marian Jeffrey, whose home the Keats brothers had all visited, and who was supposed locally to have been in love with John. Her verses, published later under her married name of Prowse, are not unlike the sonnet, nor, in a minor key, are they far off some of Keats's own.

That, for this month, is all we know. It cannot have been all gloom. In a letter of November 24th to Rice, another friend whom he had not seen since the first half of October, Keats spoke of "one or two rather pleasant occasions" which he had enjoyed since that time. Possibly the wording is reminiscent and these included some of the "pleasant hours" which he had hoped to spend, and perhaps did spend, with Isabella Jones, for Rice was a member of a racy man-of-the-world set, and good audience for such matters. Otherwise we hear little of Keats, much of the sympathy of his friends, particularly Brown. It was Brown who wrote to Woodhouse on December 1st, "Mr Keats requests me to inform you his brother Thomas died this morning at 8 o'Clock quietly & without pain—"[4] Brown had woken that morning to find Keats beside him, silently holding his hand. Neither needed to speak; when Brown at last broke the silence, it was to invite Keats to come and lodge immediately with him at Wentworth Place.[5]

Tom was buried on Monday, December 7th, at St. Stephen's, Coleman Street. For the next ten days, a whirl of engagements and visits was arranged by Keats's friends to relieve his mind.

"I have been everywhere." It was the Regency answer to grief, stoical and worldly, though not necessarily the right answer for Keats, who even in happier times felt the constraint of having to smother his feelings when in company. Yet as a rough cure it seems to have worked. The funeral too brought a welcome though short-lived relaxation by Abbey, and Keats was able to visit his sister twice in one week. He was accompanied once by Mrs. Dilke, and on the second occasion by Haslam, the quiet looker-on, who had also written off to George and Georgiana, to spare Keats the pain of being the first to break the news. There was a visit by Haydon, in fine talking form, and a call from another artist, Archer. We also hear of a meeting with Charles Lamb. For most social occasions Brown was his companion. Apart from one round of calls in Town—Mrs. Wylie, Hazlitt, and probably the Reynolds family—Keats had this cheerful rough-and-ready humorist at his side. Together they saw Kean acting in John Howard Payne's new tragedy of *Brutus*; they visited Leigh Hunt and went with him to a party at Novello's; and on Friday, December 11th, they went up Downshire Hill to Elm Cottage, to visit Mrs. Brawne and her daughter Fanny.[6]

Though a first visit to her home, this was not a first meeting. Carlino Brown, Charles's son, seemed to suggest it was, by saying later that his father introduced Keats to Miss Brawne soon after Keats had come to live with him at Wentworth Place,[7] but other evidence confirms that they met earlier and at the Dilkes. Mrs. Brawne had rented Brown's half of Wentworth Place during the summer. Hampstead being such a small place, Keats and his future fiancée could have met at any time after his return from Scotland, but there were good reasons why the meeting was delayed. The Dilkes' household (where, according to Dilke himself, they "no doubt" met)[8] was exceptionally disorganized at this time. Dilke himself was away ill during September; no sooner was he back than his wife fell ill and was away for October. Keats hardly left Tom, and then generally to go to Town. He did not see Miss Brawne till very late in the year, and it is certain that he cannot have done so till November. It can be inferred from a later letter between Keats and her that Severn was present at their first meeting;[9] Severn had gone down in September with a severe attack of typhus (probably typhoid). He was still convalescent in October, and can hardly have been about again in Hampstead until November.

Fanny Brawne, when Keats met her in November, was eighteen and a quarter, and looked younger. Both she and Keats were the eldest children of their families, and both, before they were ten, had seen their fathers die in the early thirties, Thomas Keats in an accident and Samuel Brawne of consumption; by a coincidence not so strange in the great days of coaching, both had had a grandfather who was a prosperous stable-keeper. There the resemblance ended, for Fanny's mother, Frances Brawne, after whom she was named, was still living, a widow of forty-seven. It is not unlikely that Fanny inherited from her mother an appearance and manner that was young for her age, for Mrs. Brawne had been six years older than her husband, and Fanny herself eventually married a man over eleven years her junior.

Fanny was not conventionally good-looking, but she was everything that is meant by the word unusual. With her warm brown hair, brilliant blue eyes, and exceptionally white skin, she at once attracted attention. She was brilliantly animated in company, and produced an effect which is described at various times in her life as dazzling. She also was able to make the best of herself by what appears to have been the abiding passion of her life, dressmaking. It is even possible that she did this professionally, for there were ups and downs in her fortunes, both now and in the later years. She had a quick mind and a taste for the theatre, but there is no evidence that she read greatly at this time, though she was, much later, a reader of the *London Magazine*. Book-lists which have been produced to show what she and Keats read together date in reality from two years later, when he had left for Italy.[10] The only connection between her and poetry at this time is a schoolgirl couplet written in French; fluent French was one of her accomplishments. Keats himself said that she was not attracted to him for his poetry. Her adolescent passion for the serious works of Byron did not commend itself to his taste.

There is no reason to suppose that his description of her and her behaviour, in the letter he now started to George and Georgiana, was not a perfectly sincere one. It was not an attempt to disguise his own feelings, but a straightforward account of how Fanny Brawne appeared to him at this stage:

> She is about my height—with a fine style of countenance of the lengthen'd sort—she wants sentiment in every feature—she manages to make her hair look well—her nostrills are fine—though a little painful—her mouth is bad and good—her Profil is better than her full-face which indeed is not full but pale and thin without showing any bone—Her shape is very graceful and so are her movements—her Arms are good her hands badish—her feet tolerable—she is not seventeen—but she is ignorant— monstrous in her behaviour flying out in all directions, calling people such names—that I was forced lately to make use of the term *Minx*—this is I think not from any innate vice but from a penchant she has for acting stylishly. I am however tired of such style and shall decline any more of it.

This, written in the middle of December, sounds reasonably enough like an impression after about a month's acquaintance. It is interesting to compare it with her impression, twenty years later,[11] of her early acquaintance with him:

> His conversation was in the highest degree interesting, and his spirits good, excepting at moments when anxiety regarding his brother's health dejected them.

The meeting then took place before Tom's death, sometime in this grey month of November.[12] This is confirmed by the tone of Keats's first remarks about her to George on December 16th:

> Mrs Brawne who took Brown's house for the Summer, still resides in Hampstead—she is a very nice woman—and her daughter senior is I think beautiful and elegant, graceful, silly, fashionable and strange we have a little tiff now and then—and she behaves a little better, or I must have sheered off—

This sounds like a fairly, though not entirely recent acquaintance, especially when we remember that at this time he was about eighteen months out in his estimate of her age—an unlikely situation if he had known the family any length of time. In fact the first and strongest impressions he had of her were that she was very young and that she was petite. Both, in spite of her extravagant social manner, were points of strong attraction. George after all had married a girl of sixteen; there was something in the Keats make-up which preferred immaturity in women, and this was intensified in John by self-consciousness about his short stature. "An imperial woman" like Charmian was remote, and love for such a one a "cry to take the moon home". Isabella Jones, however warm and generous, was cultured and self-assured, a woman of the world. Her moods and prohibitions, though he respected them, evidently puzzled him; she remained an enigma to him.

Fanny Brawne, in spite of her fashionable manners and her penchant for "acting stylishly", was certainly neither remote nor enigmatic; her more extravagant behaviour was probably a sign that she was far from being self-assured, and was trying to overcome her immature appearance. No letter from her to Keats survives; but what can be gathered from his own letters to her, six months later, indicates that hers were ingenuous in feeling and conventional in phrase. The contrast between her and Isabella is pointed by the way in which both received the same piece of news two years later. Both were shown Severn's letter from Naples, in which he wrote that the sight of Keats's sufferings had just caused him to shed, unseen by Keats, a "shower of tears". Fanny Brawne commented[13]

> how lowering to the spirits it must have been when Mr Severn who I never imagined it was possible for any thing to make unhappy, who I never saw for ten minutes serious, says he was so overcome . . .

Isabella Jones remarked[14]

> I never saw so much egotism and selfishness displayed under the mask of feeling and friendship—I got through the first letter, pretty well; I did not like his flood of tears "en parenthese" . . .

These are certainly two points of view, the simple and the sophisticated.

How far Keats fell in love at first sight must remain unsure. Men generally tell their fiancées that they did, and Keats was not free from this normal human habit. The impression left by his first words about her is not unlike the account he gave later:[15]

> The very first week I knew you I wrote myself your vassal; but burnt the Letter as the very next time I thought you manifested some dislike to me.

This may well have been the occasion when Fanny was "monstrous in her behaviour".

The attraction was certainly there; but it has not been enough appreciated that Keats's description of Fanny, oddly flattering and unflattering, lies in that part of his letter to George which he always reserved for "a little quizzing"—i.e. amusing gossip—with his sister-in-law. There is no reason to suppose, since it occurs about other subjects in all the letters, that this was a deep-laid and roundabout scheme for introducing a serious topic to his brother. The subject of Fanny Brawne and her unprepossessing girl-friend, Caroline Robinson, to whom Keats and Brown seem to have been boisterously rude, appears in the same breath as "the thing Kingston"—Wordsworth's acquaintance, the pompous Controller of Stamps, whom Lamb had so baited at Haydon's famous party a year before, taking a candle to "look at that gentleman's organs". In the next sentence Keats remarks, "I shall insinuate some of these Creatures into a Comedy some day". That he still thought of Fanny Brawne at this time as a creature in a comedy is shown by the nickname he applied to her several weeks later—Millamant.[16]

At any rate Keats, by Thursday, December 17th, was "tired of such style", and also of the overdone gaiety of the past ten days. Poetry had gone by the board. On this Thursday, however, the weather was fine and frosty, the house for once quiet, and Bentley, his former landlord of No. 1 Well Walk, had just staggered in with a clothes-basket of Keats's books from his old lodgings. Unpacking them had been a reminder to Keats; he must begin again with his own poetry. "I live under an everlasting restraint—never relieved except when I am composing—so I will write away."

(*Hyperion* Book II, 101-end)

5

LEIGH HUNT AND ROBERT BURTON

AND write away he did. The next morning, he speaks of *Hyperion*—and of other poems:[1]

> I think you knew before you left England that my next
> subject would be "the fall of Hyperion" I went on a little
> with it last night—but it will take some time to get into
> the vein again. I will not give you any extracts because
> I wish the whole to make an impression—I have however
> a few Poems which you will like and I will copy out on
> the next sheet.

He did not, in fact, copy these poems until just over a fortnight
later, when he transcribed in full the poems *Fancy* and *Bards of
Passion*; but it is certain that both these poems were written
on December 17th, perhaps in preparation for making his
pen less "goutty" for the beginning of the third book of
Hyperion. The day before there is no mention of them, nor of
"the Shadow of an idea"; the day after, they are there, full-
grown. If 150 lines in a day, as well as the attempt to restart
the long poem that night, may seem astonishing, we have again
to remember how fast Keats worked, especially at times when
the current of his spirit had been unnaturally dammed up.

Nor is that all. With the poems before him in the fortnight
before he sent them abroad, Keats made fair way into the
third book of *Hyperion*. Seen side by side with the minor
poems, the first sixty lines show complete evidence of having
been composed at the same time and in the same mood.
Perhaps only the early lines, alluding plainly to Tom's death,
were the work of this first evening:

> A solitary sorrow best befits
> Thy lips, and antheming a lonely grief.

Yet the rest followed quickly. It is not merely that these lines share a large poetic vocabulary with the two poems. It might be argued that roses, nightingales, lilies, lawns, bubbles, blushes, rustles, whispers, wine and lips are commonplaces of poetry, and that words such as "antheming", "goblet", or "melodious" might occur anywhere; but when we look at what Keats cancelled in his draft of *Hyperion*, and see that the faint-lipped shells of that poem were originally, like "Autumn's fruitage" in *Fancy*, red-lipped; that Hyperion himself, like Fancy too, originally *roamed* rather than "wandered forth"; that the calm-throated nightingale of *Hyperion* was originally partnered by a sleek-throated mouse in *Fancy*—then there can be no doubt that the larger fragment and the smaller poems were written in the same primary burst of inspiration.

What had touched off the spark? The alternating current of attraction and repulsion aroused by Fanny Brawne had something to do with it. There is a strong note of

> If she be not so to me,
> What care I how fair she be

about *Fancy*. Yet from the literary side there is one certain influence, neglected until now because it has been dismissed as trivial by Keats himself. What seems a triviality to a great poet often makes a great poem; even a poet's dislikes may resolve themselves in verse, and so it is here. Nothing, in fact, better illustrates how Keats could transmute the commonplace into unconscious gold than his work on December 17th, 1818.

It is sad to think that the base metal upon which Keats unconsciously went to work was Leigh Hunt. Keats owed some of the best as well as the worst of his life to Hunt, and he had, in the end, a fair appreciation of the older writer; but at this moment, Hunt had reached the low-watermark of his opinion. Hunt's habit, which Keats had noted, of damning the best things by his association with them, had now a specially bitter taste in Keats's mouth; he had damned Keats himself with the critics, for it was Keats's known association with Hunt which had produced the bad reviews of *Endymion*. Hunt never stood lower with Keats, in fact, than at the unfortunate party to

which he had recently taken him and Brown. Brown did not
hide his disgust, while Keats reproduced the party in a dialogue
which so strongly reminds one of Blake's satire *An Island in the
Moon*, that it is worth printing it in a rather more regular
dramatic form than Keats's hasty letter-writing had time to
achieve:[2]

> *Scene: a little parlour. Enter Hunt, Gattie (Ollier's brother-
> in-law), Hazlitt, Mrs. Novello, Ollier.*

GATTIE Ha! Hunt! Got into your new house? Ha!
Mrs. Novello, seen "Altham and His Wife"?

MRS. N. Yes (*with a grin*). It's Mr. Hunt's, isn't it?

GATTIE Hunt's? No! Ha! Mr. Ollier, I congratulate
you upon the highest compliment I ever heard
paid to the book! . . . Mr. Hazlitt, I hope you
are well?

HAZLITT Yes, sir . . . no, sir . . .

HUNT (*singing at the piano*) La Biondina! (*ad lib*) Hazlitt,
did you ever hear this? (*sings*) La Biondina!
(*ad lib*).

HAZLITT Oh no, sir . . . I never . . .

OLLIER Do, Hunt, give it us over again! Divino!

GATTIE Divino! Hunt, when does your Pocket Book
come out?

HUNT (*singing*) What is this absorbs me quite? (*to the
others*) O, we are spinning on a little; we shall
floridize soon, I hope. Such a thing was very
much wanting. People think of nothing but
money-getting. Now, for me, I am rather
inclined to the liberal side of things. I am
reckoned lax in my Christian principles. . . .

Keats's gift of satire was never better; all the most unfortunate
side of Hunt's style, personal and literary, is expressed in the
word "floridize", and its full significance had just been laid
bare to the world in the Pocket Book mentioned in the dialogue.

This was *The Literary Pocket Book* for 1819, a copy of which
was given and inscribed to Keats by Hunt himself. In form,
the diary—for that is what it is—is a small red leather wallet

with a tuck-in flap, rather like a bank pass-book.[3] In content, it consists of twelve essays on the months of the year, each headed by a stanza from Spenser's *The Faerie Queene*, Book VII, Canto vii; then there is the diary, with blank pages opposite for memoranda; a list of famous artistic and literary anniversaries; a compendium of the principal events, centres, and places of artistic interest in London, and finally an anthology of poems, including some of Keats's own. It is an ordinary Christmas gift-book, innocuous enough if it were not for the opening essays, which explain why Keats found the book, as he said, "full of the most sickening stuff you can imagine". To see what this stuff was, it is only necessary to read a few paragraphs from Hunt's opening essay on January:

> ...January is the coldest month of the year, the winter having now strengthened by continuance. To those, however, who cultivate their health and imagination, life has always enjoyments and nature is full of beauties. The frost sets our victorious firesides sparkling; and with our feet upon a good warm rug, we may either double enjoy the company of friends, or get into summer landscapes in our books, or sit and hear
>
> > The excluded tempest idly rave along
> > > Thomson
>
> Our wisest ancestors—those of Shakespeare's time—who understood most things better than we, and whom we begin to understand better than any of their posterity— knew how to take the roughly kind hint of nature, and kept up their Christmas festivities through the whole of this month. They got a little and enjoyed everything, instead of getting everything and enjoying a little. . . .
>
> Even to observe nature is to enjoy her. He is infinitely mistaken, who thinks there is nothing worth seeing in winter-time out of doors, because the sun is not warm and the streets are muddy. Let him get, by dint of good exercise, out of the streets, and he shall find enough. In the warm neighbourhood of the towns he may still watch the field-fares, thrushes, and blackbirds: the titmouse seeking its food through the straw-thatch; the red-wings, field-fares, skylarks, and tit-larks upon the same errand over wet meadows; the sparrows, and yellow-hammers, and chaffinches, still beautiful, though mute, gleaning

from the straw and chaff in the farm-yards; and the ring-dove, always poetical . . .

. . . But the very frost itself is a world of pleasure and fairy beauty. The snow dances down to earth, filling all the airy vacancy with a giddy whiteness; and minutely inspected, every particle is a chrystal star, the delight perhaps of myriads of invisible eyes. The ice (hereafter destined to "temper dulcet creams" for us in the heat of summer) affords a new and rare pastime for the skaiter. . . .

So the cosy, facile prose runs on, like water dripping from a lukewarm tap, full of tea-party sentiment and, perhaps even worse, an affected heartiness. This is Hunt at his least creditable, and in judging him, we should not forget how much better he could write. We should also not forget that here, obviously, is the germ of much of the thought and expression of Keats's two poems. The imagination which defies the frost and, seated by a warm fireside, gets "into summer landscapes" is first-cousin to Keats's Fancy, who is capable of bringing him, as the poem says, "All delights of summer weather", though Fancy is mercifully free from the suburban touch of the good warm rug. The winter birds lend their help to the picture, and though Hunt may not precisely have known a titmouse from a tit-lark, he sent his creatures, like Keats's,

Foraging for sticks and straw.

Even Hunt's ice-creams helped Keats in *Fancy* to see Persephone's eye as dulcet. In the middle of this, "Our wisest ancestors—those of Shakespeare's time" give a natural lead to the Bards of Passion and of Mirth, double-lived as the company of friends is double enjoyed in the essay, and lending us their wisdom and teaching in the same way. As for "the ring-dove, always poetical", that useful bird, together with the Thomson quotation, was reserved for another, later poem.

So much for the content and much of the verbal feeling of the poems. Their rhythm and form—"a sort of rondeau" as Keats called it—show a different source and strain. It is natural to think of Milton's *L'Allegro* as a source, but what was the source of *L'Allegro* itself? Whatever modern critics may have decided, this is the criticism that Keats read:[4]

It will be no detraction from the powers of Milton's original genius and invention, to remark, that he seems to have borrowed the subject of *L'Allegro* and *Il Penseroso*, together with some particular thoughts, expressions, and rhymes, more especially the idea of a contrast between these two dispositions, from a forgotten poem prefixed to the first edition of BURTON'S ANATOMIE OF MELANCHOLY, entitled, "The Author's Abstract of Melancholy; or, A Dialogue between Pleasure and Pain."

That was the judgment of Warton, the eighteenth-century critic. It is to be found reprinted in the introduction to Keats's copy of *The Anatomy of Melancholy*. Burton's poem[5] is, far more truly than Keats's pair, "a sort of rondeau", or rather a double rondeau, with alternate verses of pleasure and pain, each ending with a similar refrain. The antithesis of Fancy and Pleasure in the same poem by Keats, with their returning refrains, is, quite apart from the identical metre, a clear echo of this. So are the words, especially when the last section of *Fancy*, which Keats cancelled before publication, is compared with Burton's poem. Burton's

> No gemm, no treasure like to this,
> 'Tis my delight, my crown, my bliss

and·

> I'll not change life with any King,
> I ravisht am:

have clearly made their mark; while this single stanza of Burton holds the essence and much of the substance of this part of *Fancy*:

> Me thinks I court, methinks I kiss,
> Me thinks I now embrace my mistriss.
> O blessed dayes, O sweet content,
> In Paradise my time is spent.
> Such thoughts may still my fancy move,
> So may I ever be in love.

This is the beginning of the alliance between Keats and the work which, according to Boswell, was the only book that ever got Dr. Johnson out of bed two hours earlier than he wished to rise. It weaves itself in and out of his thought and style all through the next nine months and more. It is no detraction, in Warton's phrase, from Keats's original genius and invention, to say that some of his finest subjects and their expression in both prose and poetry were taken from Burton's closely-packed pages; Burton, in fact, is the true pocket book or diary of Keats's literary life from now onwards. It is the journal which, he promised George, he would now keep regularly, and into which he proposed to copy all his poems as he wrote them. Such a journal was never made; but with Keats's edition of Burton beside us, we may make it, and trace the order and some of the inspiration of the poems as they came to him. The whole idea of *Fancy* is reinforced in the first few pages of Burton's prose introduction to the reader:[6]

> . . . *not to be a slave of one science, or dwell altogether in one subject, as most do, but to rove abroad,* centum puer artium, *to have an oar in every mans boat, to taste of every dish, and to sip of every cup:*

This is Keats's

> Sit thee there and send abroad,
> With a mind self-overawed,
> Fancy. . . .
> She will mix these pleasures up
> Like three fit wines in a cup,
> And thou shalt quaff it.

It is not only that Keats was fascinated, as many have been before and since, by dipping into Burton's highly-coloured rag-bag of verbal patterns. That indeed might have been enough for any poet with an ear for words and rhythms.[7] It is clear that Keats marked his copy of Burton as much for the *curiosa felicitas* of the words as for their meaning. Yet it would be a mistake to think that Keats merely used Burton as a verbal aperitif for his poetry. His methodical marking, and even more, his marginal notes show that he was following as much as anything the philosophic argument and the thought. Burton may not seem to us a philosophic author, and certainly not an original one; he has, as he himself said, "laboriously

collected this cento out of divers writers", and he takes pains
to show that his book is in reality a disguised anthology of the
opinions and thoughts of other writers. We might see more
of psychology than philosophy in the result, and say that more
than half the interest of the *Anatomy* lies in its being a case-book
of the author's own great and neurotic personality. Whether
as that or as philosophy, it was at once in sympathy with
Keats's needs at this time. He had a tendency to what he
himself recognized as morbidity of temperament, a tendency
"to bode ill like the raven". At the same time, he had long
felt the need to reconcile this private brooding with the outer
world by some system of what he roughly called "philosophy".
The great reality of his brother's death had now made such a
reconciliation urgent. He felt he must start afresh in thought
and feeling. He realized more clearly than before that "his
enjoyment in the different states of human society must depend
upon the Powers of his Mind" and that "the more we know the
more inadequacy we discover in the world to satisfy us". On
the New Year's Eve on which he wrote these remarks to George,
in a passage which already shows Burton's purely verbal
influence, he had been sitting down to face the world and its
problems much in the spirit in which Burton describes his own
life:[8]

> Amidst the gallantry and misery of the world, jollity,
> pride, perplexities and cares, simplicity and villany,
> subtlety, knavery, candour and integrity, mutually mixt
> and offering themselves, I rub on, *privus privatus:*

Would "the gallantry and misery of the world" allow Keats to
enjoy this solitary sensation and the rebirth of poetry which it
had brought?

(*Fancy, Bards of Passion, Hyperion* III, 1–60)

6

HUSH, HUSH AND ISABELLA JONES

KEATS at once felt the conflict of his situation. On the very morning of December 18th, with two new poems and his epic re-started, he wrote to George[1] "I must do it—I must wait at home, and let those who will come to see me. I cannot always be (how do you spell it?) trapsing." To Woodhouse he wrote even more explicitly, though with even less care about spelling:[2] "look here Woodhouse—I have a new leaf to turn over—I must work—I must read—I must write—I am unable to affrod time for new acquaintances." Woodhouse had wanted him to meet a lady novelist; but the suggestion which alarmed him was that he should go into the country with Brown, to visit Dilke's father and mother at Chichester and Laetitia Snook, Dilke's married sister, at Bedhampton, just over the Hampshire border. It was a further campaign of distraction. "They say I shall be very much amused." Reluctantly, he seems to have accepted. When Brown went off in the coach to Chichester during the week-end of December 19th-20th, it was agreed that Keats would follow at least by Christmas Day. Keats wanted to see his sister again before he left London, and this he did, walking over to Walthamstow on the frosty morning of Monday, December 21st. This may have been the occasion of a poem, for just about this time, Keats wrote the charming song *I had a Dove*. He transcribed it for George shortly afterwards, calling it "a little thing I wrote off to some Music as it was playing". Fanny Keats played the piano, and enlivened her dull and restricted life at the Abbeys by keeping livestock, rabbits and pigeons. Keats ended a nonsense poem to her, a few months later, with the lines

> Two or three dove eggs
> To hatch into sonnets—

which might well be a reference to this song.

54

At all events, Keats had to hurry back to a late dinner engagement with Haydon at the painter's studio in Lisson Grove. This was an important meeting for several unforeseen reasons. Keats let himself go, as he often did in Haydon's expansive company, and was in full cry—"rhodomontading"—when he found himself without an audience; Haydon had slipped out of the room. Keats was not offended; perhaps he guessed a reason, as we may too. Haydon was perpetually in debt; the crises in this state always grow acute towards quarter-day, now only a few days off. There was probably a dun at the door. The subject of money, unluckily for Keats, was introduced during the evening. Haydon's eye-trouble still prevented him from working at his picture of *Christ's Entry into Jerusalem*, but he had a new project of putting himself before the world, this time as a teacher. He was planning to open an exhibition in the West End of the work of his more talented pupils—the Landseers and others. This would need capital. Haydon was as much a man of the world as Brown. Both genuinely loved Keats, but some mixed motives must be suspected in the intense interest that both now began to take in him. They must have realized that a share of his dead brother's money was due now to come to John. Keats was always carried away by his own generous moods, though he had the caution to ask Haydon to "ask the rich lovers of art first" when the inevitable request for money came.[3]

Yet Haydon had, indirectly, "a treat" to give Keats at this meeting, or perhaps at a further dinner (to "bare" his "Soul"), which he hastily arranged a few days later.[4] Keats describes it as second only to Shakespeare:

> I looked over a Book of Prints taken from the fresco of the Church at Milan the name of which I forget—in it are comprised Specimens of the first and second age of art in Italy. . . . Full of Romance and the most tender feeling—magnificence of draperies beyond any I ever saw not excepting Raphael's. But Grotesque to a curious pitch—yet still making up a fine whole—even finer to me than more accomplished works—as there was left so much room for Imagination.

There is little wonder that Keats forgot the name of the church in Milan, since there is nothing in Milan that resembles his description except perhaps the Luini frescoes in the Church of San Maurizio in the Monastero Maggiore. It has been assumed that the book was the collection of engravings by Carlo Lasinio of the Campo Santo at Pisa, the work of Benozzo Gozzoli and others; this is confirmed from another source, the *Autobiography* of Leigh Hunt. It is pleasant for a change to give two examples of Hunt's prose at its sympathetic best. Hunt visited the Campo Santo frescoes themselves in 1822, a year after Keats's death. In his autobiography he wrote:[5]

> They have the germs of beauty and greatness, however obscured and stiffened; the struggle of true pictorial feeling with the inexperience of art. . . . They are like a dream of humanity during the twilight of creation.

And again:[6]

> —the profusion of attitudes, expressions, incidents, broad draperies, ornaments of all sorts, visions, mountains, ghastly-looking cities, fiends, angels, sibylline old women, dancers, virgin brides, mothers and children, princes, patriarchs, dying saints; it would be a simply blind injustice to the superabundance and truth of conception in all this multitude of imagery not to recognize the real inspirers as well as harbingers of Raphael and Michelangelo . . .

His description is longer and more vivid, for he had seen the original colours under an Italian sky, while Keats had merely studied the black-and-white approximations of the print-book; but it is clearly the same artistic experience, and one which sank deeply into Keats's imagination.

The third result of the exertions of this day was that Keats woke up the next morning with a sore throat. Much play has been made about this sore throat by Keats's biographers, but it seems to have been a simple enough though tiresome complaint which had troubled him on and off for the past year; it may even have been due, rather unromantically, to bad teeth.[7] At all events, it was enough to make him postpone the journey by coach to Chichester for another month, though it did not prevent him from going out and visiting friends during the daytime. According to the Reynolds family, with whom he cut an engagement, he spent Christmas Day with the Brawnes. Fanny Brawne recalled this day as the happiest she had then spent.[8] It was probably the first occasion on which he came alone to her house, and she was able to see him as himself, without the company of the Dilkes or Brown. Keats and the Dilkes dined with Mrs. Brawne again just over a week later; he seems to have spent a good deal of time with Dilke and his wife, who had written a charming note of warning about Keats to her parents-in-law at Chichester—"You will find him a very odd young man, but good-tempered and very clever indeed." Many of his days were unfortunately occupied by visits to the City on two fruitless quests. One was to persuade Abbey to keep Fanny Keats at school; the other was to raise money for Haydon. Both did nothing more than exasperate his former guardian, who retreated into a shell of disapproval, vagueness, and obstinacy, in which he even began to object to Keats writing letters to his own sister. He contrived to keep Keats short of cash for his own needs, so that we find the poet writing to his publisher, Taylor, begging a loan for himself and Haydon. It is not known what answer Taylor, a generous but cautious man, gave. There is talk of writing, but only one poem appears during these four weeks; it is a minor one, but connected with major work and events in the history of this year.

Among the people he visited to relieve these tedious hours in Town was Isabella Jones in Gloucester Street. Her presents of game, begun as a kindness to the invalid Tom, continued to such an extent that Keats was obliged to give some of them away to friends.[9] On Wednesday, January 20th, Keats spent the night in Town before catching the early coach the next morning for his long-postponed visit to Chichester and Bedhampton. The date, which can be inferred from a careful study of his letters both before and after the visit,[10] has a significance for Keats which has never before been explored. In his copy of the *Literary Pocket Book*, there is written a version of his lyric *Hush, hush, tread softly*. Just opposite the third stanza, in the diary-space for January 4th, there are the pencilled words "Written (*illegible*) twenty first of January". On January 21st, then, Keats broke a poetic silence of a month

by writing an extremely lively lyric about an evening flirtation
with a lady called Isabel, who has some elderly and choleric
gentleman lurking in the background.

> Hush, hush! tread softly! hush, hush, my dear!
> All the house is asleep, but we know very well
> That the jealous, the jealous old bald-pate may hear,
> Tho' you've padded his night-cap—O sweet Isabel!
> Tho' your feet are more light than a Faery's feet,
> Who dances on bubbles where brooklets meet,—
> Hush, hush! soft tiptoe! hush, hush, my dear!
> For less than a nothing the jealous can hear.
>
> No leaf doth tremble, no ripple is there
> On the river,—all's still, and the night's sleepy eye
> Closes up, and forgets all its Lethean care,
> Charm'd to death by the drone of the humming May-fly;
> And the moon, whether prudish or complaisant,
> Has fled to her bower, well knowing I want
> No light in the dusk, no torch in the gloom,
> But my Isabel's eyes, and her lips pulp'd with bloom.
>
> Lift the latch! ah gently! ah tenderly—sweet!
> We are dead if that latchet gives one little clink!
> Well done—now those lips, and a flowery seat—
> The old man may sleep, and the planets may wink;
> The shut rose shall dream of our loves and awake
> Full-blown, and such warmth for the morning's take,
> The stock-dove shall hatch her soft brace and shall coo,
> While I kiss to the melody, aching all through!

Keats's Fancy had brought him "all delights of summer
weather" with a vengeance. Yet this is not fancy at all; it is
an actual description of the place where he had first met
Isabella Jones, where they had first "warmed" to each other
and kissed. The lyric has always been dismissed as merely
fanciful for a variety of reasons. It has been called a song,
whereas Keats's rough manuscript gave it no title; it was misdated 1818 by Brown. The name Isabel has appeared to be
an assumed name, put in for the rhyme. Moreover one of the
Reynolds sisters, in her extreme old age, claimed that Keats
had composed it to a tune she played to him.[11] Yet, like every-

Song

1

Hush, hush, tread softly, hush, hush my dear,
All the house is asleep, but we know very well,
That the jealous, the jealous, old Baldpate may hear,
Though you've padded his nightcap, O sweet Isabel,
Though your feet are more light than a fairie's
Who dances on bubbles where brooklets meet.
Hush, hush, tread softly, hush, hush my dear,
For less than a nothing the jealous can hear.

2

No leaf doth tremble, no ripple is there
On the river — all's still and the night's sleepy eye
Closes up, and forgets all its Lethean care
Charmed to death by the drone of the humming may
And the moon whether prudish or complaisant,
Hath fled to her bower, well knowing, I wa[a]l
No light in the darkness no torch in the gloom,
But my Isabel's eyes and her lips pulped with bloom.

STANZAS 1 AND 2 OF KEATS'S LYRIC 'HUSH, HUSH'.

From Keats's copy of the Literary Pocket Book for
1819.

THE NEW ENGLAND BANK INN, BO PEEP, HASTINGS. From a print, circa 1820.

thing that Keats wrote in this year, it is based on real events
and living circumstances.

When he first met Isabella Jones in 1817, at the end of May
or the beginning of June, Keats had been staying at the tiny
seaside resort of Bo Peep, near Hastings. He had just finished
Book I of *Endymion*, and was collecting his thoughts for Book II.
The place had probably been recommended to him by
Haydon,[12] who had stayed three years before in the only
available accommodation there. This was the charmingly-
situated inn called *The New England Bank*, which stood on the
site of the present Western Marina station. From rising ground
near the foot of the cliff, it overlooked distant Beachy Head, the
Channel, a Martello Tower, and the only other neighbouring
building, a coastguard station. A garden, where company
might have "an excellent dish of tea and good cream al fresco"
sloped down to the rough and winding shore road, which led
from Hastings to Bexhill.[13] Across the road, a little river
flowed parallel with it for several hundred yards before taking
a sudden turn into the sea, much in the manner described by
Keats later in *Hyperion* Book II:

> like timorous brook
> That, lingering along a pebbled coast,
> Doth fear to meet the sea.

At Hastings too Isabella's old and touchy Mr. O'Callaghan
was in the habit of spending the summer,[14] and here Keats
met her. He romantically portrayed the encounter in the first
140-odd lines of *Endymion* Book II, where in similar scenery and
beside a river in early summer, among the dancing water-
flies and the wild-roses, the hero meets a somewhat enigmatic
nymph of the stream. Now, eighteen months later, his memory
revived by his new association with her, he drew the picture
much more realistically. The same images are there. The
picture of the wild-rose bud which becomes in a moment full-
blown comes from the passage in *Endymion*:

> a wild rose tree
> Pavillions him in bloom, and he doth see
> A bud which snares his fancy: lo! but now
> He plucks it, dips its stalk in the water: how
> It swells, it buds, it flowers beneath his sight;

"The evening's sleepy frown" of the riverside scene in *Endymion* has become "the night's sleepy eye" of the same scene in the lyric. In the new poem, however, the love affair has become real, warm, and tangible, while behind it is the figure of "the jealous old bald-pate", whose nightcap has to be padded—that is, he has to be given, perhaps, a stiff dose of late-night Scotch whisky—before the lovers can meet and creep through the little gate to the meadow, and kiss in safety. All this is exact and vivid; yet the importance of it is not so much that it is a new chapter in Keats's life, but that it is also closely connected with one of his finest poems, *The Eve of St. Agnes*.

Hush, hush, in fact, is a miniature rehearsal for the great poem which Keats began to write directly he arrived in Chichester. There are strong likenesses. A cancelled opening to stanza viii of *The Eve of St. Agnes* shows the lines

> She danced along with vague uneager eyes,
> Her anxious lips full pulp'd with rosy thoughts,

which at once recall

> But my Isabel's eyes, and her lips pulp'd with bloom.

In another early stanza of *St. Agnes*, Keats's first draft actually used the exclamation "Hush, hush!" itself. *The Eve of St. Agnes* is a Romeo and Juliet story of lovers surrounded by enemies and befriended by an old nurse to a happier end than Shakespeare's pair. It has often rightly been compared to Shakespeare's play, which it matches in beauty, dramatic dialogue, and romantic atmosphere. Yet it is not trivial to see how it also shares the atmosphere of the little lyric.

> We are dead if that latchet gives one little clink!

anticipates the hero and heroine of the greater poem, stealing at midnight from the sleeping hall. It is not in the least incongruous to think of Isabella's old O'Callaghan as the ancestor of "that old Lord Maurice" and the other "hot-blooded lords" whose presence threatens the safety of the lovers in *The Eve of St. Agnes*; for the poem itself was suggested by Isabella.

About two years later, probably at the time of Keats's death, Richard Woodhouse added this note to the copy of *The Eve of St. Agnes* which he had made in his MS. Book:

> St Agnes day is the 21st of January.
> The Poem was written on the suggestion of Mrs Jones.

Isabella was just the person to have suggested such a poem. Keats later spoke of *The Eve of St. Agnes* as a poem written on a popular superstition; Isabella's letters show her to have been well acquainted with such superstitions, especially those relating to friendship and love.[15] The poem has a background very like that of the tales of mystery and horror associated with the Mrs. Radcliffe school of writers. Isabella read these writers and used their phrases,[16] traces of which are to be found throughout *The Eve of St. Agnes*. Woodhouse knew her well enough, either now or later, to set her down without question as the inspirer of the poem. It seems likely enough that she suggested it to Keats on the very night of the legend, January 20th, when he visited her before his journey south, and this may account for the laconic tone in which he mentions the poem. Even to George he never forgot his promise to Isabella, and never so much as hinted who the "Hastings lady" might be. The reason why Isabella Jones is never mentioned by name in any of Keats's letters, although she suggested one of his greatest poems, is because she herself wished that she and Keats "should be acquainted without any of our common acquaintance knowing it".[17]

It is also pretty clear how much of *The Eve of St. Agnes* she suggested. Woodhouse's brief note implies that her suggestion was a poem on the subject of the legend that on St. Agnes Eve—January 20th—a girl could dream of her husband-to-be. She did not suggest the plot of the young man actually appearing and making the heroine's vision real. That plot has been plausibly traced to a story by Boccaccio;[18] and here one is reminded of the prose "Tale", spoken of by Reynolds, which Keats had still been promising to write as recently as December 18th. That plot, never to be written in prose, had been simmering in his mind for months. The explanation of *The Eve of St. Agnes* not being mentioned previously, in his letters or anywhere else, is that it was identical in plot with the prose tale. Just as the "Hastings lady" of Keats's letters is one and the same as "Mrs. Jones" of Woodhouse's note, so the mysterious tale is the same as the poem. The lady and the story are intimately mixed; for it was the legendary subject, suggested by Isabella Jones, which brought Reynolds's suggestion from Boccaccio into life and poetry in Keats's excited brain.

Isabella Jones may have brought it to life in a very particular sense. Keats spent the night of January 20th, St. Agnes Eve, in Town before catching the early-morning coach to Chichester. On January 21st he wrote the lyric recounting the successful love-affair with Isabella, and started writing *The Eve of St. Agnes*. In the latter poem, Keats insisted that the love-affair between his hero and heroine on St. Agnes Eve was actually consummated. When he revised the poem in the autumn, he got into hot water with his publishers for adding and altering lines in three places to make it clear that this was so. The lines were decorous enough, but Keats "rhodomontaded" to such an extent on the subject that it is obvious he set great store by them.[19] In fact, he does not seem to have given them up, even in the face of Taylor's threat to refuse his imprint to such a poem, until he fell ill in 1820. It was in those months of illness that he allowed Taylor and Woodhouse to do more or less what they liked with the poem in proof, and the offending phrases were expunged. His own vehemence on this point made it likely that this side of the story was a real experience. There is, too, the added incident of the luxurious feast, accompanied by music, in the heroine's room. This was entirely introduced by Keats; it does not appear either in the traditional legend of St. Agnes Eve, nor in the Boccaccio story. Keats was at pains, in some of the expunged lines, to emphasise this incident, and to enumerate

> Viands and wine and fruit and sugar'd cream,
> To touch her palate with the fine extreme
> Of relish: then soft music heard;

This is a reminder of Keats's first impression of Isabella's surroundings, the seemingly inexhaustible supply of game at her command, together with "music . . . a Case of choice Liqueurs, &c. &c. &c."

Keats was a normal young man of his time in many ways, in spite of being "a very odd young man" in others. Extraordinary as his gifts were, he was young enough and ordinary enough to make, only a few days later, the usual youthful pun on the name of the place where he was going to stay, about a young woman "here in Bed—hampton." In his "rhodomontade" about the offending passages in *St. Agnes*, he said, according to Woodhouse, "that he sh^d despise a man who should be such an eunuch in sentiment as to leave a maid, with that Character about her, in such a situation". If such a situation presented itself to him on the evening of January 20th—as we may believe by the lyric it did—it is at least possible that he lived up to his words. It is certainly one explanation of the mood of heightened and sensuous exhilaration in which he began his great poem on the following day.

(*I had a Dove* and *Hush, hush, tread softly*)

7

ST. AGNES EVE AND CHICHESTER

THE light-hearted *Hush, hush* represents the mood in which
Keats arrived at Chichester; he may even have written it
in the coach, for it goes to a galloping rhythm. The day on
which he travelled was fine, sunny, and not too cold, and
Chichester, in the late afternoon light, has a particular charm.
The city, then as now, retained its original Roman plan of
four streets at right angles, North, South, East, and West, with
its 12th century cathedral in the south-west quarter, and its
fine Tudor market-cross where the four roads met. The houses
had been largely rebuilt in the eighteenth century, when the
bounty on corn and the demand for wool by the northern
manufacturing towns brought great prosperity to this city near
the sheep-breeding downs and in the middle of arable lands,
where, as Cobbett observed, the corn ripened earlier than in
any other part of England. These "new-built" houses, as
their deeds describe them, made Chichester the Georgian
City that it has been called today, and their warm red brick,
beautifully-proportioned lines, and the dignity of their door-
ways and fanlights still witness to the good taste of their local
architects. At evening, the regular streets glow with a well-
tempered urbanity. Keats would have seen the city first as he
came over the spur of the downs and entered by North Gate,
to be met at one of the many coaching-inns in the centre of
the city by Charles Brown, for his host was old and his hostess,
particularly in winter, delicate. Together they walked along
East Street, and actually passed again outside the city walls,
where Keats found himself in the somewhat curious eastern
entrance to the city.

This was the projection outside the city walls of the parish
of St. Pancras; it had once housed the traditional industry of
needle-making, but its buildings had been practically levelled to
the ground by the siege-guns of the Cromwellians in the Civil

War. There was, however, at that time, a relic of the ancient industry, which Keats would have seen, and which is described in some MS. reminiscences of an old Chichester resident:[1]

> . . . now William for many years a large building stand in that place, called the darnen needles you must know that the road on each side of that building was very narrow, as you went from the east street to the St. Pancrase or the Hornet there was only just room for one trap to pass at a time. . . .

Passing to the right of this oddly-named building—later corrupted to "the Dardanelles" and pulled down about a hundred years ago—Keats found himself outside the house rented by Mr. and Mrs. Dilke. It still stands, No. 11 Eastgate Square, then known as Hornet Square, owing to its proximity to the thoroughfare still called The Hornet and mentioned above.

This was one of a small row of tall red-brick houses built about 1780 by a local architect, Thomas Andrewes, who was responsible eleven years later for rebuilding in the same style Chichester's beautiful little theatre, now a warehouse. On December 8th, 1813, an auctioneer's bill gives a complete picture of the house in which Keats was to stay.[2] It was bought by Stephen Wooldridge, a brewer, who let it to the Dilkes in the following summer, a comfortable dwelling for a retired couple ". . . containing in the Basement, excellent Cellarage—Ground Floor, a neat Entrance, Eating Room, 17 ft. 3 in. by 14 ft. 9 in., stucco cornice, and marble chimney piece, dadoed and papered, opening into a handsome Breakfast Room, 18 ft. 6 in. by 10 ft. 9 in. with a semi bay window, Kitchen, Scullery, Wash-house, and a Pantry, with a large Servant's Room over the same. First Floor, a handsome Drawing Room, 18 ft. 8 in. by 17 ft. 6 in. stucco cornice, marble chimney piece, dadoed and papered in compartments, a Bed Chamber annexed, three airy Attics, a good GARDEN, well planted with Fruit Trees, and a Building with a Pit sunk for a Hot House. . ." Even the auctioneer's prose, though, hardly does justice to its delightful situation. From one of the "airy attics", which were doubtless used as spare bedrooms, Keats would have a view, if at the front, right from one side of the city to the other, back along the entire length of East Street, past the Cross, as far as the separate Bell Tower, the unique feature of Chichester Cathedral; from the back, he would look over open orchards as far as the village of Whyke with its ancient church of St. Rumbold.

This house where *The Eve of St. Agnes* was begun is also the setting for the hilarious events described in the joint letter by Brown and Keats now in the Keats Museum.[3] It was into the handsome breakfast room, now a tailor's cutting-room, that Brown burst, wearing Mrs. Dilke's hood, which he had snatched up in the hall outside, and looking "more like an 'oman than I ever could think it possible." The stay in Chichester was dominated by Brown's sense of humour, to which Keats seems to have responded gratefully; he was, as had been intended, "very much amused". So were his hosts; for Brown, as appears elsewhere, had a genius for charming elderly people. In his month's stay, he seems to have made himself a favourite not only with the Dilkes but also with their circle of Chichester society; and that circle revolved round one occupation, card-playing, which provoked Brown to a string of puns. "The family", he wrote, "are *shuffling* to carriage folks for acquaintances, *cutting* their old friends, and *dealing* out pride and folly, while we allow they have got the *odd trick*, but dispute their *honours*." He was accepted by the elderly ladies and retired gentlemen of Chichester, whose Loo tables seem to have formed quite a large item of the city's manufacture.[4]

About these Chichester characters Brown had woven a legend; he was, of course, in love with all the elderly ladies and they were in love with him—"so happy! I have been smiled on by the fair ones, the Lacy's, the Price's, and the Mullins's". Keats must share all this; he played Loo, and so off he went to the card-parties to be introduced to the elderly fair ones. The most important of them, by her position in Chichester society, was Miss Sarah Mullins. Brown called her Mullings; Keats, even more deplorably, Muggins. Brown was pining for her; she had persuaded him to shave his whiskers, so that his face looked like the sign of the full moon. Miss Mullins, the daughter of a former Mayor of the city, lived in West Street, just north of the Cathedral. It has not been possible to find her house, though it may have been one of those near the Bell Tower which were pulled down about a hundred years ago. Poor Miss Mullins, Brown's "fair one", was at that time seventy-two, but the two kindly young men sat solemnly playing cards with her, in the shadow of the Cathedral, till late in the evening: "we sit it out" wrote Keats "till ten o'clock."

Where, then, in this atmosphere of good-natured ragging does *The Eve of St. Agnes* appear—"the only complete and perfect long poem which Keats composed in the course of his life",[5] as one critic, not given to exaggeration, has called it? Poems of this stature and intensity do not spring from nowhere; but it is true, as the same critic has remarked, that "in the minute records of Keats's life, however, there is no mention of *The Eve of St. Agnes* before it was composed".[6] Yet the poem starts at once, fully-assured, perfect, and complete:

> St. Agnes' Eve—Ah, bitter chill it was!
> The owl, for all his feathers, was a-cold;
> The hare limp'd trembling through the frozen grass,
> And silent was the flock in woolly fold:
> Numb were the Beadsman's fingers while he told
> His rosary, and while his frosted breath,
> Like pious incense from a censer old,
> Seem'd taking flight for heaven, without a death,
> Past the sweet Virgin's picture, while his prayer he saith.

The clue lies in the form of the poem;[7] this is quite plainly the nine-line stanza of Spenser's *Faerie Queene*, and it is noteworthy that it is the only time, apart from acknowledged imitations of Spenser, that Keats ever uses it on his own account. Spenser, his first poet, was always in his mind, and indeed, the first words he wrote in the joint letter at this time were a joking quotation from *The Faerie Queene*;[8] but there was one particular reason why that poem should be at his command now. Hunt's essays in *The Literary Pocket Book* had each started with a stanza from *The Faerie Queene*. The essay on January is headed by the stanza beginning

> Then came old Ianuary, wrapped well
> In many weeds to keep the cold away;
> Yet he did quake and quiver like to quell,
> And blowe his nayles to warme them if he may:
> For they were numbd. . . .

Here is form and matter for the opening of the poem, the Spenserian stanza, and the personified figure of January, Keats's Beadsman with numbed fingers; not without a hint too of the stanza a little earlier in Spenser's poem, not quoted by Hunt, but close enough to remind Keats, in which the figure of Winter appears

> Chattering his teeth for cold that did him chill,
> Whil'st on his hoary beard his breath did freese;

Then, too, Hunt's cosy insistence on the inevitable coldness of January weather throughout his essay probably added to the chilly picture in Keats's mind, which was certainly not taken from the exceptionally mild weather of this January, 1819.

Apart from weather, there is the larger picture of the whole human scene in the opening stanzas of the poem, the visual counterpoint of the old hermit with his chapel and penitential devotions, and the rout of brilliantly-dressed lords and ladies. These contrasting pictures are set side by side like one of those Italian primitives in which different parts of a narrative are all portrayed in the same continuous fresco, so that all aspects of the same story are at once visible as if taking place at the same time. This, in fact, is what it is. It is the memory of the deep impression made on Keats's mind by the Campo Santo engravings which Haydon had shown him, and especially of the most celebrated as well as the most primitive of them all, the Penances of the Anchorites and the Triumph of Death. These frescoes, which show in multiple pictures the legends of the saints jostling side by side with a great dramatic conception—the gay rout of courtiers of a medieval court suddenly being shown the vision of naked corpses lying in coffins to remind them of their own death—are again described in some of Hunt's better prose:[9]

> The manner in which some of the hoary saints in these pictures pore over their books, and carry their decrepit old age, full of a bent and absorbed feebleness—the set limbs of the warriors on horseback—the sidelong unequivocal looks of some of the ladies playing on harps, and conscious of their ornaments—the people of fashion . . .

Here, seen only recently by Keats, was the juxtaposition of the aged saint, the coffined dead, and the figures of revelry, all "the timbrels and the thronged resort" even down to the details of the musical instruments carried by the medieval court ladies. Moreover, the engravings had impressed him, as he said, with their "magnificence of draperies", and it is on these draperies that Keats was always most insistent when discussing the poem with his publishers. Speaking of future plans for other poems he wrote,[10] "I wish to diffuse the colouring of St. Agnes eve throughout a Poem in which Character & Sentiment would be figures to such drapery", and again, on a proof correction in stanza vii, "I do not use *train* for *concourse of passers by* but for *Skirts* sweeping along the floor."

So much for the form and the matter of the poem; Hunt and Haydon, between them, can claim a great deal of indirect influence, while, for the twin elements of the story, first Reynolds and then Isabella must be regarded as the begetters. A successful love-affair with Isabella, with, at the same time, the lively excitement of the flirtation with Fanny Brawne, combined in the sensuous love-atmosphere of the poem; but as the poem went on, and the details of its setting began to form in Keats's mind, another decidedly different lady also took a hand.

Miss Sarah Mullins presided over one of Keats's two "old Dowager card parties" in Chichester, and Keats himself says he had a second hostess.[11] According to Brown's catalogue of the fair ones of the City, it rests between a Mrs. Lacy and a Mrs. Price. There does not seem to be any record of any old lady called Price at this time. Luckily Keats himself has left us a positive clue. In the first draft of stanza xii of *The Eve of St. Agnes* "that old Lord Maurice", the heroine's dangerous relative described by the nurse, was originally written "old Lord Maurice Lacey". Somebody called Lacy was in Keats's mind at this time, and there is a very good candidate. Just at this time, a Mrs. Lacy moved into a house in the Cathedral Close.[12] She disappears again four years later, which makes her almost certainly the Mrs. Mary Lacy, who was buried in December, 1823, just inside that central part of the Cloisters which is known as the Paradise, not far from the memorial tablet to Miss Mullins. Mrs. Lacy was just 70 in 1819, and

she was evidently one of the card-playing circle. She had lost
her husband in 1814, but a year or so later we find her having
her card-table relined.[13] It seems almost certain that it was
her house which Keats visited, and this visit is likely to have
had remarkable results; for Mrs. Lacy occupied one of the
most striking of the few genuine medieval buildings left in
Chichester.

This was the huge hall, probably the old Gildenhall of the
City, and now known as the Crypt, which dates from the early
12th century, and above it, the Hall of the Priest Vicars Choral,
which replaced an earlier upper storey in the late 14th century.
Mrs. Lacy's actual dwelling quarters were reached by a door
at street level, next to the Crypt or the Vaults as they were then
known, leading up by a winding staircase to the east end of
the Vicars' Hall, overlooking South Street. The whole building,
a stone's throw from the Cathedral Cloisters, lay at an angle
of the Vicars' Close, another square or cloister. The deed[14]
which describes her actual rooms might itself be a prose version
of some of the early lines of Keats's poem:

> . . . all that Tenement at the North Angle of the Close
> or Square late the Cloysters of the said Vicars containing
> several Chambers and Rooms over the Great Cellar afore-
> said of the said Vicars with a little Closet or Study over
> the Church Yard Stile called the Stone Stile one Kitchen
> and Wash house with the Stairs leading up to the said
> Rooms. . . .

It is reasonably certain that Keats visited this remarkable
set of medieval rooms. Even more remarkable are the rooms
and apartments to which his hostess had access. At street level,
there appears to have been a door into the "Great Cellar" of
the deed, which, as the name suggests, had been used for a
long time as a wine-cellar, and had retained the name of the
White Horse Cellar, from the White Horse Inn opposite, since
the later part of the 17th century. At the same time that Mrs.
Lacy moved into the rooms above, these cellars were rented
by a former neighbour of hers from another parish, and it
looks as though the arrangement was made between them.
This neighbour was a wine-merchant named Parker, and his
local brand of milk-punch was well-known. A visit to Mrs.

Lacy could hardly pass without Keats at least peering through the connecting door into the huge vaults with their "broad hall pillars", and the wine-merchant's trade-card preserves for us the sight that he saw there.

When Keats reached the upper rooms occupied by Mrs. Lacy the identification of this medieval architecture with the setting of the poem became even more precise. The "several Chambers and Rooms" were not all occupied by his hostess; some were already sub-let, but she paid the general land-tax for them, and so presumably had the right of entry. Her own dwelling-rooms were partitioned off from the rest by a fine piece of panelling with a connecting door. Once through this door, Keats would stand in the main body of the medieval dining-hall. This splendid room with its beamed ceiling stretched, with its kitchens at the west end, for about seventy feet, but it too had been partitioned off. The part immediately adjoining Mrs. Lacy seems to have been let to a carpenter. It included, according to a visitor[15] to the town, "a small room, apparently intended for confession, rising two steps above the floor . . . , and entered by a narrow stone doorway." One is at once led to the "little moonlight room" of stanza xiii of the poem; but there is more certain proof than that.

This tiny room was not, and had never been used, as a confessional. It was the *pulpitum*, or stone pulpit, from which the appropriate lessons were read at meal-times to the medieval Vicars as they dined in Hall. It is entered from the main hall by a narrow arch, just as described in the poem. Some time shortly after it was built, the Priest Vicars evidently found that whoever was reading the lessons could not see to do so; the only window, looking out into the Vicars' Close, was set low down and at his back so that he was standing in his own light. They therefore had a projection built above the little cell-like pulpit, and set high up in it a stone lattice window. In Keats's original draft of the stanza which describes this room, he wrote the fifth line

Pale latticed high, and silent as a tomb.

He did not change "high" to "chill" until the following autumn, when, in revising the poem, he also used the word in the first stanza to intensify the effect of the cold. As always in a poet's work, he altered the original exact description of the room where he had been to a more general one; but although Time has worked its alterations too, and the high latticed window no longer exists above the little *pulpitum*, a lucky chance has preserved for us exactly what Keats saw. Some time before 1870, when the projection seems to have been pulled down during alterations, Sir Gilbert Scott, who was working on the Cathedral, made a water-colour sketch of the *pulpitum* from the Close outside. This sketch shows the high latticed window exactly as it appears in Keats's line. It is perhaps appropriate that a famous architect should have helped to preserve evidence of the intense medieval atmosphere which pervades the first thirteen stanzas of *The Eve of St. Agnes*. When all verbal debts to Shakespeare, Spenser, and even the romances of Mrs. Radcliffe are reckoned, the architecture of the opening stanzas of the poem is real and accurate, and this must spring from the actual contact between his creative imagination and the thing itself, during Keats's brief stay in Chichester.

(*The Eve of St. Agnes*, stanzas I to XIII)

8

ST. AGNES EVE AND STANSTED

ARCHITECTURE alone can hardly be the godfather of a great poem; it may well be asked if Keats was doing little more than go to parties with ancient ladies in even more ancient buildings. Something must be due to the reading, the intense "study" which always accompanied his work on any poem; there is also the new-found companion to his thought and philosophy, Burton and the *Anatomy*. Just as traces of Shakespeare, Spenser, and Mrs. Radcliffe jostle for recognition throughout *The Eve of St. Agnes*, Robert Burton is in the field too. In a poem which mixes folklore and richness of imagery, it would be surprising if he did not suggest much to Keats's mind. The one thing he cannot have suggested, however, is the part for which he is most often given credit—that is, the legend of St. Agnes herself. In all Burton's immense parade of characters in fact and fiction, ranging from the obstinate Swiss naturalist Gesner to Aretine's imaginary courtesan Lucretia, the name of St. Agnes is never once mentioned.[1]

Yet though Keats did not take the general legend from Burton's crammed pages, the magic and superstition with which he loaded Isabella's original suggestion are obviously to be found in an early chapter of the *Anatomy*, precisely where one would expect to discover them, in the subsection of the book entitled *A Digression of the nature of Spirits*.[2] This chapter, to start with, makes one of the most important contributions to the poem by deciding Keats on his hero's name. It gave him the first impulse to chose the name Porphyro, which he retained in spite of a period when a rather Shelley-like Lionel intervened. It has never before been decided where Porphyro emerged, though Madeline clearly came from Keats's known fondness for the name "Magdalen"; the general opinion has been that Keats was drawing on a memory of Porphyrion, one of the minor Titans in *Hyperion*. In the *Digression of the nature of Spirits* however, one of the chief sources that Burton quotes is the neo-Platonist Porphyrius, who appears on the first page. His later appearances in this chapter, at least half a dozen in all, are usually under the more familiar title of Porphyry, and at one point Burton treats him to the type of inversion in parenthesis—"(saith Porphyry)"—which Keats has directly echoed in stanza xvii with his "Quoth Porphyro", where the verb too was originally "Says" and then "Swear'th" in successive alterations.

When Burton proceeds to the legends of spirits, provided by Porphyry and others, his book and these stanzas of the poem march almost page by page together.[3] Yet Keats's inspiration could never be entirely bookish, particularly at this time. He came down to Chichester to enjoy himself, and his senses were alive to external things. On Saturday, January 23rd, tempted by another fine though windy day, he and Brown decided to walk the thirteen miles to Bedhampton, where Keats was to spend the remainder of his stay. It was a walk which left them in the highest spirits. Every two or three miles they passed the head of each of the several inlets of Chichester Harbour which spread, like the outstretched fingers of a hand, far inland. The sparkle of sun and water and the little hamlets and cottages of the road were a fitting introduction for Keats to the beautiful Georgian mill-house, standing between the upper and lower mill where a little stream runs into the tidal waters of Langstone Harbour. The mill-pond where the swans still float, the garden bridge built by John Snook's old father, and the portly shape of the miller himself, John Snook the Second, promised a comforting and comfortable retreat. Snook, like his father before him, "a man of real worth and unaffected piety", was a homely person[4] and the small talk of religion, politics, and farming was the right commonplace background to that intensity which the creation of a long poem imposes on the poet's day-by-day life.

Brown was still with him, to stay the week-end and to return to London on Tuesday, and it was probably to his continued and well-meaning efforts to provide diversion that Keats owed the memorable excursion which he took on Monday, January 25th. How important this was, and what it was, is hinted by the original version of a single line in the poem. In all manuscripts of *The Eve of St. Agnes*, the first line of stanza xvii runs

I will not harm her, by the great St Paul

and it is probable that the final printed version of the line was made not by Keats but by his publishers, who altered the line to end, "by all saints I swear". There is a good reason why the poet clung obstinately to an unlikely Early Father of the Church for his hero to swear by. Keats used and kept the image which referred to a particular occasion in his own life—the day celebrating the Conversion of St. Paul. On that Saturday at Mr. Snook's house, he and Brown read, in that week's copy of *The Hampshire Telegraph and Sussex Chronicle*, the following advertisement:[5]

STANSTED CHAPEL

The Consecration of the Chapel in Stansted Park will take place on Monday the 25th instant (being the Holyday of the Conversion of St. Paul). . . .—Notice is hereby given, that the Doors will be shut, and the Chapel kept empty . . . 'till the commencement of the Service, when no one will be admitted within the Walls without a ticket. . . . As it is requisite that the Clergy should appear in their Canonicals, a Room will be provided for their accommodation.

"Tomorrow", wrote Brown that Sunday, "we shall go to Sanstead (sic) to see Mr. Way's Chapel consecrated by the two Bigwigs of Gloucester & St. Davids." It was a momentous decision.

At first sight, even allowing for Brown's persuasion, it seems a curious expedition for Keats to make. Though not as publicly anti-clerical as Shelley or Leigh Hunt, he had an almost abnormal loathing of the clergy themselves and of religious ceremonies. He used this very occasion as the theme for a diatribe against the clergy in his letter describing it to George. His going was due to the remarkable reputation of Stansted House itself, or, perhaps, to anyone interested in human nature, the still more remarkable reputation of its owner. A poet who enjoyed "light and shade", and who took a delight in the human oddity of such people as Haydon, could not fail to be curious about the Reverend Lewis Way.

Way, originally a barrister, had inherited a fortune of £300,000 from someone of the same name, not even a relative. He had bought Stansted Park, an estate of 5,500 acres on the borders of Hampshire and Sussex, for just over half that sum,[6] and, inspired by hearsay of another eccentric will, had decided to turn it into a College for the Conversion of the Jews. To this end, he rebuilt the north-west corner of the old house as a chapel "in a simple and correct Gothic style"[7] and had himself ordained deacon and priest. Late in 1817, he decided to approach the Powers who were settling Europe after the Napoleonic Wars and persuade them to make special provisions for the Jewish race. This led to a year's tour of Europe, during which he had personal interviews with the Czar Alexander himself, and achieved the personal triumph of inducing the Congress of Aix-la-Chapelle to record a clause favourable to the Jews. Fresh from this, he now wished his chapel to be dedicated as the keystone of the new College.

Way was a sincerely religious man, and known in the district for more orthodox generosity, though his special passion was the subject of local gossip and some ribald humour; Keats quotes one anecdote about Way and the Jews in his letter to George. His house was the byword of the neighbourhood, and this was one of the few chances to visit it, when the grounds and the buildings would be open to the public. The grounds themselves were well worth seeing, laid out in the style of Chantilly, and embellished by the celebrated Capability Brown, but it was the house that Keats would want to see, and did see, as we can infer from his disgruntled remark that he found it "crammed with Clergy". This house was a fine classical structure, built in the late eighteenth century round a kernel of rooms which dated from a hundred years earlier. These were the so-called State apartments built on a medieval site at prodigious expense by the Earl of Scarborough, and noted by Defoe. Two of the rooms contained a set of gold-embroidered chairs, which, rumour said, had been offered to Queen Charlotte, but which her Majesty had considered too expensive. Both these rooms were hung with tapestries, among which was a famous one from Arras, variously described as

being of the halt and foraging of an army, or of the battle of
Wynandael. Even more striking were two other rooms, the
salon with its wainscoting, and the panelled oak-room in
which hung portraits of Newton and Pope and a copy of Guido
Reni's Mary Magdalene. The carving in these rooms and
probably in the passages which led to them was by Grinling
Gibbons himself, with his characteristic fruits and flowers,
together with acorns, emblems of a former owner.[8]

It hardly needs the stage-direction, so to speak, of the echo
of St. Paul in introducing this part of the poem to show what
Keats made of all this. It has often been observed that the
poem is full of anachronisms; genuine medieval atmosphere
mixes with furniture and setting of a much later date. Here,
at last, is the explanation. In the first thirteen stanzas, apart
from an armchair borrowed from a Mrs. Radcliffe romance,
there is nothing that might not be purely medieval, identical
with the genuine medieval surroundings he found in Chichester.
Now carpets, chairs, tapestries, wide staircases, curtains are
imposed, just as the properties of Stansted House imposed
themselves on his working imagination. The change of scene
is hammering in his mind as early as stanza xxi, where the
"dusky gallery" was first an "arras" and then an "oaken
passage", a jumbling together of the two types of State apart-
ment he had just seen. In fact,

The arras, rich with horseman, hawk, and hound,

reserved for a later stanza in the poem, is probably as close as
unconscious impression can get to the foraging scene he saw.
Then the "carven imageries"

Of fruits and flowers and bunches of knot-grass

are a perfectly literal description of any of Grinling Gibbons's
usual decorations, shifted in this instance from wood to stone.
Nothing, it has been rightly pointed out, could be finer than
Keats's imaginative use of colour and of richness of materials
and texture all through these stanzas; it does not detract from
the fullness of his imagination to suggest that the rich designs
and hues he saw in tapestries, chairs, and bed-hangings—

there was the inevitable bed with its Elizabethan legend—
may have added at least a "broad golden fringe" to the margins
of the picture he was painting. Even "the wide stairs" of the
end of the poem, so different from the low-arched ways of the
earlier part, have their parallel in the grand staircase at
Stansted.

He came primarily to see the house; but the price of visiting
the house was, of course, to attend the consecration in the
Chapel, and here, perhaps, all unsought, the greatest treasure
was gathered. On the morning of Monday, January 25th,
Keats and Brown set out, taking with them an eleven-year-old
boy, their host's younger son, John Snook the Third. They
drove in a chaise to Stansted Park, a distance of five miles, all
slightly uphill. The horse was slow and even the volatile
Brown could not urge it on. "Brown drove, but the horse did
not mind him."[10] One of Keats's American biographers[11] has
added the picture of a dreary grey dripping English day, to
match the slowness of the journey. Nothing could be further
from fact. It was one of those remarkable days, typical of
this stretch of coast, where the wind snakes inland along the
narrow tentacles of the tidal creeks. The south-west gale,
which had kept every single ship penned up in Portsmouth
Harbour for the past three weeks, was blowing itself out with a
final, devastating fury.[12] Huge and startling gusts bowled the
clouds along; sudden squalls of bullet-like rain alternated with
flashing intervals of sun. There was enough drama in sky and
on land for twenty poems, and this storm, with its counterpart
in the later stanzas of the poem, has left us at least one unforgettable line:

And the long carpets rose along the gusty floor.

In the clash and buffeting of such weather, they arrived,
late, to find the little Chapel crammed to the doors with three
times as many people as it would normally hold. Three
hundred "of the most respectable gentry" were there, and
about forty clergy.[13] After his slow journey, the odds are that
Keats only just got inside the Chapel porch, in spite of Brown's
persuasiveness and the bargaining power of having a small
boy with them. From this draughty vantage, they watched

the ceremony. Keats found it "not amusing"—one of his classic understatements. It was certainly very long, and must have lasted from eleven o'clock until a late dinner-time. It was conducted by Bishop Ryder of Gloucester and Bishop Burgess of St. David's, two friends, whom Way himself had persuaded to become joint patrons of the London Society for the Conversion of the Jews. Burgess had opened the newly-built chancel of the Chapel three and a half years before, but on this occasion he contented himself with preaching the sermon—unfortunately lost—while Ryder performed the major part of the ceremony.

Keats was unlikely to appreciate that he was watching two of the leading churchmen of his age. His position near the porch, through which the wind whistled down his neck, may have had something to do with his diatribe against the clergy there. These, in full canonicals, sat snugly up in the chancel, some, no doubt, allowing their attention to wander to the entertainment to follow, whose cooking they had already smelt while changing into their vestments in the house. Keats, we need not doubt, allowed his attention to wander too. There is little evidence that he listened to any of the numerous lessons, epistles, and gospels[14]—both matins and communion service were included in the ceremony—though it would be strange if the two very striking and beautiful passages[15] appointed for this particular day of the Feast of the Conversion of St. Paul did not have some effect.

Yet it was not so much Keats's ears that were receptive as his eyes. He stood or sat just inside the porch, in the ante-chapel on the south-west side of the chancel. From here it would be most convenient for him to slip out and see a part of the ceremony which he described to George, the consecration of the burial-ground, which took place through the vestry-window on the south-east, so that the Bishop of Gloucester should not run the risk of getting wet in one of the sudden showers. From here, too, he looked across at the north windows of the Chapel, and specially at those opposite him, in the north-west corner. These windows had been designed by Way himself in a neo-Gothic style. They are set high in the wall, and each window contains three arches; the windows are diamond-paned with a good deal of clear glass, but in the centre of each arch, there is a rosette containing a shield. This shield-shaped centrepiece in the middle of each arch is filled with coloured glass, "embellished with the arms and cognizances of the Fitzalans and subsequent proprietors"—that is, of the Arundel family, who had probably built some of the older part of the Chapel late in the fifteenth century. The three arches of the window opposite Keats contained, heraldically described, these coats of arms:[16]

1. Azure a lion rampant and a border or. *Belesme,*
                                       Earl of Arundel.
2. Gules a lion rampant or. *Albini,* Earl of Arundel.
3. Barry of 8 or and gules. *Alan Fitzalan.*

Keats, in his first attempt at the famous stanzas xxiv and xxv, produced something that may be approximately written thus:

A Casement tripple arch'd and diamonded
With many coloured glass fronted the Moon
In midst w(h)ereof a shi(e)lded scutcheon shed
High blushing gules; and she kneeled saintly down
And inly prayed for grace and heavenly boon;
The blood red gules fell on her silver cross
And her white hands devout

This incomplete stanza is, of course, the basis of the final form of stanzas xxiv and xxv; but what is most striking is that this very early draft is an almost exact description of the windows opposite which Keats spent two or three hours in Stansted Chapel. They are triple-arched and the panes are diamond-shaped; in the middle of each arch is "a shielded scutcheon", and those which were nearest to Keats's line of· vision contained, as their major colour, the "blood red gules" which so impressed him that, in this early draft, he mentioned them twice in three lines. Moreover, there is no difficulty about the often-argued question whether moonlight would throw the colour of the glass; Keats saw the colour come and go in the sudden flashes of sunlight from outside, the bars of deep red, the amethyst of the heraldic azure, perhaps even falling on the pectoral cross of one of the Bishops. The glass of the windows which Keats saw was unfortunately blown out during the last

war; but to this day, the armorial bearings of the modern glass
in the south windows of the Chapel give exactly this effect.[17]

> Rose-bloom fell on her hands, together prest,
> And on her silver cross soft amethyst.

Once more, the wonder is not that Keats's unconscious eye
should be so influenced, but that his conscious art should work
so magnificently upon the picture that his experience presented
to him. We must also thank—though it is a backhanded
blessing—his uncomfortable and draughty position; for it was
from here he brought back the haunting sore throat to such
an extent that, as he himself said, he hardly went outside the
gate again for the rest of his stay at Bedhampton. In the
kindly quiet presence of his hosts, with Brown gone back to
London the next day, he was able to assemble, assort, transmute the experiences he had gathered on this Monday, and
add to them such wonderful pictures as

> And still she slept an azure-lidded sleep,
> In blanched linen, smooth, and lavender'd,
> While he from forth the closet brought a heap
> Of candied apple, quince, and plum, and gourd;
> With jellies soother than the creamy curd,
> And lucent syrops tinct with cinnamon;
> Manna and dates in argosy transferr'd
> From Fez; and spiced dainties, every one,
> From silken Samarcand to cedar'd Lebanon

Quiet and leisure gave him time for reading too, his beloved
"study". It is tempting to see in this famous stanza xxx,
describing the feast brought by his hero, some of the homely
country comforts, fruits, jellies, and junkets, which his hostess
brought out to soothe her young visitor's throat. It is more
to the point, though, to notice that not many pages further on
from where we last found him reading Burton's *Anatomy*,
"gourds", "apples, plums", and "Spices" including "cinnamon,
dates, sugar"—the last a cancelled attribute of the feast—all
come within the space of two pages.[18] In the middle of this
catalogue, too, Burton adds the comment

> Cardan makes that a cause of their continual sickness
> at Fessa in Africk, *because they live so much on fruits,*

Fessa, or Fez as Burton names it a few pages later, seems always to have been in Keats's mind when he was drafting this stanza, and there seems little doubt how it got there. Once more the *Literary Pocket Book* may have contributed its "dulcet creams", quoted by Hunt from Milton. The line from Thomson's *The Seasons*, also quoted by Leigh Hunt,

> The excluded tempest idly rave long

certainly seems to have returned, perhaps at an idle glance, while Keats was writing of his storm in the later stanzas. Yet the Stansted Chapel ceremony itself can be said to have had literally the last word. When Keats opened his host's copy of *The Hampshire Telegraph and Sussex Chronicle* for Monday, February 1st, he read an account of the occasion couched in language very different from his own satirical description to George a fortnight later; but at least he learnt that the banquet at the house, which followed the cold and lengthy consecration, had been, as the feast of his own hero and heroine was to be, "sumptuous".[19]

> These delicates he heap'd with glowing hand
> On golden dishes and in baskets bright
> Of wreathed silver: sumptuous they stand
> In the retired quiet of the night. . . .

Quiet, in his own candlelit upper room at the mill-house, Keats worked with an intensity only to be guessed at by the sight of his much-scored manuscript; while the wind, swirling up the estuary, rattled the dark window-pane, he completed one of the world's greatest narrative poems.

(The Eve of St. Agnes, stanzas XIV to end)

9

ST. VALENTINE AND ST. MARK

K EATS was back in Hampstead on Thursday, February
4th.[1] He was determined to take no chances with his
throat, and to avoid going out for the next fortnight, though
actually his good resolution only lasted nine days. Everything
was much the same. Haydon's exhibition of his pupils' work
had opened on February 1st. It had a good press, so Keats
might feel justified in dismissing the painter from his conscience
for a while. Dilke was tediously preoccupied about a school for
his son Charley, now nearly nine. He and Brown gardened,
while the latter, as usual, was engaged in humorous writing,
convinced that it would bring him a sudden windfall. Mrs.
Dilke had the Misses Reynolds staying with her, "all very dull",
according to Keats, who had never forgiven them over Jane
Cox. Fanny Brawne was a caller, and with her Keats continued to have "a chat and a tiff".[2] The disfavour with which
she too was viewed by the Reynolds sisters probably dates from
these days, for there was evidently a three-cornered flirtation
going on between her, Keats, and Brown. Part of the light
verse which Brown was hatching at this time was a Valentine
addressed to her. She was flattered, and remembered it well
enough to repeat it to her children many years later.[3]

> Whene'er we chance to meet
> You know the reason why
> You pass me in the street
> And toss your head on high—
>
> Because my walking stick
> Is not a dandy twig
> Because my boots are thick,
> Because I wear a wig

Because you think my coat
Too often has been worn,
And the tie about my throat
Is at the corners torn. . . .

To see me thus equipped
What folly to be haughty!
Pray were you never whipped
At school for being naughty?

Keats, here as in Chichester, chimed in with the rough humour
of the bald-headed and somewhat coarse-minded Brown; if he
did not actually call Fanny a naughty schoolgirl, he certainly
did something which showed a similar attitude of mind. This
too in its own curious way was a Valentine.

It seems probable that he had received a letter from her
while he was at Chichester and Bedhampton,[4] a teasing and
flirtatious one, to judge by the message, in which he included
her, written from Bedhampton—"Remember me to Wentworth
Place and Elm Cottage—not forgetting Millamant——".
Either then or when he returned, he gave her a strange present.
This was his copy of Hunt's *Literary Pocket Book*. When we
remember Keats's very unflattering opinion of this little publication, it can only seem that he did not rate Fanny's taste very
high. The book, however, was as good as new; Hunt had
written on the fly-leaf and added a number of proof-corrections,
but Keats had not made a single mark in it. The first entry
was made by Fanny in her distinctly youthful hand; it is an
astonishing one. It shows that Keats at this time had made her
a present of a totally unexpected piece of verse. It is the lyric
Hush, hush.

Before trying to understand why he did this, it must be
noticed that she does not seem likely to have taken the poem
seriously, nor to have herself fully understood its purport. She
wrote it out rather like an exercise, with a good deal of crossing
out and re-writing; in the last stanza she seems to have lost
interest in what she was copying, or to have been in a hurry,
for not only mis-writing but mis-spelling and actual mistakes
occur, and any attempt at punctuation practically disappears.
Yet the question remains what Keats thought he was doing,

in giving or showing to Fanny a lyric which described in literal detail his love-affair with Isabella.

The explanation seems to be the odd mixture of unsure feelings and bravado which, as he himself said, he was always apt to show towards women—"evil thoughts, malice spleen" and all the other "insults" which, he said, he was always impelled to indulge in their presence. As recently as Christmas he had had a return of this contemptuous feeling about women, and had felt constrained then to apologise to his sister-in-law about it—"forgive me little George you know I don't mean to put you in the mess". The only other person he had said he did not include "in the mess" of this antagonism to women had been Isabella, with whom, as with Georgiana, he felt a calm and friendly feeling. Fanny, on the other hand, had aroused this antagonism, which was only the other side of a strong attraction, in a flash. His instinct was, in the language of his day, to "smoke" her. To give her a book which he thought worthless, and to show her a poem which, unknown to her, recorded a love-affair with another lady may not seem admirable conduct; but it was much in the style of his bosom-companion, Brown, who used to put indecent verses among Keats's papers, in order, he said, to prevent young women prying among them.

The excitement of this kind of flirtation does not seem to have prevented him from finishing *The Eve of St. Agnes*, and doing the inevitable tidying-up which a long poem entails, but he had another preoccupation, less pleasant. At Bedhampton, he had received a letter from his sister from which he learnt that not only would Abbey not let her remain at school, but that he was objecting to Keats's own letters to her. Keats wrote Abbey himself "a rather plain-spoken letter" about this, and about money-matters. His throat was improving more quickly than he had expected, and he determined to follow the letter by a visit to Town, his first since the day, just over three weeks before, when he had caught the coach to Chichester. This was on Saturday, February 13th, and it was a crowded day. Apart from Abbey, Keats went to see the family lawyer and met various acquaintances including Hazlitt's wife and "that little Nero her son". A chance meeting with Woodhouse led to the lawyer taking him off to split a bottle of claret. He also, though he does not at once say so, visited Isabella Jones in Gloucester Street.[5] When he returned home that evening he started writing a new poem.

It was *The Eve of St. Mark*, another poem with what he himself called a "mother Radcliff" title.[6] Once more, Isabella had provided him with a popular superstition in the Gothic vein. The legend of St. Mark's Eve (April 24th) told how anyone standing in the church porch on that night would see the phantasm of all who were to die in that coming year. It was as promising a legend as that of St. Agnes, and it is probable that she suggested it to him in her enthusiasm after he had read her the draft of *The Eve of St. Agnes*. The form of the new poem is quite different, however, and may show what Keats and Isabella were reading together, those "matters of taste" in which, he had said, he hoped to instruct her.

> Upon a Sabbath-day it fell;
> Twice holy was the Sabbath-bell,
> That call'd the folk to evening prayer;
> The city streets were clean and fair
> From wholesome drench of April rains;
> And, on the western window panes,
> The chilly sunset faintly told
> Of unmatured green vallies cold,
> Of the green thorny bloomless hedge,
> Of rivers new with spring-tide sedge,
> Of primroses by shelter'd rills,
> And daisies on the aguish hills.
> Twice holy was the Sabbath-bell;
> The silent streets were crowded well
> With staid and pious companies,
> Warm from their fire-side orat'ries;
> And moving, with demurest air,
> To even-song and vesper prayer.
> Each arched porch, and entry low,
> Was fill'd with patient folk and slow,
> With whispers hush, and shuffling feet,
> While play'd the organ loud and sweet.

The style is that of the imitation-medieval poems of Chatterton, the strange gifted boy to whose memory Keats had dedicated his own *Endymion*. Chatterton is the first poet he would have wished to have introduced to a new and receptive reader, and the hand of Chatterton is clearly here. The opening and the metre of the poem is that of Chatterton's *The Unknown Knight, or The Tournament*, a poem avowedly "In Imitation of our Old Poets"—

> The mattin-bell had sounded long,
> The cocks had sang their morning song,

and the prime source is Chatterton's most considerable work in this vein, the drama of *Aella*. Keats even borrowed from this drama the name of his own heroine in the poem, Bertha. There is no doubt[7] that Bertha's city of the first twenty-two lines is Chichester, which he had just visited. It is worth noting also how much the weather of the poem's opening echoes the actual weather of January, 1819. It is not much like the 24th of April, when the poem is supposed to be taking place; it does resemble this January when the season was abnormally forward though still treacherous, in a climate wet enough to fill the ditches, warm enough to have brought on the early Spring flowers, and in a landscape very like the five miles from Bedhampton to Stansted among small foot-hills and sheltered downland streams.

After this opening, Keats introduced into the poem his heroine, poring in her room over an illuminated manuscript. Still the journey to Stansted asserts itself directly Bertha opens her book. This book has been called a "quite impossible invention jumbling fantastically together things that could never have figured in the same manuscript",[8] stars, angels' wings, martyrs in a fiery blaze, saints, silver rays, Moses' breastplate, a seven-branched candlestick, the covenantal Ark, the Lion of St. Mark, cherubim, and golden mice. Yet what might be impossible in a manuscript[9] was not too fantastic for the mind of Lewis Way, and it is to Keats's vigil in Stansted Chapel that he owed the ingredients of the book. His nearest sight in the nave would have been the stained glass of the north-west window, but at a farther distance, he would see another set of glass in the chancel; these were the east windows, containing seven lights.[10] At the head of each of these lights is a silver star and a small winged cherub; the two northern lights are occupied by a seven-branched candlestick. In the middle lights, below the stars and cherubs, there is a rainbow and silver rays of light descending through golden clouds. Beneath is a fire in a brazier, and the Ark of the Covenant, with two long-winged Cherubim, one at each end; lying on some steps below this is the blossoming rod of Aaron. The two southern lights, though almost certainly invisible from where Keats stood, contain a table of brass or gold, on which are piled the tables of the Law, together with a burning lamp. Every part of this was, according to his daughter,[11] Way's design—"The idea throughout is the Gospel Dispensation, shadowed forth in that of the Law, or 'Moses a schoolmaster leading to Christ'."

Keats can only have had a hazy notion of Way's idea; but the dimly-seen windows fall into a pattern clearly reproduced in the poem. All that he saw at the other end of the chapel is there—stars, angels' wings, the seven-branched candlestick, silver rays, a fiery blaze, the Ark of the Covenant and its attendant Cherubim. He has merely introduced saints and martyrs and the symbol of St. Mark; some memory may have occurred here of the very striking *Martyrdom of St. Ephesus* (in a large brazier) which he had seen in the book of prints from the Campo Santo. As for the breastplate, Keats's MSS. show that he was never quite sure whether it belonged to Aaron or Moses, and he was probably not tall enough to have seen, from the back of the congregation, Aaron's *rod* lying at the foot of the middle lights of the window. The breastplate came into his head from the first lesson of the day, the fifth chapter of the Book of Wisdom, verse 18, which Keats had heard read by Mr. Way's curate:

> He shall put on righteousness as a breastplate, and
> true judgment instead of an helmet.

It is a pity that we do not have Bishop Burgess's sermon, for it is possible that there might be found also the golden mice which, according to I Samuel vi 4, were *inside* the Ark, an unlikely piece of knowledge for Keats unless he had heard it recently expounded. This deliberate transcription of windows into book is typical of Keats's way of work. His imagination, all through his poetic life, was excited by paintings and pictorial images. The unique series of pictures in Way's glass naturally stimulated his imagination, and, in memory, their dull gold, silver, flame, and azure became the colouring of a medieval manuscript. The jumble of subjects is explained by the one place in England where such a collection could be seen, as it still can be today—in Stansted Chapel.

So far the poem, with its Chatterton heroine, had been created from two recently-remembered scenes—the city of Chichester and its surroundings, and the coloured glass in the east window at Stansted. Now

> Bertha was a maiden fair,
> Dwelling in the old Minster-square;

Keats's old dowager hostess, Mrs. Lacy of Chichester, the elderly "fair one" of the joint letter, had dwelt in

> that Tenement at the North Angle of the Close or
> Square late the Cloysters of the said Vicars. . . .

It is worth examining the exact situation of this set of rooms which Keats visited. From the little window near the head of her stairs, Mrs. Lacy could see, "sidelong", like Bertha, the beautiful little collegiate Close of the Priest Vicars Choral. This was at that time a perfect enclosed quadrangle of mainly medieval buildings in all their "rich antiquity" something like the present Vicars' Close at Wells. It was probably founded upon an older monastic quadrangle, and was thus quite literally a "Minster-square", with its own lodge-gate, within whose confines the Priest Vicars were supposed to keep their semi-collegiate rules. Beyond this square, and the jumble of buildings in the main Cathedral Close, stretched the wide gardens of the Bishop's Palace, with open land beyond. Prints of Keats's time show many more trees than at present, and it is interesting to note that some of the old trees in the Bishop's Garden are, as they are in Keats's poem, elms and sycamores. The whole situation of the little square, the Close, and the gardens on the south side of the tall Cathedral,

> So shelter'd by the mighty pile

E

is exactly that of Chichester. In the poem the beauty of old Chichester still lives, as some of its surrounding circumstances do to this day—the jackdaws that still nest in the separate bell-tower of the Cathedral, and the echoing steps which still ring out under the hollow arch, all that now remains of Mrs. Lacy's little Closet room over "the Church Yard Stile called the Stone Stile".

When we turn our eyes inward from the medieval Close of Chichester to the interior of Bertha's room, it is clear that we are in a different place and age. It is also clear, from the numerous cancelled lines in the MS. versions, that Keats made something of a fresh start here. There is a preoccupation with exact detail, the exact look of the coal, for example, which Bertha was poking, the exact effect of her shadow on the wall, which suggests, more even than any other part of the poem, an actual experience. Keats wrote the whole fragment, on some more precise information which we have from Woodhouse, between Saturday, February 13th, and Wednesday the 17th.[12] Much of it was therefore written at Hampstead, sitting working, as Keats says, with Brown; but on the Wednesday he was in Town again. He called on Haslam and Mrs. Wylie, finding them both out, and since Woodhouse almost certainly got his exactly-dated information from Isabella, it can be presumed that Keats again called on her. In the rooms in Gloucester Street, he found Bertha's room, with

The parrot's cage, and panel square;—

the square panelling and the parrot which he had noticed the first time he entered her rooms. The whole tone and circumstance of Bertha's room, with its naturalistic detail, is like his description of the Gloucester Street room when he noted down its details in October, at the time of the *Bright Star* sonnet— "a very tasty sort of place". The fire-screen is strangely fashionable for "the homely room" of Bertha, and there is an interesting point about the meticulous way in which Keats has described it. Its details must have been explained to Keats by word of mouth; for among all its oriental designs—"doves of Siam" and so on—he writes "Lima mice", apparently thus borrowing some creatures, unknown to zoology, from Peru.

What his hostess had obviously and correctly said to him must have been the East Indian "lemur mice", which he had then transcribed phonetically. There is at least a plausible reason why Isabella should have an East Indian lacquer-work screen, if her friendship with Mrs. Colonel Green is presumed; Lieut-Colonel Green had served 25 years in the East, and the screen may have been a present from him or his wife.

What Bertha read by firelight on "the legend page" is what Keats afterwards called "an imitation of the Authors in Chaucer's time." It is more skilful than Chatterton had been. Written in full—one fragment was for a long time separated from the rest of the MS.—it actually deals with the legend and main subject of the poem. Yet a line or two after this passage, the poem comes to a full stop. After working steadily at it for five days, Keats never again took it up. Even from the first he seems to have had a premonition that he would not finish it. Writing to his brother on the second day of composition, he promises to send the poem in his next journal letter "if I should have finished it". This remark must be taken as implying some doubt from the start. In fact, a few days later he stopped writing and put the poem away so securely that he did not even get out the fragment to send George until a whole seven months had passed.

Something must have gone oddly wrong. It was partly that the whole poem had been suggested to him from outside. He did not have a strong original impulse, like the original "Tale" of the lovers in *St. Agnes*, to carry the legendary plot forward. There is also something in the way Keats composed this poem, which makes it differ from almost any other poem that he wrote during this year. It appears, in contrast with most of his poems, as a sequence of impressions, not stimulated by things immediately happening at hand, but by things remembered, even though they are remembered at fairly short range. It recreates, in order, the city of Chichester, the windows at Stansted, Mrs. Lacy's surroundings, Isabella's room, and Keats's reading of Chatterton with her. It is a fairly deliberate series of what we might call flash-backs, and these are done in literal detail. Keats does not transmute "particular circumstances" in Woodhouse's sense of immediate experience. It is a type of poetry that Keats seldom practised, the poetry of deliberate recollection. Even its Wordsworthian simplicity is perhaps evidence that it was composed in a way generally foreign to Keats, more according to Wordsworth's doctrine of recollected emotion or experience. It is a "made" poem, and it comes to an end when Keats has exhausted the impressions out of which such a poem could be made—five scenes from his recent life. When he had come to an end of these impressions, he came to the end of the poem. It could perhaps never have been finished.

There may be a deeper cause why, on the Wednesday, in the middle of a line, he should stop dead. If there was, he gave no direct hint of it. Outwardly, he was specially cheerful. On Thursday, February 18th, he and Brown went next door to the Dilkes to celebrate Charley's ninth birthday. Fanny Brawne and her mother were there, and they all stayed up till after ten, talking and joking. It is true that the newspapers had given him a sudden twinge of conscience—Haydon! The painter's exhibition of his pupils' work, so Keats read, had been such a success that it was re-opening next Monday for another fortnight. Keats hastily wrote off an apologetic but still light-hearted note.[13] This was on the Friday; on Saturday, February 20th, there was a dinner at the Dilkes with Reynolds and Rice, always lively company, on some of the game that Isabella had provided. Nothing here suggests any great crisis or agitation; yet that is only on the surface. It was at this exact time that Keats wrote to George,[14] in words which may well have had a deeper meaning than even he intended, "they are very shallow people who take every thing literally. A Man's life of any worth is a continual allegory—and very few eyes can see the Mystery of his life." The next six weeks of Keats's life are a plunge into the darkness of that mystery.

(*The Eve of St. Mark*)

10

DISSIPATION AND DARKNESS

ON Monday, February 22nd, Haydon called on Keats. He does not say how Keats was, but another caller at about this time has left his impression. This was Charles Cowden Clarke, the son of Keats's headmaster at Enfield, and the strongest formative influence on his early reading. Clarke found Keats apparently in good spirits and health. He heard from Keats how he had, some days previously, had a stand-up fight with a butcher's boy who was tormenting a kitten, and had thrashed his opponent. This story, typical of Keats, would appeal to Clarke, who had known him at school as a champion fighter before he had turned with equal enthusiasm to poetry. Clarke listened to the recently-finished *The Eve of St. Agnes*,[1] and was delighted, especially when Keats told him that the line

The hall door shuts again, and all the noise is gone.

was a memory from his schooldays, when he used to hear music coming from the headmaster's house.

The accident that Clarke and Haydon both saw Keats at this time is important; for when Haydon's autobiography and memoirs appeared long after Keats's death, there were some passages in the latter to which Clarke took bitter exception. The painter had reflected on the way in which Keats faced the troubles of his life and career:[2]

Poor fellow! his genius had no sooner begun to bud than hatred and malice spat their poison on its leaves, and sensitive and young it shrivelled beneath their effusions. Unable to bear the sneers of ignorance or the attacks of envy, not having strength of mind enough to buckle himself together like a porcupine and present nothing but

prickles to his enemies, he began to despond, and flew to
dissipation as a relief, which after a temporary elevation
of spirits plunged him into deeper despondency than ever.
For six weeks he was scarcely sober, and—to show what
a man does to gratify his appetites when once they get
the better of him—once covered his tongue and throat as
far as he could reach with cayenne pepper in order to
appreciate the 'delicious coldness of claret in all its glory'—
his own expression.

The death of his brother wounded him deeply, and it
appeared to me that he began to droop from that hour.
I was much attached to Keats, and he had a fellow-
feeling for me. I was angry because he would not bend
his great powers to some definite object, and always told
him so. Latterly he grew irritated because I would shake
my head at his irregularities and tell him that he would
destroy himself.

Clarke commented on this view of Keats,[3] in a way which has
been echoed by every biographer of the poet:

The most mean-spirited and trumpery twaddle in the
paragraph was, that Keats was so far gone in sensual
excitement as to put Cayenne pepper upon his tongue,
when taking his claret! In the first place, if the stupid
trick ever were played, I have not the slightest belief in
its serious sincerity. During my knowledge of him Keats
never purchased a bottle of claret; and, from such observation as could not escape me, I am bound to assert that his
domestic expenses never could have occasioned him a
regret or a self-reproof: and, lastly, I never perceived in
him even a tendency to imprudent indulgence.

It is clear that Clarke and Haydon were very different people.
From their tone, one would be inclined to trust Clarke. Yet
such complete disagreement between two grown men is
extraordinary. Haydon's natural style was made up of
exaggeration; but he seldom, if ever, invented outright. There
was usually more than a grain of truth in his wildest growths.
Besides, he was now seeing very much more of Keats than
Clarke was. He had interested motives, for he wanted money;
but this very fact meant that he was following Keats's daily

movements with keen interest. Clarke had not seen Keats for a long time before this meeting—"for God knows when", Keats wrote[4]—and he never saw him again. At a meeting where the younger man read a long poem, and the elder naturally dwelt on their happy early days together, it is not likely that Keats would reveal himself exactly as he was. On one specific point, in fact, Clarke could not have been more wrong. Only a few days before this meeting, Keats had actually written to George,[5] "now I like Claret—whenever I can have Claret I must drink it,—'tis the only palate affair that I am at all sensual in."

Both views then are partial and partisan. Clarke wanted Keats to appear still as a clean-limbed schoolboy, full of manly and heroic action; Haydon wanted himself to appear as the wise friend, the onlooker whose advice, if taken, would have saved the situation. Yet the situation itself, into which Keats's life now entered, does seem to have many more affinities with Haydon's account than Clarke's.

First, Haydon's account clearly refers to this time. It was since the death of Tom, he says, that Keats "began to droop", or, as far as his career was concerned, "began to despond". Keats's first reaction to the reviewers had been, as we have seen, confident and firm; but it is just now that a different note begins to creep in, a tone of bitterness. Although he says "I am in no despair about them", it is clear that the unpopularity of his poems has begun to worry him. He attacks the reviews for the first time; he speaks of his hurt pride. Jealousy creeps into his mind, and fixes itself upon the successes of Lord Byron. He notes that Murray's have sold four thousand copies of Byron. He exclaims, "You see what it is to be under six foot and not a lord"—i.e. Byron. He comments, "Lord Byron cuts a figure—but he is not figurative——". All this is at just this time in February. A month later he is still talking of his poems having been "fly-blown on the Reviewshambles". It is a very different tone from the previous autumn, and it can only be due to one thing. *Endymion* had stopped selling; "my poem has not at all succeeded——". Hessey's optimism, late in October, that the book had begun to "move," was unfounded; the members of the reading public whom Taylor and Woodhouse had tried to interest had not been enough.

There is no more depressing moment than when an author visits his publisher and sees row upon row of his own unsold books. That was what Keats saw just at this time in February. It may have had much to do with his failure to get on with *Hyperion* or to finish *The Eve of St. Mark*—the uncut, clean, yet "fly-blown" copies of his last long poem, with the dust beginning to settle upon them. Bad reviews had made him take Haydon's advice and emulate the porcupine; but bad sales, neglect, the books lying there unread, was quite a different matter. His depression is obvious from this moment, though it is not so obvious that he at once "flew to dissipation". Yet one curious fact about Haydon's account is that, in the midst of its many vague terms, there are islands of precise observation. The phrase "For six weeks" is one of these. There is a strange exactness about this. "Six" cannot have been only for alliteration. "Seven" would have done as well, or, more naturally, "a month or so". Haydon seems to be dating by some definite landmarks in time.

The opening of this six weeks' period can only have been this week-end of February 20th-21st. There is no suggestion, from Haydon or anyone else, that Keats was drinking between the death of his brother and that time. Brown said in January that Keats had benefited from "a strict forbearance from a third glass of wine", and Keats wrote on February 19th that he never now drank more than three glasses of wine and never any spirits and water. It cannot have been at any later time, for on April 13th Keats received from Haydon a letter of unreasonable reproach, which drove the two men apart, except for occasional meetings, until Keats left the country for Italy. Haydon does not, of course, mention this, nor the contents of the letter, a characteristic complaint that Keats had let him down over money. This is what makes his account suspect; he is anxious to picture himself not as the disappointed borrower but as the disinterested best friend.

Yet if we do assume the six weeks to have started at this week-end in February, there is a very natural time for it to end. Exactly six weeks later, Dilke, self-harassed by worry over his boy's fate at Westminster School, moved himself and his wife to Westminster itself, in order to be near young Charley. Just before he left on April 3rd, he was given a farewell party in the form of a bachelor claret-feast at which Keats, Brown, Reynolds, and four others were present. Keats comments "We all got a little tipsy—but pleasantly so—I enjoy Claret to a degree." At this week-end of April 3rd-4th, Mrs. Brawne and her family moved into the other half of Wentworth Place instead of the Dilkes. Fanny Brawne was now next door. Some modern biographers have backed Clarke's account by pointing out how impossible it would have been to conceal any hard drinking from such near neighbours; but if Haydon's timing is literally true, the arrival of the Brawnes would have been at the exact end of the period of dissipation. Their presence may even have put an end to it.

When we look at the events of Keats's life during these six weeks from February 20th to April 3rd, Haydon's account begins to seem not so fantastic after all. It is a strange period, sketched mainly in the letter he was continuing to write to George and Georgiana. The progress of the letter itself shows that something was wrong. This was the letter[6] which Keats had promised his beloved brother and sister-in-law would be an accurate journal of his doings, accompanied by poems copied on the days that he wrote them. Yet the first part of the letter comes to a dead stop on Friday, February 19th, with no poems copied, and is not continued for about ten more days. Then, on March 2nd, he begins again, quite casually, has another ten days' gap, continues for another week, and then comes to another complete halt. He even loses one sheet of this part of the letter, and does not find it nor forward it to George till the autumn. He only copies one poem, the sonnet *Why Did I Laugh?*

Irregular letter-writing does not mean irregularities in the sense that Haydon used the word. Yet the contents of the letter indicate, in contradiction to Clarke, an acute period of gloom and doubt about himself, often verging on self-contempt and self-reproach. The only thing he can find to interest George and Georgiana, apart from a brief flash of "quizzing" for the latter about her brother Henry's sweetheart, is to copy out long passages from Hazlitt's *A Letter to William Gifford Esq.*, in which the essayist lashes the editor of the *Quarterly*. This is another instance of the bitterness about the reviews which had now invaded Keats's mind; but most of the bitterness is reserved for himself. On Saturday, March 13th, he comments "I know not why Poetry and I have been so distant lately I must make some advances soon or she will cut me entirely." On March 14th he dined with some Hampstead neighbours, the Davenports "—and had a nap. I cannot bare a day annihilated in that manner—". On Monday the 15th—"I do not know what I did on monday—nothing—nothing—nothing—I wish this was any thing extraordinary." Two days later he reproached himself with staying in bed till ten in the morning after a party with Taylor, and on the 19th till nearly eleven. Again, late rising, lack of energy, and sleeping during the day are not dissipation, but they were unusual for Keats, and he knew it.

His social life was now complicated in the extreme. He wrote to Haydon on March 8th, "all my going out has been to town, and that has been a great deal". It was. The sporadic records of these six weeks show that he was in Town on at least thirteen or fourteen days,[7] that is, one third of the time, while if we allow for the days when the gaps in his letter-writing leave us in doubt, we can safely assume that he was in Town about half the time. For all this, he seems to have done nothing there, except for one visit to the British Museum and one to a theatre. One cannot help speculating about Isabella, whom he had been visiting so often until this period; there is no mention of her nor of any more presents of game. Nor, though there are several casual and half-cynical remarks about it, is there any real talk of poetry. He even speaks of taking up the medical profession again. There is only one poem, the strange, profound, and unhappy sonnet beginning "Why did I laugh tonight?"

This sonnet, which Keats wrote on about March 19th, is introduced by a set of unusual circumstances. On Thursday, March 18th, the amazingly hot weather had tempted Keats and Brown to play cricket on Hampstead Heath. Bumpy pitches, even with underhand bowling, were a danger to anyone as short as Keats, and he got a black eye. Brown applied leeches, and, almost certainly, after the fashion of the day, administered laudanum. The next day was Keats's longest lie in bed, till eleven. In this sleepy state, he had a half-waking vision.

Neither Poetry, nor Ambition, nor Love have any alertness of countenance as they pass by me: they seem rather like three figures on a greek vase—a Man and two women whom no one but myself could distinguish in their disguisement.

At the moment when he wrote these words, a message was put into his hands from his devoted friend Haslam. It told him that Haslam's father, who had been in a coma for some time, was hourly expected to die. Keats, still writing to George, launched into a philosophic discourse on life and death, and how "superior beings" in some other existence might regard the tragi-comedy of human affairs. This meditation may owe something to the evening spent three days before with the philosophic Taylor, one of whose remarks is quoted by Keats; but in expression as well as thought, it derives from Keats's reading of Burton. It is difficult to say whether Keats's prose or Burton's is the more delightful:

I go amongst the buildings of a city and I see a Man hurrying along—to what? the Creature has a purpose and his eyes are bright with it.

Burton, after a meditation on how misfortunes come unawares, exactly parallel to Keats's thoughts on receiving Haslam's note, wrote:[8]

Our towns, our cities, . . . our villages are like molehills, and men as so many emmets, busie, busie still, going to and fro, in and out, and crossing one anothers projects.

But Keats develops his argument—"straining", as he says, "at particles of light in the midst of a great darkness" to a poetic pitch that Burton never attained. He introduces the sonnet:

I did not intend to have sent you the following sonnet— but look over the last two pages and ask yourselves whether I have not that in me which will well bear the buffets of the world. It will be the best comment on my sonnet; it will show you that it was written with no Agony but that of ignorance; with no thirst of any thing but Knowledge when pushed to the point though the first steps to it were throug(h) my human passions—they went away, and I wrote with my Mind—and perhaps I must confess a little bit of my heart—

> Why did I laugh tonight? No voice will tell:
> No God no Deamon of severe response
> Deigns to reply from heaven or from Hell.—
> Then to my human heart I turn at once—
> Heart! thou and I are here sad and alone;
> Say, wherefore did I laugh? O mortal pain!
> O Darkness! Darkness! ever must I moan
> To question Heaven and Hell and Heart in vain!
> Why did I laugh? I know this being's lease
> My fancy to its utmost blisses spreads:
> Yet could I on this very midnight cease
> And the world's gaudy ensigns see in shreds.
> Verse, fame and Beauty are intense indeed
> But Death intenser—Death is Life's high mead.

Before considering what this turmoil of mind and heart, which produced the sonnet, may have been, it must be noticed that, whatever it was, it also produced a sudden fine addition to the almost-forgotten *Hyperion*. It is the last part of that fragment ever to be written by Keats; on March 8th,[9] he had cynically described himself as "being in a sort of cui bono temper, not exactly on the road to an epic poem", and a few moments later he exclaimed, in the same vein, "I will not spoil my love of gloom by writing an Ode of Darkness!" At the same time he made a resolution "never to write for the sake of writing or making a poem", which may mark his final resolve not to go on with such a "made" poem as *The Eve of St. Mark*. Yet ten days later, he not only wrote his Ode to Darkness (in sonnet form), but continued his epic poem in a final brilliant burst. The inspiration is clearly that of the sonnet, especially when his words introducing the sonnet are remembered. The speech of Apollo himself is full of echoes of Keats's own mood and manner in this crisis. There are the same rhetorical questions, the same reiteration of "dark, dark" —"darkness, darkness"—and the mental state is exactly repeated, "with no Agony but that of ignorance"—

> In fearless yet in aching ignorance

The agonies which fill Apollo's brain

>   as if some blithe wine,
>   Or bright elixir peerless I had drunk,

are the agony which filled Keats's mind and which produced the philosophy of the letter and the sonnet.

Keats conquered the agony of this crisis—"I went to bed, and enjoyed an uninterrupted Sleep—Sane I went to bed and sane I arose." He found his relief by doing exactly what he had done on September 21st, 1818; it may even have saved his sanity to "plunge into abstract images to ease myself". Thus, strangely enough, the last sixty or seventy lines of *Hyperion* were probably written in the same mood and under the same need as the first. This is specially so, once more, of Apollo's speech. Keats himself told Woodhouse[10] that this speech seemed to come to him as he wrote it, like something from a power outside himself. "It seemed to come by chance or magic—to be as it were something given to him." These lines and the sonnet purged and cleared his overwrought soul, at least for the moment. There is an astonishing likeness between this and, on another plane, Haydon's account of Keats's bouts of dissipation at this time, "which after a temporary elevation of spirits, plunged him into deeper desspondency than ever". For the sudden break in the clouds which produced this double flash of poetry in the middle of March did not last. There is a bitter letter to Severn at the end of the month about the joint trials of artist and poet. The whole pattern of these six weeks, and particularly of this month of March, favours the essential truth of Haydon's account. The painter was watching the poet with alarm. Quarter-day was again coming close; Haydon's appeals became passionately urgent. "Before the 20th if you could help me it would be nectar and manna and all the blessings of gratified thirst." When he finally denounced Keats, it was for leading him on "step by step, day by day". The way he put this monstrous accusation itself clearly shows that he had watched daily and with horror the spectacle of Keats, elusive, often in Town, doing no work, raising no money, caught in the whirlpool of some passionate crisis of his own, behaving in a way that, to the agitated and egotistical painter, could only seem "scarcely sober".

He could not see that Keats's over-indulgence in claret-feasts was only an outward symbol of a deep inward emotion which had thrown him off balance. Its nature is wrapped in his own silence, but the solution may very well lie in the sonnet and the circumstances leading to it. Poetry, Ambition, Love—Verse, Fame, and Beauty—so a poet may rationalize and generalize; but when a young man daydreams, under the relaxing effects of a drug, about a man and two women "whom no one but myself could distinguish in their disguisement", it is not likely that these are merely the figures on a vase. It is likely that, in his heart of hearts, they are more concrete than the abstractions into which he habitually turns them. The man is himself, and the women are not two abstract figures, but two flesh-and-blood women.

This may seem crude, but it fits the facts as we know them. Keats had been seeing much of two women—Fanny Brawne and Isabella Jones. His "chat and a tiff" with Fanny had been going on for a long time—too long now not to be serious. Isabella, though beautiful too, was associated in his mind with poetry—she had suggested two great poems—and "fame", from their earliest association "when the *Fire* of his imagination appeared agitated with a *Thirst* for *fame*——".[11] He knew he would have to make some emotional decision. He knew on February 20th, at the beginning of these dark six weeks, that Fanny Brawne was coming to live next door to him in exactly six weeks' time. Part of the answer to this indecision was to escape to Town, to plunge into dissipation which, though it may have had some origin in literary disappointment, must have had this deeper emotional core. Then, perhaps, something was going wrong between himself and Isabella. He may have begun to feel he was being "made" to write poems; his natural answer would be, in defiance, to write nothing. Better death than compulsion, either in love or literature, however intense the temptations of either:

But Death intenser—Death is Life's high mead.

His strange disgust with the idea of Fame, the resentment of being made what he later called "a versifying Pet-lamb"[12] seems to spring from some particular personal reason. The exhilaration which had produced *The Eve of St. Agnes* had somehow, somewhere gone rotten at the source. He may have found something wearing, almost dishonourable in the association with Isabella, which had to be maintained "without any of our common acquaintance knowing it." Though Keats could be as free in his behaviour as any of his friends, and "as much like the Holy Ghost", in his brother's picturesque phrase,[13] as any conventional picture of goodness, he had a very highly developed sense of honour. It led him to be punctilious about Isabella's request; it may have led him to consider it, as the circumstances continued, to be not only irksome but wrong.

(*Sonnet:* Why Did I Laugh? *Hyperion* III, 61-end)

11

LIGHT VERSE AND PARODIES

BETWEEN Sunday, April 4th, and Sunday, April 11th, there is one of the few weeks in Keats's life for which we have a complete and unbroken blank. There can be no doubt that Fanny Brawne had much to do with it. This was the first week in which she came to live in the house next door to Keats. Yet that is not to say that he did nothing during this week but battle against or drift with the tide of his love. Much of the week was spent in intensive reading; Keats had once more plunged into an earnest and methodical study of Burton. To judge by parallels in his letters, by the middle of March he had only apparently reached page 160 of the *Anatomy*, which, with the introductory pages, would put him only about halfway through the first volume; yet by the end of April, we can judge, by even clearer parallels between the *Anatomy* and the subjects and substance of his own poems, that he had finished this first volume and had even embarked on the second. It was not Keats's habit to skip. All this points to intensive reading, and as Keats laments all through March about his idleness, it is likely that it was in this week that he began to give himself the "great shake" which he himself said would be needed to get himself going again. Early the next week, he said, "I was whole I had begun reading again". Whatever his personal life, his imagination was once more swimming on the flood of Burton's overflowing monologue.

If this week was occupied with reading, the next began with Keats listening to a live monologue by the greatest living talker of his time—Samuel Taylor Coleridge. This meeting, which took place on Sunday, April 11th, is extremely well-known, and many theories have been built about its influence on Keats. In spite of its familiarity, it is worth quoting the account of it which Keats gives at the tail-end of a section of a letter to George, written late at night on Thursday, April 15th.[1]

Last Sunday I took a Walk towards highgate and in the lane that winds by the side of Lord Mansfield's park I met Mr Green our Demonstrator at Guy's in conversation with Coleridge—I joined them, after enquiring by a look whether it would be agreeable—I walked with him a(t) his alderman-after-dinner pace for near two miles I suppose. In those two Miles he broached a thousand things—let me see if I can give you a list—Nightingales, Poetry—on Poetical Sensation—Metaphysics—Different genera and species of Dreams—Nightmare—a dream accompanied ~~with~~ by a sense of touch—single and double touch—A dream related—First and second consciousness— the difference explained between will and Volition—so m(an)y metaphysicians from a want of smoking the second consciousness — Monsters — the Kraken — Mermaids — Southey believes in them—Southey's belief too much diluted—A Ghost story—Good morning—I heard his voice as he came towards me—I heard it as he moved away—I had heard it all the interval—if it may be called so. He was civil enough to ask me to call on him at Highgate.

Of the many imaginary expansions of this monologue from Keats's brief yet penetrating synopsis—including a suppositious dialogue based on the pleasing fancy that Keats *did* make use of the invitation to Highgate—by far the most likely and convincing has been made by Dr. H. W. Garrod, from his deep knowledge of the characteristic channels of Coleridge's thoughts and ideas. Yet, on the evidence we have, even he allows[2] that "Keats' light-hearted—perhaps even contemptuous—account of the Highgate conversation suggests, certainly, that the whole left upon his mind no very powerful impression." Though a great deal may be indirectly attributed to this meeting—the first inklings of the Nightingale Ode, for instance —there is no evidence that Keats took it and the Coleridgean monologue as anything but the subject for a joke. Once again, it is worth noting that his account of it is placed right at the end of this section of the letter, the position he always reserved for "a little quizzing".

On the next day, Monday, April 12th, Keats wrote to his sister at Walthamstow.[3] Though he naturally did not reveal to his young sister the deeper places of his heart, he spoke plainly of one of the other matters which was unsettling his mind and paralysing his writing—the prolonged silence from George. However, he wrote cheerfully and sensibly to Fanny, promised to order her some pot-plants, and to buy her, next time he passed Tassie's shop in Leicester Square, some of the imitation jewellery which was then so popular. He repeated his idea of spending the summer in lodgings at Westminster, where, in fact, he went that same afternoon to dine with the Dilkes for the first time in their new quarters, 25 Great Smith Street. Tuesday, April 13th, was a day of mixed experience. The morning's post brought the unwelcome letter from Haydon, in which the painter accused him of having let him down over the promised loan. Keats replied at once, reasonably but with considerable coldness. It sounds as if he had anticipated having to make such a reply, and knew in advance what he should say. In the evening, another anticipated trial turned out well. Keats went to a dance-party given at 27 Lamb's Conduit Street by Sawrey, the doctor who had attended Tom. In spite of misgivings he enjoyed himself. Reynolds was there, always good company. Keats liked his hostess; besides her, he met one of the prettiest girls he had ever seen, and clearly enjoyed her company and conversation.[4] It would be interesting to know the name of this fresh young woman, who could so much attract the poet's eye and ear in the middle of the complex of emotions which he was then undergoing.

It is almost certain that he stayed the night in Town, probably at Taylor's, where he was to be found on the Wednesday morning. Here he heard two pieces of interesting news, one literary, and the other personal. The first was one of Taylor & Hessey's most successful scoops. Taylor put into Keats's hands a copy of a book which was to appear under their imprint the following day. This was Reynolds's parody of Wordsworth's poem, *Peter Bell*, whose impending publication had been announced. The book is a brilliant piece of anticipation, as well as a superb parody. Reynolds knew his Wordsworth well, but it may not have been all luck that he hit on the exact metre and stanza-form of the poem. Wordsworth had composed it many years before, and Reynolds may have got wind of its form. At all events, the exaggeratedly simple diction and homespun philosophy made up a side of Wordsworth which Keats could never bring himself to admire, and the parody had a special relish for him. Even more to his present taste was Taylor's other news. Morris Birkbeck, the founder of the American settlement where Keats believed George and Georgiana to be, was one of Taylor's authors. Taylor had just seen one of Birkbeck's sons, and learnt that he was leaving Town to join his father in America on April 21st or 22nd. Here was a chance for Keats to send his letters direct to George by a safe courier. On the next morning, Thursday the 15th, Keats hurried round to his old lodgings at Well Walk, to retrieve the remaining letters that had passed between him, Tom, George and Georgiana, in case any should be worth enclosing in the packet to America, as he had done at the end of October in the first packet. He sorted them, and sat down that evening at Wentworth Place to continue his own letter to George for the first time for four weeks.

It is a curious continuation. To start with, it is evidently written very late at night. The reason may have been that concentration was difficult during the daytime. This was not solely due to Fanny Brawne next door. Brown, whose school-boy nature always expanded towards small boys, had had his rowdy pair of nephews staying with him, as they had done in the Christmas holidays. There were disadvantages in this mutual housekeeping, and to a poet, abnormally sensitive to rhythm and sound, this was one. "They make a bit of a racket" is probably another of Keats's understatements, and though he only mentions their voices—"wasps stings"—it is likely they had other instruments to torture his ears in a small house. Bedtime brought relief, though evident exhaustion; the letter is weary, and the poetry composed in it a strange farrago.

These midnight couplets, "a little extempore" as Keats called them, start in the middle of some unexplained fairy-tale:

> When they were come unto the Faery's Court
> They rang—no one at home—all gone to sport
> And dance and kiss and love as faerys do
> For Fa(e)ries be as human lovers true—
> Amid the woods they were so lone and wild
> Where even the Robin feels himself exild
> And where the very brooks as if affraid
> Hurry along to some less magic shade.

The lines go on to describe a vain princess in dainty "blue silver'd" slippers, with three attendants, an Ape, a Dwarf, and a Fool, all of whom were once princes who have been changed into these shapes for various offences against the fairies. The Ape is particularly ugly with his long jaw, and is the butt of the party, on whom the vixenish little princess unleashes her sharp tongue. The Fool, whose crime was that

> He fell a snoring at a faery Ball

does not say much, but the Dwarf tries to save the situation by rhyming. After they have all gone into the Fairy Court, the princess's mule contrives to get his bridle stolen by the "Monkey men" in the woods, and trots off, at which Keats concludes "Brown is gone to bed—and I am tired of rhyming", as well he might be.

Obviously it was a joke, the kind of joke which could be understood at a glance by George and Georgiana. The only possible explanation is that the joke was a strictly family one, suggested by the family letters Keats had just been handling. The characters are, in fact, the Keats family. It is "a little quizzing" for Georgiana. She is the vain Princess in dainty slippers; Keats, next day, in a similar prose piece for her, asks "What sort of shoes have you to fit those pretty feet of yours?" The scene is both Fairyland (that is, the world of their childhood family language) and America. The clue to this is "The Monkey-men" of the poem, who live among the trees; this is made clear by another joking remark the next day in the same prose "quizzing" to Georgiana—"now you might easily distill some whiskey—and going into the woods set up a whiskey shop for the Monkeys." The rhyming Dwarf is Keats. Family humour often allows terms that would be intolerable outside, and his height had probably earned him this brotherly nickname from childhood. The Fool is Tomfool—Tom, of whom he had just been reminded by the letters. Again, family humour has its own rules. He is the lightest characterized of the four, and the reference to his death—

> He fell a snoring at a faery Ball

is only a grotesque turn of "He is not dead but sleepeth". The real ragging is reserved, as it was to be in the next day's writing, for George—the Ape. The miniature of George does show a rather long jaw and upper lip. Keats himself mentions this upper lip in an earlier letter. It was typical family humour to call him the Ape, and to make fun of his supposed ugliness to his wife, who, as later letters show, was quite capable of "quizzing" Keats back in her turn. The humorous reference to their marriage is couched in the slightly arch terms the Keats set used about young women—"picklock'd a faery's boudour"—and carries the typical middle-class joke about husbands after marriage—

> now no king
> But ape—

As for the mule, he was taken from Robertson's *History of America*, an old school prize, which Keats was just now re-reading, and so is completely in the American picture.[5] One astonishing modernism—"And they had had it"—makes the whole composition resemble even more the dialect of the sort of family language, unintelligible to outsiders, which all young people have always used, and perhaps always will. At all events, in these purely personal verses, Keats was writing himself back into some sort of poetic form, although, as he said that same night, "I cannot do it yet with any pleasure."

Yet these extempore couplets are important in the development of his style, for they are a kind of poetic signpost pointing to a new area of reading. Charles Brown said that Keats wrote *Lamia*, which he began in the middle of June, "after much study of Dryden's versification".[6] It is now, in the middle of April, that his intense "study" of Dryden begins; the *Extempore* is his first essay in the style of Dryden, and signals the beginning of this study. He began[7] to read the poems of Dryden, not so much the great political and religious satires such as *Absalom and Achitophel* or *The Hind and the Panther*, but the volumes containing the addresses and odes on various subjects, the prologues and epilogues to the plays, and, more specially, Dryden's translations and modernizations from Chaucer, Boccaccio, Ovid and others. The whole tone of the extempore couplets is that of Dryden. The opening recalls Dryden's *Prologue to the Duchess* (of York) on her return from Scotland.

> When factious Rage to cruel Exile drove
> The Queen of Beauty, and the Court of Love,
> The Muses droop'd with their forsaken Arts,
> And the sad Cupids broke their useless Darts.
> Our fruitful Plains to Wilds and Deserts turn'd,
> Like Eden's Face when banish'd Man it mourned:

Keats's couplets on the Princess, vain of her beauty, have the exact ring of Dryden, and echo his *Ode to Mrs. Anne Killigrew*.

> Beauty alone cou'd Beauty take so right.

The light verse of April 15th was a more important essay than he knew.

The next morning, Friday, April 16th, Keats was still writing light verse, but with considerably more pleasure and grasp. The young Browns had just left and the house was quiet. His verses were a counterblast to some stanzas in the style of Spenser which Brown had threatened to write—there is no evidence that he did—"against Mrs Miss Brawne and me". Keats took advantage of the dull and unpromising day to parody both Spenser and Brown's mode of life. In these three stanzas, the cheerful, stout, prematurely bald, stubble-chinned, self-indulgent, hard-drinking and lecherous Brown was described, detail by detail, in a catalogue of opposites. Parodies were already in the air, and it is reasonable to suppose that both Brown and Keats were inspired by Reynolds's jeu d'esprit on Wordsworth. On Saturday, the 17th, Keats went out with Rice, Reynolds, and their friend Martin to the first night of "a new dull and half-damn'd Opera" at Covent Garden, an adaptation of *The Heart of Midlothian* with music by the prolific composer, Henry Bishop. Once again, he seems to have spent the night at Taylor's, and stopped there all Sunday with Woodhouse, passing "a quiet Sort of pleasant day".

This occasion, there is practically no doubt, is when Keats composed his own parody of Wordsworth—not his first, for he had parodied Wordsworth's poem *Written in March, while resting on the Bridge at the Foot of Brother's Water* eighteen months before.[8] Keats's sonnet, *The House of Mourning Written by Mr. Scott*, has never before been recognized[9] for what it is—a simple parody of Wordsworth's sonnet *Composed in the Valley, near Dover, on the Day of Landing*. Wordsworth's sonnet, which is addressed to his sister, and referred to in her journal, began

> Dear fellow Traveller! Here we are once more.
> The cock that crows, the smoke that curls, that sound
> Of Bells, those Boys that on yon meadow ground
> In white-sleev'd shirts are playing by the score,
> And even this little River's gentle roar,
> All, all are English.

Keats's parody reads

> The House of Mourning written by Mr. Scott—
> A sermon at the Magdalen,—a tear
> Dropt on a greasy novel,—want of cheer
> After a walk uphill to a friend's cot,—
> Tea with a maiden lady,—a curs'd lot
> Of worthy poems with the author near,—
> A patron lord,—a drunkenness from beer,—
> Haydon's great picture,—a cold coffee pot
> At midnight when the Muse is ripe for labour,—
> The voice of Mr. Coleridge,—a french bonnet,
> Before you in the pit,—a pipe and tabour,—
> A damn'd inseperable flute and neighbour,—
> All these are vile,—but viler Wordsworth's sonnet
> On Dover: Dover! who *could* write upon it?

His parody, like Wordsworth's poem, is a catalogue; using the technique of his own Spenserian stanzas on Brown, he has made it not a catalogue of smug and cosy likes, but a list of *dislikes*. Just as Wordsworth's list culminates complacently, "All, all are English", so Keats's concludes, "All these are vile", and proceeds, as a final stroke, to add Wordsworth's own sonnet to the list. It is a parody, in its smaller scale, as trenchant as Reynolds's.

That it was written at this time is self-evident from the second half of the poem. All these seven lines refer to matters which, in the previous week of Keats's life, had got on his nerves. Haydon's great picture had been made odious by the painter's letter on Tuesday; the "cold coffee pot at midnight" reflects his chilly boredom scribbling verses late at night on

Wednesday. The voice of Mr. Coleridge had fascinated and exasperated him on the Sunday; he had been in the pit of the theatre—he could seldom afford more—the previous evening. All the early part of the week his ears had been assaulted by the racket of Brown's nephews; it is reasonable to attribute to them a drum and penny whistle. Who was the neighbour who could not be separated from playing the flute? A not too unlikely guess places this as Sam Brawne, Keats's new neighbour and Fanny's brother.[10]

One other conjecture may be made. It is only the lines from number 8 onwards that refer, directly or indirectly, to Keats's experiences during the past week. The rest seem to have little to do with him. It is possible that they were composed by Woodhouse and that the sonnet was therefore a joint composition, existing as it does only in the lawyer's handwriting. Many of the first seven lines contain matters which might well be special hates of a publisher or a publisher's reader, as Woodhouse was. *The House of Mourning* itself was a long, dull, and not very successful poem published by Taylor and Hessey themselves in 1817; unsold copies were probably on the shelves around them. "A curs'd lot of worthy poems with the author near" speaks for itself—a publisher's nightmare. "A tear Dropt on a greasy novel" may voice the good-class publisher's contempt for the average reading public. Taylor & Hessey too suffered from "patron lords", such as Lord Radstock, Clare's patron, who were apt to take literary matters alarmingly into their own hands, while Woodhouse, a connoisseur of claret, whose relations were in the wine business, would be the first to deplore "a drunkenness from beer". It would be only just if the man who preserved so much of Keats should himself be preserved—if only in these few lines that cap an unexpectedly light-hearted week.

(*An Extempore* (When they were come unto the Faery's Court)
Spenserian Stanzas on C. A. Brown
Sonnet: The House of Mourning written by Mr. Scott.)

12

LA BELLE DAME AND THE FALSE FLORIMEL

FEW famous poems make such an abrupt appearance in the world as *La Belle Dame Sans Merci*. Keats's continuation of his letter to George provides this remarkable introduction:[1]

> I have been very much pleased with the Panorama of the Ships at the north Pole—with the icebergs, the Mountains, the Bears, the Walrus—the seals, the Penguins —and a large whale floating back above water—it is impossible to describe the place—Wednesday Evening—

> La belle dame sans merci—
> O what can ail thee Knight at arms
> Alone and palely loitering?

There follows what is obviously a first or a very early draft of the poem, then a light-hearted apology for the last line of the eighth stanza,

> With kisses four.

This is followed in turn by the unfinished *Song of Four Fairies*, then by one of Keats's most profound philosophical meditations on "The vale of Soul-making", after which he concludes for the night:

> There now I think what with Poetry and Theology you may thank your Stars that my pen is not very long winded —Yesterday I received two Letters from your Mother and Henry which I shall send by young Birkbeck with this—

What is the origin of this magical poem, if indeed magic can have an origin? What had happened to Keats in the three days since he spent the quiet, pleasant Sunday writing his

parody of Wordsworth—for the reference to Birkbeck and the
letters clearly fixes the "Wednesday evening" of *La Belle Dame*
as Wednesday, April 21st? Nothing we may discover about
these three days will explain how such a poem comes into being;
but there is much that may, in Woodhouse's words, add to the
"beauty and Interest" of the poem.

On Monday, April 19th, Keats was once more in Town. He
was now alternating fallow weeks of reading and writing at
home with a fevered activity among his friends in London.
On this day, he simply did not leave himself time to do all that
he had intended. He went to Leicester Square, almost certainly to buy the imitation gems he had promised his sister.
While there, his eye was caught by an advertisement which
had appeared that day.[2]

> Henry Aston's Panorama, a novel scene representing the
> north coast of Spitzbergen, magnificent appearance of the
> ice, critical situation of the vessels, and natural history of
> the country.

Keats paid his shilling and lingered here for some time, "much
pleased" with these marvels, and quite absorbed by them; it
was with a shock that he realised that he had forgotten two
things. One was a promised visit to Mrs. Wylie, the other that
he had invited Taylor (as a return for his hospitality), Woodhouse and Reynolds to come back to dinner at Hampstead
with himself and Brown. He cut down his visit to Mrs. Wylie
to half an hour, made his apologies, and dashed home. It was
a bachelor party. After dinner they began to play cards,
probably Brag, which Brown mentions later as playing in the
company of Reynolds.

It was Woodhouse's first visit to Wentworth Place, and he
came for a purpose. It is not too much to imagine him often
being the odd man out as the other four played, and browsing
to some effect among Keats's rough drafts of poems; for owing
to the sudden storm which came on, the guests stayed playing
all night. In that time, Woodhouse evidently extracted from
Keats the manuscripts of *The Eve of St. Agnes* and of the unfinished *Hyperion;* according to his careful notes, he started
copying both these poems from Keats's manuscripts on the

very next day, Tuesday, April 20th, and this was obviously the occasion on which they came into his hands. Since *The Eve of St. Mark* follows immediately in Woodhouse's note-book, and also bears his note "Copied from J.K.'s M.S.", it seems clear that on this evening he received from Keats's hands the manuscripts of all three poems. He must have returned to his chambers in the Temple tired but well-satisfied with his all-night sitting.

Reynolds too had reason to be pleased. During the evening he extracted from Keats the promise that he would see that a review of the *Peter Bell* parody appeared in the next Sunday's *Examiner*: this, Reynolds must have known, would probably mean a review by Keats himself. Taylor seems to have mixed card-playing with religion and philosophy. Keats's thoughts often turned to theology after a visit to or from his philosophical publisher, and it is to Taylor that we may owe some of Keats's "vale of Soul-making", which follows *La Belle Dame* in the letter to George. Brown, the overgrown schoolboy, clearly conceived a schoolboy jealousy of Woodhouse—"one of his funny odd dislikes", Keats called it. He saw in the lawyer a much more methodical rival to himself as Boswell to the young poet. As for Keats, the next day found him completely knocked up with lack of sleep, smoke (Taylor was a cigar-smoker), and probably drink. He could not write a line and felt "not worth sixpence".

By the morning of Wednesday, April 21st, he felt at least enough recovered to resume his letter to George. The Wylies had sent him their letters the day before, and he wanted to add more before giving the whole packet to young Birkbeck. He also wrote his promised review of Reynolds's parody. It was a tactful notice,[3] attributing part of Reynolds's success to his real, though concealed, admiration of Wordsworth's poetry, and in it Keats drew his images, complimentary both to the poet and the parodist, from Spenser:

> This false florimel has hurried from the press and obtruded herself into public notice while for ought we know the real one may be still wandering about the woods and mountains. Let us hope she may soon appear and make good her right to the magic girdle. The Pamphleteering

Archimage we can perceive has rather a splenetic love
than a downright hatred to real florimels—

The reference is to the *Faerie Queene*, Books III, IV, and V, and
in particular to Book III, where the Witch, when her son's
love for the heroine Florimel is disappointed, makes him an
unreal double of that lady; "this false florimel" then appears to
others in place of the heroine, just as Reynolds's parody had
appeared to the public in place of Wordsworth's poem. Keats
made a fair copy of the review and sent it off to Leigh Hunt.
Then the same evening,[4] he wrote *La Belle Dame* and the poetry
and prose which accompanied it in the letter to George.

No other poem that Keats ever wrote shows so clearly the
coming-together of the mingled elements of the life he was
leading—experience, reading, thought and emotion. The
threads are closely woven, but once they are untangled, they
lie plainly visible. First, there are his own manuscripts, which
he must have at least glanced through when he handed them
to Woodhouse two nights earlier. The title, *La Belle Dame Sans
Merci*, is itself taken from *The Eve of St. Agnes*, stanza XXXIII,
line 4, where it is mentioned as the tune which Porphyro
plays to Madeline. Porphyro's feast for Madeline too gives
its "manna"—in the manuscript "manna wild"—to La Belle
Dame's

> "And honey wild, and manna dew,"

The influence of the fresh sight, which Keats had taken, of
The Eve of St. Mark is also clear. "Vallies cold", "sedge",
"aguish hills" set the scene for *St. Mark* just as the same or very
similar words do for *La Belle Dame*, while in both the heroine
looks "sidelong". Keats had a fondness for certain poetic
words—"sidelong" was one of them—but it is noticeable that
a more unusual word "aguish" is taken from *St. Mark* and
repeated in the *Song of Four Fairies*, written the same night.
Moreover, the knight's sleeping vision in *La Belle Dame* is not
unlike the legendary vision in *St. Mark*

> Of ilka gent and ilka carle
> Whom colde Deathe hath in parle.

Keats's recent glance at his two great poems certainly influenced his choice of words for the ballad; an even stronger influence was his habitual and steady reading of *The Anatomy of Melancholy*. One would now expect him to have arrived at about page 300 of the first volume. On pages 280–284 and thereabouts, Burton is dealing with the four different types of Melancholy, which he divides in the traditional way according to the four medieval "humours" of the body—hot, cold, moist, dry. Here, of course, is the idea of the *Song of Four Fairies*; but more particularly Burton deals in these pages, which Keats was reading, with those who suffer from the symptoms of the cold "humour" of melancholy,[5]

> That wandered in the woods sad all alone,
> Forsaking mens society, making great moan
> they delight in floods and waters, desert places, to walk alone in orchards, gardens, private walks back-lanes. . . . He forsook the city, and lived in groves and hollow trees, upon a green bank by a brook side, or confluence of waters, all day long, and all night. . . . They are much given to weeping, and delight in waters, ponds, pools, rivers, fishing, fowling . . . they are pale of colour, slothful, apt to sleep, much troubled with the head-ach.

Keats's knight-at-arms,

> Alone and palely loitering,

is clearly of this kind. His delusion lasts "all day long" in Burton's exact words; he seeks the neighbourhood of waters,

> Forsaking mens society, making great moan,

pale and "apt to sleep". Keats's hero is a character straight from Burton's case-book.

The title and expression of the poem owe much to *St. Agnes* and *St. Mark* and its hero, both in words and temperament, derives from Burton. Its heroine has been endlessly debated. She is Woman, Fanny Brawne, the premonition of Death, according to taste. She may be all of these things, but how she came into the poet's mind may be seen by recalling how he spent the day on which he actually wrote the poem, Wednesday, April 21st. He spent it in writing, correcting, and carefully revising his review for *The Examiner*.

La Belle Dame is taken from that review. She is, at least in part, the "false Florimel" of the *Faerie Queene*. Like the false Florimel she too is unreal, a phantom who disappears. Either the story of Florimel was vividly present in Keats's mind when he wrote, or, like a good reviewer, he looked up his references; for there is every sort of parallel between this part of the *Faerie Queene* and *La Belle Dame*. The false Florimel even meets

> An armed knight, upon a courser strong,

who rides away with her; but the clearest resemblance in words and whole phrases is that between *La Belle Dame* and part of the single stanza of Spenser's poem which describes the real Florimel and the besotted son of the Witch:[6]

> Girlonds of flowres sometimes for her fair hed
> He fine would dight; sometimes the squirell wild
> He brought to her in bands, as conquered
> To be her thrall. . . .

These passages were suggested by the review he wrote that morning; the subject of the review, Reynolds's parody, also left its mark on *La Belle Dame*. Keats said that the parody had "an inveterate cadence" of the real thing in some of its stanzas, and it is just that cadence that he himself has caught, the ballad-metre which he had not used since his Scottish poems the previous summer. The whole poem has a Wordsworthian simplicity. It even has Wordsworthian echoes.

> Her hair was long, her foot was light,
> And her eyes were wild.

is pure Wordsworth. These occur not because of some subconscious memory of Wordsworth himself, but because of the "false florimel" of Wordsworth's style which he had just been reading that morning. Moreover, he felt uneasy that his own poem might be open to the same objection and parody as

Wordsworth's. His laughing excuse for the line "With kisses four" was made because he felt it was too much like one of Wordsworth's less happy exactitudes,[7] such as

> I've measured it from side to side:
> 'Tis three feet long, and two feet wide.

Keats was conscious of his debt to Wordsworth in this poem, but conscious too that his ballad had, like the parody, "an inveterate cadence" of the older poet.

So far, every element in the poem can be related in some way to Keats's life, work and reading in the previous forty-eight hours. Yet there is another series of elements, associated with the week before, yet still working perhaps more powerfully than anything else in Keats's mind at this time. Six days before he wrote *La Belle Dame*, Keats had fetched home a bundle of letters from Well Walk.[8] These contained, as well as a letter from George to Georgiana, the two remaining letters from Keats to Tom —numbers five and six of the series of seven from the Scottish tour. Once more he re-read these letters to his dead brother, and once more they had their haunting and powerful effect on his imagination. A passage in Letter 5, about Loch Awe, which had previously struck him, was followed by an even more evocative section:

> Yesterday our walk was of this description—the near Hills were not very lofty but many of their steeps beautifully wooded—the distant Mountains in the Hebrides very grand the Saltwater Lakes coming up between Crags and Islands fulltided and scarcely ruffled—sometimes appearing as one large Lake.

Here is the lake-setting of *La Belle Dame* among the cold hills, while from a description in Letter 6 of the burial place of the Scottish kings on the Island of Iona, Keats gained the vision of the later stanzas of the poem:

> I saw pale Kings and princes too,
> Pale warriors, death pale were they all.

This spider-web of suggestions in Keats's mind seems to weave and cross from every point a pattern that makes the

whole delicate poem. Yet one point has so far been omitted—
the one which accounts for the passion and meaning of the
poem as a whole. It is rash to risk an exact meaning for so
rare and instinctive a poem as this seems to be, yet its words
and form have many links with his daily life, and so may their
meaning. The passion shown in the poem has only one parallel
in the story of the few days before Keats wrote. This is the
complicated emotion he felt over a strange discovery which he
picked up together with the other papers at Well Walk.

In Autumn, 1816, when Keats and Tom were staying at
Margate, a precociously-clever schoolfellow, Charles Jeremiah
Wells, had sent Tom some love-letters which purported to
come from a girl called Amena Bellefila. From the one sur-
viving letter, it seems impossible that he meant it as a genuine
full-blooded hoax; it is a joke so obvious that it seems certain it
was meant to be found out. The major part of the letter sets
out to be only one thing—a parody of the romantic mock-
Spenserian language used by the Keats boys and their circle.
What is more, it is a parody of the style and subject-matter of
Keats's own early poetry. It is written, in fact, very skilfully
in a sort of disguised blank verse, with occasional rhyme, but
always sidestepping into prose rhythms when one tries to pin
it down for more than two or three lines as poetry. It would
be tedious to quote it all—Wells must have had plenty of time
on his hands to compose this, which is part of only one letter—
but the following is a fair specimen:[9]

> Now would dame Fortune Fickle Jade grant me but my
> request Id prove to the(e) whether I could be ungrateful
> this Instant would I bind about thy Loins a Cuirass a
> Shield & Sword Id give to the(e) Tempered with my
> Virgin Blessing upon thy head so honorable would I place
> a shining Brazen Helmet and on the top shou'd be in form
> of an Innocent Dove mine own high Honour as sign that I
> can trust it to the Keeping the Shield shou'd be a mass
> of Shining Adament where on engraven is the name of
> thy Fair Love and on thy many couloured breast Plait
> should be stampt a holy cross in sign that thy mind as tis
> was Purity and in thy right hand thou shoulds't wield a
> spear like the one that thundering Ajax thro his superior
> in Spirit Noble Hector pierced & thou shouldst wear the

Sword that the high Britomartis wielded & with the Vow
of holy Maid shouds't thou be shielded and I my self
(pardon my presumption) woud like to (be) thy Squire
thy Page for I can ride & scour a Field as swift as did the
brave Camilla spoke of by *famous Homer* and I would
fearless hunt the Tushed Boar of Inde or oer the Moss of
Lapland would pursue the Bounding reindeer for a pure
heart doth make me fearless fit Squire to so Noble Virtuous
Knight onward with thee I'd travel cheering thy heart
with Melody of Voice and with Guitarr well strung by
Cupid God of Love would lull thy restless heart into a
melodious slumber and when that Cloyd I from my breast
would take a reeden pipe & whistle the sweet tunes and
lulabies to thy sore Love oppressed heart . . .

This apparently pointless jumble is packed with pointed
references to some of the worst lines, couplets, and stanzas of
Keats's own youthful poems. The beginning at once recalls
his *Specimen of an Induction to a Poem*—

> And that bright lance, against the fretted wall,
> Beneath the shade of stately banneral,
> Is slung with shining cuirass, sword, and shield. . . .

Further down, the jingle of an internal rhyme—

> & thou shouldst wear the Sword that the high Brito-
> martis wielded & with the Vow of holy Maid shouds't
> thou be shielded

signals a direct parody of one of Keats's least fortunate immature stanzas:[10]

> Hast thou a steed with a mane richly flowing?
>   Hast thou a sword that thine enemy's smart is?
> Hast thou a trumpet rich melodies blowing?
>   And wear'st thou the shield of the fam'd Britomartis?

In later passages of the mock-heroic prose, several of the
familiar characters of Keats's early work appear—"young
Calidore", William Wallace, on whom Keats had perpetrated
the couplet

> Of him whose name's to ev'ry heart a solace,
> High-minded and unbending William Wallace

together with Keats's youthful fancy for lying, in imagination,
on "violet beds", and many more of his poetic clichés. Even
the lines he wrote for his brother to give as a Valentine to
Georgiana are parodied, particularly those beginning

> Hadst thou liv'd when chivalry
> Lifted up her lance on high,
> Tell me what thou wouldst have been?
> Ah! I see the silver sheen
> Of thy broider'd, floating vest
> Cov'ring half thine ivory breast;
> Which, O heavens! I should see,
> But that cruel destiny
> Has placed a golden cuirass there;
> Keeping secret what is fair.

Such skits on verses that must have been common property in
the Keats circle suggest that Wells only intended a harmless if
clumsy joke. Yet this was not how it appeared to Keats, in
the half-insane outburst when he read through this and at
least one other such letter on Friday, April 16th, 1819:

> The instigations to this diabolical scheme were vanity,
> and love of intrigue. It was no thoughtless hoax—but
> a cruel deception on a sanguine Temperament, with every
> show of friendship. I do not think death too bad for the
> villain—The world would look upon it in a different light
> should I expose it—they would call it a frolic—so I must
> be wary—but I consider it my duty to be prudently
> revengeful. I will hang over his head like a sword by a
> hair. I will be opium to his vanity—if I cannot injure his
> interests—He is a rat and he shall have ratsbane to his
> vanity[11]—I will harm him all I possibly can—I have no
> doubt I shall be able to do so—Let us leave him to his
> misery alone, except when we can throw in a little more—

Every man has a blank patch in his sense of humour and
self-knowledge. Poor Tom's was probably about women, if he
indeed took stuff such as this seriously; Keats's blind spot was

probably about his early and private poems. The violence of the letter can only be explained by a complete lack of proportion in his usually balanced nature. It would be shocking and disgraceful, if we did not realise that behind it was undoubtedly the injured vanity of a poet. He would not have been human if some such element did not now and again peep its "boar's tushes"—another of his favourite expressions, parodied here by Wells—through his remarkably mature composure. Yet Keats, ultimately, was the gainer by the storm of passion that this literary trick roused in him.

Tom had been deceived by the false Amena, who had offered to be a squire

> to so Noble Virtuous Knight,

to travel with him, to love him, and to lull him to sleep. The knight of the poem is deceived by the "false florimel" of a chance meeting. The passion in the poem is Keats's passion at his own and Tom's deception, Tom in ill-health, whom he had seen dying—

> I see a lilly on thy brow,

"*death's* lilly" as he first wrote it. The story of *La Belle Dame* is, among all its other elements, the story of Keats's dead brother and the cruel deception that first his friends, and then life itself, had played upon him—the delivery of his youth to disappointment and Death. It gains for us its poignancy and immortal quality from a circumstance unseen to Keats—that within two years he himself was to go the way of his brother and to join him among the death-pale crowd.

(La Belle Dame Sans Merci. Song of Four Fairies)

13

SONNETS AND THE FIRST ODE

APRIL 21st ushers in another period of silence in Keats's personal life. The two Wylie brothers visited him on Sunday, April 25th, on the same day as his review was printed by Hunt in *The Examiner*. The next glimpse we have is of a moment on Friday, April 30th, when he and Brown sit opposite each other, copying out the sonnets and poems which Keats had written in the last few days, together with some older ones which Brown had unearthed.[1] Brown had been stung by his meeting with Woodhouse to keep closer records, and, in fact, he afterwards was of great assistance to the lawyer, and overcame his initial dislike. For Keats, the period of silence had been a period of production. The spring, beautiful and forward this year, had, as he hoped, roused him up; to these days belong several sonnets and the first of his great odes, the *Ode to Psyche*.

Keats introduced this ode in his letter to George in these words[2]—

> The following Poem—the last I have written is the first and the only one with which I have taken even moderate pains. I have for the most part dash'd of(f) my lines in a hurry. This I have done leisurely—I think it reads the more richly for it and will I hope encourage me to write other thing(s) in even a more peac(e)able and healthy spirit. You must recollect that Psyche was not embodied as a goddess before the time of Apuleius the Platonist who lived after the A(u)gustan age, and consequently the Goddess was never worshipped or sacrificed to with any of the ancient fervour—and perhaps never thought of in the old religion—I am more orthodox that to let a he(a)then Goddess be so neglected—

Keats's remark that this poem is the last he has written must be taken, together with his statement that it was composed leisurely, to mean that it is the latest to be completed. His introduction to George echoes the tone of a passage in *The Anatomy of Melancholy* which he was reading much earlier in the month:[3]

> ... they will flock afar off to hear him, as they did, in Apuleius, to see Psyche ... many mortal men came to see fair Psyche, the glory of her age: they did admire her, command, desire her for her divine beauty, and gaze upon her, but, as on a picture: none would marry her, *quod indotata:* fair Psyche had no money.

Keats's idea that Psyche was "so neglected" is clearly derived, though he gives different reasons for it, from Burton. He seems, as he said, to have taken pains to work out this idea, and this probably involved a reading of some translation of Apuleius himself.

At all events, he does not seem to have started the poem until just after the memorable night of April 21st, but there are close links that show he did start it then, and that the ode was begun in an aftermath of the mood which had produced *La Belle Dame* and its accompanying poem. The "moss-lain" Dryads, who are "lull'd to sleep" belong to the verbal pattern of the first poem, while there are also verbal likenesses to the *Song of Four Fairies*. The two have a common vocabulary, "Vesper", "Zephyr", "couches", "fans" and so on, and they have a common source too. The Scotch letters 5 and 6 also contributed their colour and atmosphere to the classical ode.

Yet for the very fact that he was writing an ode at all, Keats's new and intense reading of Dryden must be held responsible. Dryden favoured this form, and produced some fine poems in it, of which the *Ode to Mrs. Anne Killigrew* is one of the best. Keats had already echoed Dryden, and this ode in particular, in his light-hearted *Extempore*; now he was beginning to follow the model of Dryden in his more serious poems. The seventeenth-century writers, with their balance of verbal felicity and well-expressed thought, have always been a happy hunting-ground for later poets. Keats was now applying his intensive study to two such writers, Burton with his prose from the first half of the seventeenth century, and Dryden with his poetry from the second half. Burton and Dryden form no bad mental

field for a poet's grazing, especially for a poet who already had
a general acquaintance with the Latin classics, in which both
writers are steeped. Together they guided one of Keats's
most fruitful and imaginative periods of work in the late
spring and early summer of 1819. When Brown, in Keats's
words, rummaged up the sonnets that Keats had been writing
at this time, he copied out the first fruits of this new alliance
in Keats's mind. All these poems can roughly be defined as
offshoots from his reading of Burton and Dryden; they take
their subjects and expression largely from Burton and Dryden,
with the exception of the interesting but unsatisfying sonnet
On the Sonnet, which seems to be a pure experiment, and to
derive from no source, conscious or unconscious. The others
show all kinds of variants of this admittedly very variable
formula. *To Sleep*, for instance, derives its thought and some
of its expression from the specific passage he was reading in the
Anatomy, entitled *Waking and terrible dreams rectified*. Keats was
always most affected by other poetry in quotation. Here his
inspiration for the tone and movement of the sonnet are the
lines quoted by Burton,[4]

> Sleep, rest of things, O pleasing deity,
> Peace of the soul, which cares dost crucifie,
> Weary bodies refresh and mollifie.

Burton calls it "sweet moistning sleep"; Keats, in a draft,
spoke of "Its sweet-death dews". His beautiful sestet, beginning

> Then save me, or the passed day will shine
> Upon my pillow, breeding many woes

echoes the sense of Burton's[5]

> for the most part our speeches in the day time cause our
> phantasy to work upon the like in our sleep;

while the lovely last line may be compared with Burton's[6]

> "God Morpheus . . . with a horn and ivory box".

The most interesting of Keats's sonnets at this time, from
every point of view except that of poetic achievement—which

is no more, it must be said, than mediocre—are the pair *On Fame*. Reading on in his second volume of Burton, Keats was specially struck with the chapter providing the Melancholy man with remedies *Against Envie, Livor, Emulation, Hatred, Ambition, Self-love, and all other Affections.*[7] He marked with approval down the margin the last paragraph of this chapter beginning

> I was once so mad to bussell abroad, and seek about for preferment, tyre my self, and trouble all my friends;

Just before this paragraph, he read the phrase, "I have learned, *in what state so ever I am, therewith to be contented*", and as a tail-piece to the whole chapter, this couplet, translated from Prudentius:

> Mine haven's found: Fortune and Hope, adieu!
> Mock others now: for I have done with you.

This alone would seem to account for the sentiment and particularly the final couplet of his first sonnet; but Keats also found a surprising confirmation of his mood in Dryden. He was reading Dryden's *Prologues and Epilogues*. Dryden's epilogue to his play *The Conquest of Grenada* has a passage beginning[8]

> Fame, like a little Mistriss of the Town,
> Is gaind with ease; but then she's lost as soon;
> For, as those taudry Misses, soon or late,
> Jilt such as keep 'em at the highest rate . . .
> So, Fame is false to all that keep her long;
> And turns up to the Fop that's brisk and young.

A few lines later, Keats read

> 'Twill be high time to bid his Muse adieu:
> Well he may please himself, but never you.

What Keats wrote he derived without question from his reading in the two books:

> Fame, like a wayward girl, will still be coy
> To those who woo her with too slavish knees,
> But makes surrender to some thoughtless boy,

> And dotes the more upon a heart at ease;
> She is a Gipsey, will not speak to those
> Who have not learnt to be content without her;
> A Jilt, whose ear was never whisper'd close,
> Who thinks they scandal her who talk about her;
> A very Gipsey is she, Nilus-born,
> Sister-in-law to jealous Potiphar;
> Ye love-sick Bards! repay her scorn for scorn;
> Ye Artists lovelorn! madmen that ye are!
> Make your best bow to her and bid adieu,
> Then, if she likes it, she will follow you.

So Burton and Dryden chime together to a remarkable degree in this sonnet, and they must also have chimed with some feeling in his own life, for him to be so sensitive to their echo. He was writing about something, someone, some real and living situation; we may not have all the clues, but we must give him the credit for having real and not trivial feelings, which appear again in the second sonnet on Fame, written, he says, while Brown was copying the first into a note-book. This also has its echoes from Burton[9] and Dryden, but inspiration was closer at hand than that.

He wrote this sonnet on the fine early summer day of April 30th at Wentworth Place; the setting, when all reading is considered, was his real new inspiration. He was living with Fanny Brawne next door, at a wall's thickness; French windows opened into the garden from her house just as they did from his. Here was the setting for the *Ode to Psyche*, with its hint of love always impending, just round the corner:

> A bright torch, and a casement ope at night
> To let the warm Love in.

In the sonnets there is more than one sign that he was shutting the door on a former love and inspiration, and opening it wide to another and more finally dominant influence. There is another sonnet, written a little earlier—at least by April 16th—which does not merely take its imagery from Dryden's translations of Ovid, but provides some hint of what was going on in Keats's mind at this moment. It is a key to this period, just as the sonnet *Why Did I Laugh?* is a key to the darker period in

his life a month before in the middle of March. Like that
sonnet, this one is based on a dream or a half-waking vision,
and, in the same way, the occasion is described quite frankly
in a passage from his letter to George:[10]

The fifth canto of Dante pleases me more and more—

—Keats had returned to his reading of the *Inferno* in Cary's
translation, which he had taken with him on his Scottish
tour—

> The fifth canto of Dante pleases me more and more—it
> is that one in which he meets with Paolo and Francesca—
> I had passed many days in rather a low state of mind and
> in the midst of them I dreamt of being in that region of
> Hell. The dream was one of the most delightful enjoy-
> ments I ever had in my life—I floated about the whirling
> atmosphere as it is described with a beautiful figure to
> whose lips mine were joined as it seem'd for an age—and
> in the midst of all this cold and darkness I was warm—
> even flowery tree tops sprung up and we rested on them
> sometimes with the lightness of a cloud till the wind blew
> us away again—I tried a Sonnet upon it—there are four-
> teen lines but nothing of what I felt in it—O that I could
> dream it every night—

Keats's debt to Cary's translation is clear without his
acknowledgment; he even gives the circle of Hell, in which
his figures are blown, some of the attributes, the rain for
instance, which are only found in the next circle of Hell at the
beginning of the following canto. The main image of this
sonnet is drawn again from Ovid's Metamorphoses in Dryden's
translation, this time from Book One:

> While *Hermes* pip'd, and sang, and told his tale,
> The Keeper's winking eyes began to fail. . . .

> Thus *Argus* lies in pieces, cold and pale;
> And all his hundred eyes, with all their light,
> Are clos'd at once in one perpetual night.

The long last line of the sonnet, with its extra syllables, is also taken from the occasional alexandrines with which Dryden varies the couplets of this part of the translation.

Yet this sonnet is not only another of those which show how closely Keats was reading Dryden; it reveals even more about his personal life. Just as the sonnet *Why Did I Laugh?* was born of a dreaming vision of a man and two women—himself and two loves—this new dream presented him with a clear picture of himself and one woman. The one like the other was an abstraction of the events of his life. There is now only one love in the field. Isabella has been pushed back into the shades, where she had perhaps for some time belonged. Whatever the decision was, Keats had made it, or had it made for him by circumstances. Fanny Brawne has been his near neighbour for less than a fortnight, and the balance has tipped in her direction. Melancholy haunts him, and is to haunt him through all the unforgettable poems he is about to write, a sense of the waste and tragedy of life; but as far as life goes, rightly or wrongly, he has made his choice. He now faces the world with the single problem of his love, to add to those which must always face the artist. The joy and the strange melancholy that this experience was to bring to him are both expressed and foreshadowed in this beautiful sonnet:

> As Hermes once took to his feathers light,
> When lulled Argus, baffled, swoon'd and slept,
> So on a Delphic reed, my idle spright
> So play'd, so charm'd, so conquer'd, so bereft
> The dragon-world of all its hundred eyes;
> And, seeing it asleep, so fled away,
> Not to pure Ida with its snow-cold skies,
> Nor unto Tempe, where Jove griev'd that day;
> But to that second circle of sad hell,
> Where in the gust, the whirlwind, and the flaw
> Of rain and hail-stones, lovers need not tell
> Their sorrows,—pale were the sweet lips I saw,
> Pale were the lips I kiss'd, and fair the form
> I floated with, about that melancholy storm.

> (*Ode to Psyche. Sonnets* on Sleep, Fame (2),
> on A Dream, on the Sonnet)

14

MAY AND THE TWO GREAT ODES

TO the greatest number of his ordinary readers the name
Keats at once conjures up two of his works—the *Ode to a
Nightingale* and the *Ode on a Grecian Urn*. Apart from the first
line of *Endymion* and some lines from the Chapman's Homer
sonnet, these two odes are probably quoted more commonly
than the whole of the rest of Keats's work put together.
Whether they give a true or a false impression of his whole
work is another matter, though it is certain that a reader who
only knew these 130 lines would have a good idea of Keats's
characteristic poetic style. It is a larger question whether the
philosophy of these poems is also characteristic or whether it
was a phase which Keats was passing through at the time.
This philosophy has a single, coherent, and eternal theme.
The poet sees the world as a vale of tears—though Keats,
chameleon-fashion, had denied this a fortnight earlier—in
which all human activities are subject to decay and death.
He only finds certainty and survival, or indeed truth, in ideal
beauty—in the one ode, the beauty of nature, exemplified by
the nightingale's song, in the other the eternal beauty of art,
transfixed and transfigured for ever in the Grecian Urn.

It is a philosophy which has been held by many poets
before Keats and since; one is at once reminded of W. B.
Yeats's Byzantium poems. Yet it is not entirely typical of
Keats, nor even of some of his thought just before this time.
In his letter to George he rejected, a fortnight earlier, the
"vale of tears" view of life, and substituted what he called
"the vale of Soul-making", in which he accepted the misfortune
of the world as a necessary part of the soul's evolution:[1]

> Do you not see how necessary a World of Pains and
> troubles is to school an Intelligence and make it a Soul?
> A Place where the heart must feel and suffer in a thousand
> diverse ways?

This is far more like the robust philosophy which Keats carried out in most practical affairs of his daily life. It must be asked whether there were special circumstances which made him adopt an equally valid but distinctly different philosophy when he wrote the two great odes in the month of May, 1819.

It was, in fact, on April 30th that he first drafted the Nightingale ode. Brown says that he wrote it under the plum-tree in the garden at Wentworth Place, and makes it clear that this was on the same day that the sonnets and other fugitive poems were "rummaged up" and copied.[2] It is this setting that runs like a happy summer's day through all the gamut of great poems that he now began to write—Wentworth Place, the graceful little double house, he and Brown in one half, Fanny and her family in the other. The garden plot with its ancient and still-standing mulberry, a laurestinus hedge sheltering it from the lane and passers-by, was the calm and restful setting for the work of this perfect summer. The weather itself can claim to have begotten much of these poems. He closed his letter to George:

> this is the 3d of May and everything is in delightful forwardness; the violets are not withered before the peeping of the first rose;

this flower-pattern is echoed in stanza v of the ode.

> Fast fading violets, cover'd up in leaves,
> And mid-May's eldest child
> The coming musk-rose, full of dewy wine,

Keats, again on the subject of the joyously early summer weather, wrote to his sister Fanny on the next day, the 1st of May:[3]

> O there is nothing like fine weather . . .—and, please heaven, a little claret-wine cool out of a cellar a mile deep—with a few or a good many ratifia cakes—a rocky basin to bathe in, a strawberry bed to say your prayers to Flora in . . .

This is practically a prose version of stanza ii of the ode, which he had written on the previous day,

O for a draught of vintage! that hath been
Cool'd a long age in the deep-delved earth,
Tasting of Flora and the country green,

Keàts probably went on making small but important revisions
to the poem in the early part of May before the new ode, *On a
Grecian Urn,* absorbed him. The careful Woodhouse attributed
both odes to May.

It seems certain that he was happy here at Hampstead,
anchored by the beauty of the place and his growing love for
Fanny. A slow attachment is the deepest, and so it was with
theirs. Much too must be allowed to the bachelor comfort of
Brown's house, the encouragement of his cheerful friend, the
occasional bottle from the dark little cellar that still survives
in the damp little basement, where the new maid, Irish Abigail,
was all too soon attracting the amorous attentions of Brown.
It seemed an idle life to Keats, but it was productive of great
poetry. Nor can his life at any time be called idle while he
still carried on the intensity of his habitual reading.

The Nightingale ode does not by any means describe the
sunny morning under the plum-tree when Brown saw the poet
writing it.[4] The first two stanzas might, at a stretch, be said
to have this setting, especially if one thinks of the claret-cellar
in the underground basement of Wentworth Place, but from
the last line of stanza ii onwards the setting is entirely different.
Keats is listening to the bird in the dark, at midnight, in "the
forest dim", a tangled wood of half-seen leaves and flowers,
filled with wafts of scent. Some critics have been led, perhaps
by the imaginative picture by Severn, which hangs in Keats
House, to seek another setting for Keats's experience, in
another quarter of Hampstead Heath. Yet it was not into
any actual stretch of country that Keats's imagination passed
in that summer-garden morning, but into a landscape of the
mind, which, in his reading, he had visited and enjoyed before.

Among Keats's early reading, closely allied with his enjoyment of the "old English" poems of Chatterton, was the
charming medieval verse-allegory called *The Flower and the
Leaf.* In Keats's time this poem was generally attributed to
Chaucer, and Keats quoted, as from Chaucer, five lines from
it to preface one of the most considerable poems of his own

1817 volume. At the same time, early in 1817, he wrote one
of his own minor sonnets after reading this idyll—

> This pleasant tale is like a little copse

Now after an interval of two years, in the early summer of 1819,
he was delighted to come upon it again, not this time in the
pages of Chaucer, but in the delicate and sympathetic modern-
ized translation of Dryden.

It is in Dryden's pages, as Keats read them at this time,
that he found the story, particularly its introduction, which
had such an effect on the theme and setting of the ode.[5] The
unknown writer of *The Flower and the Leaf* wanders at midnight
to seek the nightingale in a wood where

> The thick young Grass arose in fresher Green

along a path which eventually leads to

> A soft Recess, and a cool Summer Shade;

It was into this scenery that Keats wandered when he wrote

> But, in embalmed darkness guess each sweet,
> Wherewith the seasonable month endows
> The grass, the thicket, and the fruit-tree wild;
> White hawthorn, and the pastoral eglantine;

here, in a country of imagination, he listened to the song

> While thou art pouring forth thy soul abroad
> In such an ecstasy!

So too did the unknown medieval poet listen to his nightingale:

> So sweet, so shrill, so variously she sung,
> That the grove eccho'd, and the Valleys rung:
> And I so ravish'd with her heav'nly Note
> I stood intranc'd, and had no room for Thought,
> But all o'er-pow'r'd with Extasy of Bliss,
> Was in a pleasing Dream of Paradice;

So too did the older poet see the nightingale close at hand, in a couplet which gives Keats the setting and the words for his ode:

> Where stood with Eglantine the Lawrel twin'd;
> And both their native Sweets were well conjoin'd.

These are not merely isolated examples; it is clear that these lines, which almost immediately follow, gave Keats many images for his poem:

> Nor till her Lay was ended could I move,
> But wish'd to dwell for ever in the Grove.
> Only methought the time too swiftly pass'd,
> And ev'ry Note I fear'd would be the last.
> My Sight, and Smell, and Hearing were employ'd,
> And all three Senses in full Gust enjoy'd.
> And what alone did all the rest surpass,
> The sweet Possession of the Fairy Place;
> Single, and conscious to my Self alone
> Of Pleasures to th' excluded World unknown.
> Pleasures which nowhere else, were to be found,
> And all *Elysium* in a spot of Ground.

Even the famous lines from stanza ii of the Nightingale ode,

> Tasting of Flora, and the country green,
> Dance, and Provencal song, and sunburnt mirth!

follow in the sequence of the older poem, as it unfolds its story. The allegory of the medieval writer proceeds to a vision of two festal troops who appear in this place,

> Thus dancing on, and singing as they danc'd.

One is led by Diana, some of whose squires

> The Boughs of Woodbind or of Hauthorn held.

The other party is commanded by Flora. Flora's company of ladies is dressed in green, and in dancing too long in the heat of the day, which has now dawned, they become first overheated and then drenched by a thunderstorm, and have to have "their Sun-burnt Cheeks" attended to by the votaries of Diana. This, and much more, Keats read in this charming poem, which, it is worth noting, Dryden himself described in his preface as being "after the manner of the *Provencalls*".

Thus Keats unconsciously took from this source a great deal of the woodland setting and many verbal echoes for his nightingale's song, which, like that of *The Flower and the Leaf*, was not the melancholy strain of most poets, but a solvent for care and grief. In Burton's *Anatomy*, he was also reading about the similar properties of wine which[6]

> *glads the heart of man*, Psal. 104.15; *hilaritatis dulce seminarium*. Helenas boule, the sole nectar of the Gods, or that true nepenthes. . . which puts away care and grief.

The theme of wine and of Bacchus in the poem is certainly derived from Burton; even more certainly is the lovely description of the nightingale's song as "thy high requiem". A page later[7] in Burton there follows the Latin line,

> Bacchus et afflictis requiem mortalibus affert.

The page of Burton on which this quotation occurs is headed by one of Keats's approving pencilled ticks in the margin, a sure sign that the whole passage had pleased him. The next time he makes this mark of approval, some forty pages later, is at the head of a passage just as surely connected with the *Ode on a Grecian Urn*. The general setting of the Nightingale ode had been inspired by Dryden, and some of its details by Burton. With the *Ode on a Grecian Urn*, the position was reversed. Burton provided Keats with hints for the main theme and much of the general philosophy. The passage he had now reached and noted was near the beginning of Burton's great *Third Partition* on *Love-Melancholy* which was to absorb Keats all through the summer. The chapter which early won his approval was the section on *Pleasant Objects of Love*:[8]

> Pleasant objects are infinite, whether they be such as have life, or be without life. Inanimate are countries, provinces, towers, towns, cities, as he said, *Pulcherrimam*

THE WHITE HORSE CELLAR (NOW CALLED THE CRYPT), SOUTH STREET, CHICHESTER. From a wine-merchant's trade-card, circa 1830.

THE PULPITUM, THE VICARS' HALL, CHICHESTER.
From a photograph of a water-colour sketch by Sir Gilbert
Scott, painted sometime before 1870.

STANZA 3 OF KEATS'S LYRIC 'HUSH, HUSH'.
From Keats's copy of the Literary Pocket Book for
1819.

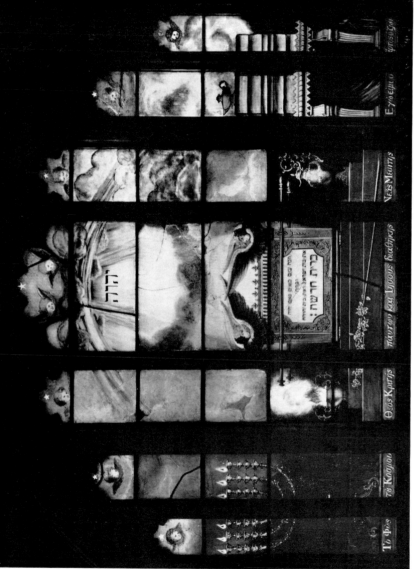

THE EAST WINDOWS, STANSTED CHAPEL.

W. ROBERTSON, D.D.

Sir Jos. Reynolds pinx!   *London. Published by S.A.& H.Oddy June 1. 1808.*   *Mackenzie sculp.*

FRONTISPIECE OF 'THE HISTORY OF AMERICA' BY WILLIAM
ROBERTSON (which Keats possessed).

John Lerius the Burgundian *cap.* 8. *hist. navigat. in Brasil.*
is altogether on my side. For whereas (saith he) at our coming
to Brasil, we found both men and women naked as they were
born, without any covering, so much as of their privities,
and could not be perswaded, by our Frenchmen that lived a
year with them, to wear any, [a] *Many will think that our so*
long commerce with naked women, must needs be a great
provocation to lust; but he concludes otherwise, that their
nakedness did much less entice them to lasciviousness, then
our womens cloaths. *And I dare boldly affirm,* (saith he)
that those glittering attires, counterfeit colours, headgears,
curled hairs, plaited coats, cloaks, gowns, costly stomachers,
guarded and loose garments, and all those other coutrements,
wherewith our country-women counterfeit a beauty, and so
curiously set out themselves, cause more inconvenience in this
kinde, then that Barbarian homeliness, although they be no
whit inferior unto them in beauty. I could evince the truth
of this by many other arguments; but I appeal (saith he) *to my*
companions at that present, which were all of the same mind.
His country-man Montague in his Essayes, is of the same
opinion; and so are many others; out of whose assertions
thus much in brief we may conclude: that beauty is more
beholding to art then nature; and stronger provocations pro-
ceed from outward ornaments, then such as nature hath provided. It is true that those fair sparkling eys, white neck, coral
lips, turgent paps, rose-coloured cheeks, &c. of themselves are
potent enticers; but when a comely, artificial, well-composed
look, pleasing gesture, an affected carriage shall be added, it
must needs be far more forcible then it was, when those
curious needle-works, variety of colours, purest dyes, jewels,
spangles, pendants, lawn, lace, tiffanies, fair and fine linnen,
embroideries, calamistrations, oyntments, &c. shall be added,
they will make the veriest dowdy a goddess, when nature
shall be furthered by art. For it is not the eye of it self
that entiseth to lust, but an *adulterous eye,* as Peter terms it,
2. epist. 2. 14. a wanton, a rolling, lascivious eye: A wandring eye, which Isaiah taxeth, 3. 16. Christ himself, and
the Virgin Mary had most beautiful eys, as amiable eys as any
persons, saith [b] Barradius, that ever lived; but withall so
modest, so chaste, that whosoever looked on them, was freed
from that passion of burning lust; if we may believe [c] Gerson

[a] Multi tacite opinantur commercium illud adeo frequens cum Barbaris nudis, ac
presertim cum fœminis, ad libidinem provocare, at minus multo noxia illorum nuditas
quam nostrarum fœminarum cultus. Ausim asseverare splendidum illum cultum,
fucos, &c.   [b] Harmo. evangel. lib. 6. cap. 6.   [c] Serm. de concep. virg. Physio-
gnomia virginis omnes movet ad castitatem.

"Beware of the rustling of silks and the creaking of shoes"

A PAGE FROM KEATS'S COPY OF BURTON'S 'THE ANATOMY OF
MELANCHOLY'.

ISABELLA JONES'S HANDWRITING.   From a letter to John Taylor, dated April 14th, 1821.

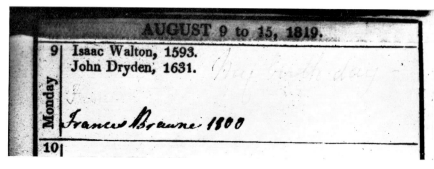

Early 1819 (ink) and late 1820 (pencil).

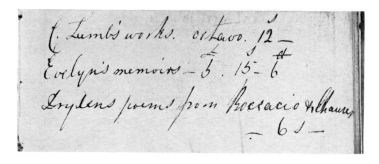

Late 1820.

FANNY BRAWNE'S HANDWRITING.
From Keats's copy of the Literary Pocket Book for 1819.

insulam videmus, etiam cum non videmus; we see a fair island by description, when we see it not. The sun never saw a fairer city, *Thessala Tempe*.

The verbal echo of "Tempe", in Keats's line

In Tempe or the dales of Arcady

was no coincidence; Keats went on to develop the thought of his reading, and to construct a poem, once more, on the lines of Burton's philosophy. For Burton, after previously quoting Plato to show that Beauty is a good in itself, proceeds through this section and that which follows—*Honest Objects of Love*—to develop the Platonic theme that Good and Beauty and Wisdom are identical, that virtue is a good and a beauty in itself, and is the only way of expressing an eternal truth:[9]

> No beauty leaves such an impression, strikes so deep, or links the souls of men closer than virtue.
> Non, per deos, aut pictor posset,
> Aut statuarius ullus, fingere
> Talem pulchritudinem, qualem virtus habet:

and, a line or two later,

> vertue's lustre never fades, is ever fresh and green, *semper viva* to all succeeding ages.

"Beauty is truth, truth beauty"—the old philosopher has practically said it; only Keats, with that precision which great poetry affords, has fixed it in five words for ever.

Much of the actual verbal expression comes from Dryden, but the thought is here in Burton. Many other influences can be traced,[10] but his immediate reading of Burton and Dryden is stamped all over the thought and the verbal expression of this ode. Burton suggested the philosophic solution to Keats's dilemma. Yet the dilemma itself is not to be found anywhere in Keats's reading. There must have been something in his life which caused him to abandon, or at any rate to lose sight of the philosophy of the "vale of Soul-making", and feel in his own words in this ode "a heart high-sorrowful and cloy'd".

Something in his life had strangely saddened his view of a May morning.

What had happened was this. On May 13th the long-expected letter arrived from George in America. The contents have not survived—the letter was destroyed by accident soon after Keats read it—but they were evidently ominous. "I have had good news (tho' 'tis a queerish world in which such things are call'd good)" was the best that Keats could find to say about his brother and sister-in-law. They had altered their plans and had not gone to Morris Birkbeck's settlement. Instead George was investing his capital in some trading concern in Hendersonville, Kentucky, and was evidently needing more money. To Keats, who had always regarded his brother, though younger than himself, as the family sheet-anchor, it seemed that he himself must now take up his role of elder brother, and become what he hated being most, a responsible man of affairs. He began talking, not very happily, of trying to get a job. According to Fanny Brawne,[11] he wrote to George offering all the financial help that was in his power. This letter, like George's, has not survived, and there is evidence that Keats dashed it off so impetuously that he half-forgot he had sent it.[12]

These circumstances are enough by themselves to show why, in this month of May, Keats's world had, as he said, "taken on a quakerish look",[13]

> Where but to think is to be full of sorrow
> And leaden-eyed despairs.

The torment of thoughts, the fever and fret of business—to these was added the burden of mortality, of Love's decay and death. Keats had been reminded of his dead brother so much a few weeks before that he had enshrined his memory in an imperishable lyric. In the Nightingale ode he wrote the line

> Where youth grows pale, and spectre-thin, and dies;

with Tom still in mind. This world was the world in which youth dies. It was also the world disfigured by disease,

> Where Beauty cannot keep her lustrous eyes

Keats spoke of his life as a time when "the death or sickness of some one has always spoilt my hours". The order may be significant. Tom had died the previous December. By this May, Isabella Jones had fallen ill; she wrote at the end of this month to Taylor:[14]

> You once favoured me with the most amusing and delightful letter I ever read (Love epistles excepted) and that at a time when perhaps I did not feel its value, being blest then with better health; now I request that you will in charity write . . .

She left Town this summer not for Bo Peep, but for Tunbridge Wells, to take the cure there. She spoke in the same letter of "*our* favourite *Endymion*". It is unlikely that Keats was still seeing her at this time, but, in going to see his own portrait by Severn in the Royal Academy, he must have seen hers; it is also likely that he would hear the news of her illness through Taylor, Reynolds, or one of their mutual friends. Among all the uncertainties of their friendship, we at least know that she was a beautiful woman, and that there is no other woman friend of Keats who was both a beauty and who had suffered illness in this month. Fanny Brawne, though her name is not mentioned any more than Isabella's, seems to have been in radiant health.

That was the third and most vital complication in Keats's life. Fanny said distinctly, of the time when Keats wrote his offer of help to George, "At that time he was not engaged to me".[15] Yet an engagement or at least an "understanding" must have been imminent. Six weeks later he complained that she had recently "so entrammelled" him.[16] This all points to his being on the brink of some such understanding with her in May. Her nearness had cast the die in her favour, and brought some relief to him. Neither of the great odes could have been written by a man against whom all the world had turned. They are the work of a man overpowered, in the midst of distress, by the joy of a greater beauty than even he can express:[17] "I want a brighter word than bright, a fairer word than fair." Those were his feelings a few weeks later, and we can take them as at least beginning their intensity now. Fanny Brawne was the solvent for his distressed state.

Yet it is unlikely that this was more than an unofficial engagement, an "understanding", for the idea of formal engagement and marriage to her, perhaps to anyone, was bound to put thorns about his path. His uneasy and ambivalent feelings about women and about sex in general still haunted his inward being. There is not one single external event that we can pin down to this month; his private life is suddenly silent. Yet much can be seen in the marginal notes in his copy of Burton's *Anatomy*, made between the two passages which he ticked, the one connected with the first ode and the other with the second. These marginalia, therefore, belong to this exact time, and give us an indication, and an alarming one, of the state of his inner mind.

On the second page of the great compendium on *Love-Melancholy*, which Keats was just beginning to read, Burton remarks that "an old, a grave, discreet man is fittest to discourse of love matters". Keats comments[18]

> I could relate here a storry or two about old women—
> Old Men are innocents—old women are herodesses in
> these matters. Old Men let them pass with half attention
> but (not impiously I say it) old women like mary lay up
> these things and ponder them in their hearts.

Fifteen pages later, he bursts out, after some of Burton's definitions of the objects of love:[19]

> Here is the old plague spot: the pestilence, the raw scro-
> fula. I mean that there is nothing disgraces me in my
> own eyes so much as being one of a race of eyes, nose and
> mouth beings in a planet called the earth who all from
> Plato to Wesley have always mingled goatish, winnyish,
> lustful love with the abstract adoration of the deity. I
> don't understand greek—is the Love of God and the Love
> of women expressed by the same word in Greek? I hope
> my little mind is wrong—if not I could—Has Plato
> separated these loves?[20]

On the next page, following Burton's argument, he adds:

> Ha! I see how they endeavour to divide—but there appears
> to be a horrid relationship.

Much could be said about these lengthy marginal notes, and
the state of mind that they reveal; at a time when so little is
known about the rest of his life, it is perhaps as well not to
exaggerate them, certainly not to paint a whole picture from
them. Yet, coming at this time, they do not show a favourable
attitude of mind towards any sort of conventional engagement
to be married; on the contrary, they show a violence on the
subject of sex, at whose origins we can only guess.

(*Ode to a Nightingale. Ode on a Grecian Urn*)

15

TWO LESSER ODES AND *LAMIA*

KEATS'S disturbed state of mind at the end of May is
reflected in the two odes he wrote then, *On Melancholy* and
On Indolence. Both these odes, too, reflect a slight exhaustion of
poetic power and invention. Just as *The Eve of St. Mark* was
written on the backwash of effort after the great *Eve of St. Agnes*,
so these two odes are a minor counterpart of the great odes of
May. In both of them Keats searched backward in his experience, instead of taking the living moment which provided his
usual vital inspiration.

In spite of its title, the *Ode On Melancholy* takes hardly any
verbal inspiration from the pages of Burton which he was
reading at this time, though some of Burton's remedies for
head-melancholy, "nightshade", "piony seeds", and other
recipes for anointing the temples, are faintly echoed. Its debt
to Burton lies further back. The basis on which Keats built
the poem was a cancelled stanza of his own—

> Though you should build a bark of dead men's bones,
> And rear a phantom gibbet for a mast,
> Stitch shrouds together for a sail, with groans
> To fill it out, blood-stained and aghast;
> Although your rudder be a dragon's tail
> Long sever'd, yet still hard with agony,
> Your cordage large uprootings from the skull
> Of bald Medusa, certes you would fail
> To find the Melancholy—whether she
> Dreameth on any isle of Lethe dull. . . .

Keats did not go on with the poem on these lines. The cheerful
delights of April weather and his growing love intervened, for
these lines date from the time of his dark period in early spring.
At that time Keats had read this quotation in Burton,[1] chiming
with his mood:

O sad and odious name! a name so fell,
Is this of melancholy, brat of hell.
There born in hellish darkness doth it dwell.
The Furies brought it up, Megaera's teat,
Alecto gave it bitter milk to eat.
And all conspir'd a bane to mortal men,
To bring this devil out of that black den.

Jupiters thunderbolt, nor storm at sea,
Nor whirl-wind, doth our hearts so much dismay.
What? Am I bit by that fierce Cerberus?
Or stung by serpent so pestiferous?
Or put on shirt that's dipt in Nessus blood?
My pain's past cure; physick can do no good.

This has the cadence and feeling of Keats's cancelled stanza.
The stanzas of the ode as we have it follow this form, but do
not echo its words. The philosophy of the ode is borrowed
from a much later section of Burton, which he had only
recently been reading, entitled *Against Melancholy it self*.[2] The
moral of this passage, much of which Keats marked, is that
one must accept and make use of the advantages of Melancholy—"if we melancholy men be not as bad as he that is
worst, 'tis our dame Melancholy kept us so". Keats indeed
took this philosophy to a much finer conclusion in the last
stanza of the ode, to a creed of luxurious acceptance which
might stand as the Romantic poets' solution for the dilemmas
of life:

> His soul shall taste the sadness of her might,
> And be among her cloudy trophies hung.

Yet for all this, there is a slackening of poetic power in this
and the ode which follows, *On Indolence*. This ode can be
dated almost exactly to the first week in June. On the last
day of May, Keats was looking back into the past in a double
sense. He had just been destroying, in the last day or two, a
number of old letters and memoranda, "which had become of
no interest". It need hardly be said what interest these would
now be to us—Fanny Brawne's first notes, Isabella Jones's
letters with their well-turned phrases and elegant seal, the

long letter of family news he received in October from George and Georgiana. There is no knowing what he may have destroyed. What is certain is that he kept some letters which were a voice from a remoter past.

These were from the Jeffrey sisters of Teignmouth, and specially those from Marian, the poetess, who may have been his unknown benefactor of the previous November. On the last day of May he impulsively wrote to her. It was the natural thing to do. A remote and sympathetic friend, who knew nothing of the real state of his mind, nor the world of experience he had been through since they last met, was a source of relief to him. This sense of relief is felt throughout the letter, which is otherwise darkly clouded.[3] He had also a motive for writing. Brown, following his usual custom, was going to let Wentworth Place this summer, this time to a Jewish gentleman named Nathan Benjamin. Keats would be homeless in a few weeks' time. He wondered if Miss Jeffrey could find him cheap lodgings near Teignmouth. He told her too that he could not contemplate the job he had thought of taking, when George's news came, that of a ship's surgeon on an East Indiaman. Although he enjoyed writing to her, his depression kept returning, and towards the end of the letter he quoted Wordsworth's lament in the *Ode on Intimations of Immortality*, that

> Nothing can bring back the hour
> Of splendour in the grass and glory in the flower.

These lines, which he slightly misquoted, may mean that Keats was re-reading the elder poet's great ode at this time. If so, Wordsworth's

> The clouds that gather round the setting sun
> Do take a sober colouring from an eye
> That hath kept watch o'er man's mortality;

may well have something to do with the final lines of Keats's *Ode on Melancholy*, with their own haunting and sober beauty.

Just over a week later, on Wednesday, June 9th,[4] he wrote again to Marian Jeffrey. She had proved a friend eager to help, and had written him two letters in the meantime, suggesting suitable places near her home for him to stay. In these few days, his mood and plans had entirely changed, with the inconsistency which was both the delight and the despair of his friends. Devon, he now thought, would only remind him of the dead Tom. Still, he might consider going there later. For the moment, the Isle of Wight was to be the place. James Rice, his cheerful invalid friend, had called on Keats on Tuesday June 8th, the day before, and proposed a month's stay at Shanklin. Keats had quite given up the idea of employment as a ship's surgeon, but perversely defended it to Miss Jeffrey:

> An Indiaman is a little world. One of the great reasons that the English have produced the finest writers in the world is, that the English world has ill-treated them during their lives and foster'd them after their deaths. They have in general been trampled aside into the bye paths of life and have seen the festerings of Society.

"For all this", he added, "I will not go on board an Indiaman".

It was not only his plans that had changed, but his attitude to life too. It was more cynical and tougher, as these words would suggest. So was his attitude to his own poetry:

> I daresay my discipline is to come, and plenty of it too. I have been very idle lately, very averse to writing; both from the overpowering idea of our dead poets and from the abatement of my love of fame. I hope I am a little more of a Philosopher than I was, consequently a little less of a versifying Pet-lamb.

The rejection of Fame and the Pet-lamb remark make it clear that he has just written the *Ode on Indolence;* his next sentence but one confirms it:

> You will judge of my 1819 temper when I tell you that the thing I have most enjoyed this year has been writing an ode to Indolence.

This ode, though certainly not typical of his "1819 temper", was another piece of looking back, and it is an interesting

example of the way Keats's mind worked. He had now read
on a little further in Burton, and had come upon this quotation,
in the pages of the *Anatomy*, from his favourite *Faerie Queene*:[5]

> Hard is the doubt, and difficult to deem,
> When all three kinds of love together meet,
> And do dispart the heart with power extreme. . . .

"When all three kinds of love together meet": Keats was at
once reminded of his vision, during the dark days of March, of
the three figures on a Greek vase, the figures of a man and two
women, or Poetry, Love, and Ambition. The reminder and
the cadence of Spenser's verse compelled him to recreate the
experience, in a most unusual way for him, nearly three months
later. He began his ode:

> One morn before me were three figures seen

Yet this recreating process was touched all through with his
new mood of cynicism. All three are this time dismissed; he
will not write, he will not love, he will not strive to be

> A pet-lamb in a sentimental farce.

Something had bitten deep into him to make him say this—
and, indeed, to make him even pretend that this poem sums
up the great achievements and the great personal stresses of
1819. The least convincing part of the poem is its dismissal of
Love. Just at the time that he wrote it, he must have become
at least provisionally engaged to Fanny Brawne. It had been
a long time coming. It is evident, from his reply to her, that
Fanny Brawne, in one of her letters to the Isle of Wight,
reproached Keats with being "an age" in coming to the point.
Yet when it came it was the more complete. He turned with
relief to her, perhaps all the more because she was a contrast
from others he had known—"women whom I really think
would like to be married to a Poem and to be given away by a
Novel".[6] It is not unlikely that he had one particular woman
in mind—Isabella Jones, who had been so much associated
in his mind with the love of Fame, which he had just rejected
both in prose and in poetry. In a mood of cynicism about his

worldly prospects and of relieved adoration of beauty without any attendant complications, he turned to Fanny. For the rest, as he said, "the morrow will take care of itself".

Indeed, it seemed at first as if even the worldly prospects showed some hopeful signs. Elmes, the editor of the *Annals of the Fine Arts*, wanted to print the *Ode to a Nightingale*, and Keats wrote on June 12th promising him a final copy directly he had one. Two days later, he let Elmes have it, and went with Brown to Town. The purpose clearly was to raise money. He had put off the irksome necessity of trying to raise some of the promised money for George for a month. Now, on the verge of an engagement, he wanted funds for himself as well. Brown, equally clearly, wanted the rent.

For some reason, Keats was not able to see his former guardian about money that day. All he did was to post a letter to Fanny Keats from Lombard Street, in which he mentioned his lack of money. Two days later, on Wednesday, Keats had his interview with Abbey. The point at issue was the disposal of Tom's money.[7] Keats and George, though for different reasons, both urgently wanted their shares. Abbey, a master of obstruction, produced a trump card. First, he showed Keats a letter from George announcing that a daughter —not a son as Keats had prophesied—had been born round about May 1st. This, of course, made George's case even more urgent, and it was with a kind of perverse relish that Abbey then showed his hand. He produced a solicitor's letter from one of Keats's aunts announcing that she was going to contest their claim. A Chancery suit was pending. If Abbey advanced money now to the Keats boys and the suit eventually went against them, he himself would be heavily out of pocket. So he managed to persuade Keats by the one method he knew would be successful in that quarter—an appeal to generosity.

Yet if he had calculated on depressing John, he was very wrong. Real difficulty always acted as a spur to Keats's nature. His response to this news was twofold. First he wrote to all those friends, including Haydon, who owed him money— a total of £200 or more, according to Brown.[8] Secondly, also urged by Brown, he determined to write a new and this time successful narrative poem. By the greatest good fortune, he had just read on to this page in Burton's *Anatomy*:[9]

Philostratus, in his fourth book *de vita Apollonii* hath a memorable instance in this kinde, which I may not omit, of one Menippus Lycius, a young man 25 years of age, that going betwixt Cenchreas and Corinth, met such a phantasm in the habit of a fair gentlewoman, which taking him by the hand, carried him home to her house, in the suburbs of Corinth, and told him she was a Phoenician by birth, and if he would tarry with her, *he should hear her sing and play, and drink such wine as never any drank, and no man should molest him; but she being fair and lovely, would live and die with him, that was fair and lovely to behold.* The yong man, a philosopher, otherwise staid and discreet, able to moderate his passions, though not this of love, tarried with her a while to his great content, and at last married her, to whose wedding, amongst other guests, came Apollonius; who, by some probable conjectures, found her out to be a serpent, a lamia; and that all her furniture was like Tantalus gold, described by Homer, no substance, but meer illusions. When she saw herself descried, she wept, and desired Apollonius to be silent, but he would not be moved, and thereupon she, plate, house, and all that was in it, vanished in an instant: *many thousands took notice of this fact, for it was done in the midst of Greece.*

The choice of this story as a plot for his new poem was a shrewd one. Burton is full of good stories, though not always told at such length as this one, and there is another splendid plot on the same page. Yet Keats saw, immediately he had written it, the fascination that the Lamia story would have with the public:[10]

I am certain there is that sort of fire in it which must take hold of people in some way—give them either pleasant or unpleasant sensation. What they want is a sensation of some sort.

He was right. *Lamia* has always caught the public's imagination, although, poetically speaking, it is not always Keats at his happiest.

He started it at once, and it is reasonably certain that he had completed its prologue—that is, the events which occur antecedent to the story as Burton tells it—before he arrived in the Isle of Wight at the end of the month. For the whole narrative form of the poem, and particularly these first 170 lines, he was indebted to his close and recent reading of Dryden. The couplets are managed in exactly Dryden's manner; the opening recalls Dryden's opening to his translation of Chaucer's *Tale of the Wife of Bath;* the preliminary story of Hermes is once more modelled on Dryden's translations of Ovid. Yet Keats struck gold again in Burton for the most famous passage in the poem, his first description of the snake-heroine. Reading on only twenty pages from where he had found the original story, he came upon this magnificent example of Burton's prose, which he marked heavily down the margin:[11]

> Whiteness in the lilly, red in the rose, purple in the violet, a lustre in all things without life, the cleer light of the moon, the bright beams of the sun, splendor of gold, purple, sparkling diamond, the excellent feature of the horse, the majesty of the lion, the colour of birds, peacocks tails, the silver scales of fish, we behold with singular delight and admiration.

This, falling pat when he had written only forty lines of the poem, and wished to produce his first great effect, must have seemed like an omen. Nothing is more assured than the glittering lines he then wrote:

> She was a gordian shape of dazzling hue,
> Vermilion-spotted, golden, green, and blue;
> Striped like a zebra, freckled like a pard,
> Eyed like a peacock, and all crimson barr'd;
> And full of silver moons, that, as she breathed,
> Dissolv'd, or brighter shone. . . .

A new mood of confidence filled him; cynicism and doubt vanished. Though he had neither the money to get married nor to help George, he felt able to face the world. He told Fanny Brawne,[12] just before the last week-end in June, that he would not return to London unless he had achieved something to change his fortunes. Brown had suggested another source for money. In a month, when Rice's time was up, he would join Keats at Shanklin. Together they would collaborate in a tragedy; with his knowledge of the theatre and Keats's power of verse they would take the London stage by storm. Buoyed with these hopes, Keats left London on Sunday, June 27th, and arrived at Shanklin on the following day; he was on the brink of the most intense period of creative effort of even this crowded year.

(Ode on Melancholy. Ode on Indolence.
Lamia, Part I, 1–170)

16

LAMIA AND A SONNET REVISED

K EATS had every reason to feel optimistic about the setting he had chosen for this intensive attack on his work. He had visited Shanklin for the day two years before, when he was just beginning *Endymion,* and had carried away delightful memories. The country in this south-east corner of the Isle of Wight was some of the most beautiful on the South Coast. The water, which Swinburne was later to make the setting for his poems about swimming, has often the deep blue and purple of the Cornish inlets. The downs, rising here to nearly 800 feet, the highest in the Island, descend to the sea in dazzling white cliffs. Small rivulets cut through the soft chalk in the steep valleys, known by the expressive local name of chines. Keats had been enchanted by the beauty and the solitude of the place. As he remembered it, there were only a few fisher-men's huts, perched on the slopes above the sea; the human beings were vastly outnumbered by the primroses and cowslips.

It is evident that his hopes received a shock. He had seen the Island out of season; then as now, it was quite a different place in the height of summer. Shanklin Chine was full of sight-seers with spy-glasses; the heat filled the narrow valley with mists, which Keats convinced himself were unhealthy; since his tour in the Scottish mountains, the downs looked puny; the picturesque cottages provided only narrow coffin-like apartments for visitors.

However, Keats and Rice settled in one of these cottages a little way back from the sea. Keats's action on their first clear evening there might be taken as an omen. He wrote a passion-ate letter, too passionate to send, to Fanny Brawne.[1] Passion and poetry were to fight out between them the next few months. Poetry, indeed, had plenty besides to fight against. Although Keats said he did not spend a day without "sprawling some blank verse" (the tragedy) or "tagging some rhymes"

(*Lamia*)², distractions settled on him like a swarm of wasps. A minor one, which he mentioned later, was the voice of the old lady across the way; people who live by the sea are always apt to shout, and Keats was sensitive to noise. After having nursed Tom he was also sensitive to illness, and Rice's illness weighed upon him, despite the latter's perpetual good nature. Nor was he well himself; he had caught a cold on the coach coming down.

Far from money worries being left behind in London, they pursued him with double force. On Tuesday, July 6th, he was forwarded another letter from George. This contained even more specific matters of business. George was in such urgent need of capital that Keats wrote off to Abbey the next day. He did not pursue the fruitless matter of Tom's share; but he asked to have a statement of whatever money was credited to himself, so that he could lend it to George. He also urged that George's available capital should be speedily released to him. On the same day he wrote a short letter to George. This letter has not survived, so, although it evidently repeated its offer to help, we do not know whether Keats announced his recent attachment to Fanny or concealed it, thinking that it would embarrass George still further. On the whole, the only phrase of the letter which has survived suggests that he did tell George:³

> However I shod like to enjoy what the competences of life procure, I am in no wise dashed at a difference prospect.

"What the competences of life procure" may well have included the prospect of a wife; Keats comforted himself at the same time by recalling that he could at least earn an everyday living by falling back on the old plan of becoming a doctor.

He was also writing and receiving love-letters once a week regularly. Much of what Fanny Brawne wrote to him can be inferred from his replies to her. As he had noticed six months before, she had a very young manner for her age. In her first letter she asked if it depended on "horrid people"—that is, Abbey and the aunt—whether their engagement was to develop. She also scolded him for his loving tribute to her beauty—"I want a brighter word than bright, a fairer word than fair." She then excuses herself, and brings him effectually to heel, by saying that she is afraid he will think that she does not love him. This was a normal flirtatious gambit, but Keats responded with high seriousness. He was very much in love. He made it clear too that conventional love at a respectful distance was not what his ardent and sensuous nature required. He wished their love, he said, to be "moistened and bedewed with Pleasures".

This Drydenesque phrase is a reminder that, in the middle of discouragement and distraction of every kind, he was working at a remarkable rate. In under a fortnight he had finished, he said, an act of the play, long before Brown had come to join him. This probably sounds more impressive than it was. Most amateur playwrights are hazy in speaking of acts and scenes. It appears from the manuscript that what Keats meant was a long first scene, which had to be substantially cut and revised when the more professional Brown came to look at it. Yet it is undeniable that in the same short time, he had also finished the whole of the first part of *Lamia*. With every sort of interruption, by ill-health, love, and business, this may probably be reckoned one of the greatest feats of concentration in his life. What is more, the style of the poem began to be more his own, and to lose the cadence which it had acquired from Dryden. Lines such as

About a young bird's flutter from a wood

are pure Keats. The direct echoes of Dryden are few; those that exist show that Keats was now reading, appropriately, Dryden's translation of Ovid's *Ars Amoris;* he was also reading, by other signs and even more appropriately, the section of Burton called *Beauty a Cause of Love-Melancholy*.[4] For the dialogue of his two lovers when they met, he was partly indebted to the curious coincidence that in this section of the *Anatomy* there is a dialogue, part of which he marked, between two lovers. One of these has a name which is only one letter different from his own hero—Lycias.[5]

This chapter of Burton on *Beauty a Cause of Love-Melancholy* ends with a pleasing fable, the moral of which is that there is nothing which attracts man's instinct so much as a beautiful woman.[6] Keats has been frequently hauled over the coals for the passage near the end of the First Part of *Lamia*, which says exactly this. It was certainly not a sentiment which, at this time, he would wish to excuse; his letters to Fanny are full of it.[7] The reason is the chiming-in with his mood of the simple and worldly fables of Burton rather than the Byronic cynicism of which he has been accused. Besides, he seemed to have worked through the mood of cynicism of the previous month. He had now learnt, he said, to "look upon the affairs of the world with a healthy deliberation".

Yet the second half of July was not as happy as the first. There was bound to be a reaction after the concentrated work on *Lamia*, but this was made worse by the unfortunate effect of Rice's ill-health. Rice was one of Keats's favourite friends, and he was at his kindliest here, doing the housekeeping and local marketing, and generally making it possible for Keats to work undisturbed; but Keats's own words tell what the trouble was:[8]

> He was unwell and I was not in very good health: and I am affraid we made each other worse by acting upon each others spirits. We would grow as melancholy as need be.

On July 13th, Keats felt in an "irritable state of health". On the 14th he received a letter from Fanny Brawne saying that she too had been ill. He took the letter to bed, and when he found her name on the seal obliterated the next morning, he took it at first as an evil omen. That evening when he wrote to her, something of his former cynical mood had returned, together with a bitterness about his own poems. The next day, the 16th, one of his prime causes of worry burst out. Abbey had ignored his last urgent letter. He wrote again,[9] demanding the greatest amount that he could afford to lend George, and making arrangements for Haslam to call on Abbey and expedite matters. To Fanny, he wrote that he would see her in London within a month. He probably contemplated a return to Town for both reasons. At all events, he was thoroughly unsettled.

A curtain of silence falls on Keats for a short time; when it rises it is on a scene full of smoke. In the tiny living-room of the cottage, four men were playing cards and smoking, night and morning—Keats, Rice, Brown, and the publisher Martin, who had come to take Rice away. Brown, as usual, had brought his own ebullient atmosphere. Martin had brought his sister, who lodged for a time with three friends in a cottage over the way. The whole tempo and scheme of Keats's life had abruptly changed again. Brown had brought papers and books, and was ready to drive on with the tragedy in double harness, providing the plot scene by scene while Keats wrote the dialogue. He had read and approved of the first part of *Lamia*, and had inspired Keats with new confidence.

It is as well at this point to look at the first part of *Lamia*, that is, of the main story as a whole. Some attempts have been made to try and identify the main characters—Lycius, Lamia, Apollonius—with the tense situation in which Keats now found his own life. This is tempting, but difficult to justify. Keats kept very close to the story as he found it in Burton, the story which, he knew, "must take hold of people in some way" just as it had taken hold of him. It is the most consciously artistic of all his productions, and he was not likely to allow unconscious autobiography to stray in. Yet there is a set of curious parallels, not with the present but with the past.

Many of the incidental touches in the meeting of Lycius and Lamia are like the meeting, nine months before, of Keats and Isabella Jones. First, Lycius passes her and then turns back to her, just as Keats had done in Theobald's Road. Then she recalls how she had last seen him in the city

> 'mid baskets heaped
> Of amorous herbs and flowers, newly reaped
> Late on that eve,

just as Isabella had previously seen Keats with George at Covent Garden. Then comes the wonderful passage of their walk back through the suburbs of Corinth:

> Men, women, rich and poor, in the cool hours,
> Shuffled their sandals o'er the pavement white,
> Companion'd or alone; while many a light
> Flared, here and there, from wealthy festivals,

> And threw their moving shadows on the walls,
> Or found them cluster'd in the corniced shade
> Of some arch'd temple door, or dusky colonnade.

This is identical in feeling and even in expression with Keats's words:

> As we went along, some times through shabby, some times through decent Streets I had my guessing at work, not knowing what it would be and prepared to meet any surprise—

They pass old Apollonius, Lycius's friend. Lamia shrinks. Isabella had wished to avoid their common acquaintances. They arrive at her house, described in Keats's first draft as "royal-squared", echoing the square-panelling of Isabella's apartments in Gloucester Street.

This does not mean, in any sense, that Lamia *is* Isabella—any more than she *is* Fanny, or any other woman. It may mean simply that Keats was using his experience of life in an active and creative way, looking on it, as he said, "with a healthy deliberation". One other incident suggests this. On Sunday, July 25th, when Martin had taken Rice back to Town, and the little cottage was at last quiet, Keats sat down and wrote to Fanny Brawne.[10] There is no doubt that she is the only one in his thoughts. First-hand news of her, from Brown, had overwhelmed him; she seemed distant yet unbearably close. His mood was one of exultant humility. The words and phrases poured from him:

> . . . all I can bring you is a swooning admiration of your Beauty. . . .

> I have two luxuries to brood over in my walks, your Loveliness and the hour of my death. O that I could have possession of them both in the same minute.

> I will imagine you Venus to-night, and pray, pray, pray to your star like a He(a)then.

"Your's ever, fair Star", he ended. There is no mistaking the likeness between these phrases and the second version of the *Bright Star* sonnet, which Fanny Brawne possessed and copied.

It seems more than likely that Keats wrote the second version at this week-end. Brown had just arrived, bringing, among his papers, the note-book in which he had made his collection of Keats's sonnets. The first *Bright Star*, which Keats had written the previous October, was probably among these. Now Keats made a new version. It is one more suited for a young man, however passionate, to address to his fiancée. The sensuous images of touch and feeling are toned down:

> Cheek-pillowed on my Love's white ripening breast

becomes merely

> Pillow'd upon my fair love's ripening breast

while

> To touch for ever its warm sink and swell

turns into the less realistic and milder

> To feel for ever its soft fall and swell

Similarly, "To hear, to feel" at the beginning of the last line but one becomes the less urgent "Still, still to hear". The sonnet has taken its more decorous and better-known form:

> Bright star! would I were stedfast as thou art—
> Not in lone splendour hung aloft the night
> And watching, with eternal lids apart,
> Like nature's patient, sleepless Eremite,
> The moving waters at their priestlike task
> Of pure ablution round earth's human shores,
> Or gazing on the new soft fallen mask
> Of snow upon the mountains and the moors—
> No—yet still stedfast, still unchangeable,
> Pillow'd upon my fair love's ripening breast,
> To feel for ever its soft fall and swell,
> Awake for ever in a sweet unrest,
> Still, still to hear her tender-taken breath,
> And so live ever—or else swoon to death.

If the lyric to Isabella, *Hush, hush,* was given by Keats in a fit of bravado to Fanny, he made amends here by recasting this sonnet, inspired by his meeting with Isabella, to fit his new love. This is not to say that Keats wrote a sonnet to one woman, and altered it to suit another. The two poems are sonnets to Love, and to a particular situation in his love. Keats now found himself in a second and different situation, at a time when he was acquiring a more conscious artistic control and a power of looking steadily at his own life. His life was to become, during the two months that remained of this astonishingly creative year, primarily that of a writer with a mastery over both himself and his work. His objective view over the rewriting of this sonnet is typical of the objective view he was now taking of his life in relation to his work, a view which was to seem to Fanny a sign of harshness and to his publisher Taylor a sign of pride. A month later he was to exult in this and to justify it, the self-centred joy of a writer who knows he is writing to the top of his own powers. He was now entering on a period when writing was to blot out for a time all the distractions and chances of personal life.

(*Lamia*, Part I, 171–end. *Bright Star*, final version)

17

DRAMA AND THE MOVE TO WINCHESTER

I

"BROWN and I are pretty well harnessed again to our dogcart", wrote Keats on the last day of July. He meant, as he said, the tragedy of *Otho the Great*. The composition of this was, to say the least, curious. Every day Brown sat opposite Keats and told him the events and characters of the next scene; Keats then wrote the scene or a part of it without, Brown said, ever knowing how the whole plot of the play was going to develop. If this was really the method, it is remarkable that the play has the coherence which indeed it shows. This scheme, Brown remarked, broke down over the last act, in which he attributed both plot and writing to Keats. Allowing again for amateurs' haziness over the divisions of act and scene, we can at least be safe in considering the long last scene as being Keats's unaided work.

However odd the method, it took the friends only an exact month to write a five-act drama. It was finished by August 23rd, and that in spite of one gap of at least two or three days when Brown went off on a walking-tour by himself.

There is no doubt too that Keats did some work on what was virtually a new poem—*The Fall of Hyperion, a Dream*—during this time. As early as July 25th he had spent the whole day "in a very abstract Poem", which was always his term for anything connected with *Hyperion*, while just after he and Brown left Shanklin for Winchester, which they did on August 12th, he spoke of having been at work on *Hyperion*.[1] From the common imagery which the two poems have it is clear that he wrote the new *Hyperion* either just before the second part of *Lamia*, which he resumed at Winchester, or just after. There are decisive clues that he did most of his work on *The Fall of Hyperion* after he had finished all of *Lamia*; but it is worth remembering that much of it must have been in his mind, though not on paper, while Brown and he jogged on in their daily dogcart of *Otho the Great*.[2]

Not much can be said about this collaboration, except that the results are not as bad as they might be. Keats's treatment of Brown's plot is more like his own favourites, Beaumont and Fletcher or perhaps the lesser-known Massinger, than anything else.[3] The style has not his usual clarity; the effort of dramatic composition was so great, that he seems to have given up much of the usual reading from which he refreshed his creative mind. He seems practically to have put down Burton at the chapter which had been such a favourite with him—*Beauty a Cause of Love-Melancholy*—but it is worth noticing one echo, since it is connected with a passage in the earlier part of the tragedy for which Keats had a particular affection. This is at a point when the hero Ludolph, for some reason best known to himself (or to Brown), has been fighting in battle disguised as an Arab. He is addressed by a friend, who has penetrated the disguise, as

> Ludolph, that blast of the Hungarians,
> That Saracenic meteor of the fight,

while Ludolph, in reply, says, in words which Keats quoted to his brother:

> Not as a swordsman would I pardon claim,
> But as a son. The bronzed centurion,
> Long toil'd in foreign wars, and whose high deeds
> Are shaded in a forest of tall spears,
> Known only to his troop, hath greater plea
> Of favour with my sire than I can have.

In this chapter in Burton, which Keats had been reading before tragedy engrossed him, he had noticed[4]

> a grim Sarazan sometimes
> —— nudus membra Pyracmon,
> a martiall hirsute face pleaseth best;

while in the early part of July he had seen, in common with the rest of the south of England, the comet which for several nights had swept across the sky. For the rest, Keats seems to have been too busy to look at Burton, or perhaps much else, until he was writing the last scene of the play. By that time, he and Brown had moved to Winchester.

They went, according to Keats, to be within reach of a library, and though they did not find one, the bookshops of Winchester were a good substitute. It was not only the need for books that Keats felt. In the midst of tremendous creative effort, he was moody, restless, morbid. "I begin to dislike the very door-posts here—the names, the pebbles." "Even the senseless door-posts", he wrote in Act IV of *Otho*, "Are on the watch." It was from exactly this time, in the first half of August, that he began to feel the promptings of the disease which attacked him six months later. The tubercular infection, which he had caught from nursing Tom the previous year, had just begun to invade his system, with results that he himself vividly described.[5] "Either that gloom overspread me or I was suffering under some passionate feeling, or if I turned to versify that acerbated the poison of either sensation." The beautiful land and sea-scape meant nothing to him; he did not feel well enough to bathe. Yet with these feelings there also existed the optimism and intellectual excitement which so often go with the early stages of the disease.[6] "I am in complete cue—in the fever; . . . My Mind is heap'd to the full; stuff'd like a cricket ball——"

One of the results of this state of mind was that he grew resentful and irritable with Fanny. As Haydon said,[7] he did not "bear the little sweet arts of love with patience". In the last week in July he wrote her a passionate letter, probably enclosing the *Bright Star* sonnet. She replied archly that "she must not have" any more such letters. She also told him something of her own doings, and mentioned staying out late at night. This is the first hint of her fondness for dancing, with which some biographers of Keats have made great play, and it arises from a very natural set of circumstances. Keats, in this summer of 1819, now seemed likely to stay away for an indefinite time. He showed no signs of even a fleeting visit to Hampstead. The engagement between them at this stage was of the nature of an "understanding" and need not prevent her enjoying the normal fashionable pursuits of her circle. In this very summer, these had received a welcome innovation. Under an energetic new Mess President, the Royal Artillery Mess at Woolwich had begun to give some of the best balls in London.[8] The Artillery band played for them, and at least four were organised during the summer season, of which they became one of the most widely advertised and popular features. Mrs. Brawne had an acquaintance among military men, and Fanny was taken to these dances.[9] It was probably one of these which she mentioned in the letter, without giving exact particulars, for Keats, in his reply, asked her, "What fairing is it?". That she told him, and that he did not approve, is likely from his next letter, which he wrote from Winchester. He went out of his way to say, "I am no officer in yawning quarters", and the whole letter takes on a tone which he himself called "flint-worded". In fact, when he arrived at Winchester, he did not at first write to her at all. He had a string of business letters to send off, almost certainly about George's affairs, for though Abbey had replied reasonably after his last urgent appeal, nothing much seemed to have been done. He was, moreover, deep in the last stages of *Otho*, his own unaided work. When he wrote to her on August 16th,[10] it was, in his mad hero's words, to

> Put on a judge's brow, and use a tongue
> Made iron-stern by habit!

His own heart, he now said, seemed made of iron. She had been offended that he had not kept his promise of coming to see her. She had told him—another familiar lover's gambit—that he might do as he pleased. He replied with cold realism that he could not do as he pleased; his life was ruled by lack of money.

It is likely that Ludolph's picture of his unfaithful bride in the last scene of the play is a picture of Fanny Brawne, drawn in exact physical detail;[11] he also echoes the tone and words of Keats's letter to her on August 16th. It would be foolish to take the parallel too far, since everything that Keats wrote was an amalgam of life and reading. On coming to Winchester, he had begun, after the long working interval, to take up Burton again; once more the 17th-century prose helped to enrich the wild and splendid setting which Keats planned for his mad hero's death-scene. In the very chapter on *Artificial allurements of love,* Keats marked several passages on women's dress, of which this is the shortest:[12]

> ... those curious needle-works, variety of colours, purest dyes, jewels, spangles, pendants, lawn, lace, tiffanies, fair and fine linnen, embroideries, calamistrations, oyntments &c.

At the bottom of the page he added his own comment from *King Lear:*

> Beware of the rustling of silks and the creaking of shoes

This was clearly in his mind for lines 85–90 of the last scene, where his hero describes his heroine as

> Sweeping into this presence, glisten'd o'er
> With emptied caskets, and her train upheld
> By ladies, habited in robes of lawn,
> Sprinkled with golden crescents, others bright
> In silks, with spangles shower'd,

There are other echoed quotations and marginal comments,[13] which show how much Keats was savouring his reading, and recreating it in his writing. He was now what he most wanted to be, a writing animal. "I am convinced more and more day by day that fine writing is next to fine doing, the top thing."[14] Filled with the joy of fine writing both in himself and others, Keats felt at the peak of his abilities. In two months, he had written well over 1500 lines; he now proposed to work for another two months at the same rate. Within a few days of reaching Winchester he had finished one play; such was his confidence that he immediately started on another.

(Otho the Great)

II

Brown relates exactly how *King Stephen* came to be written at Winchester:[15]

> As soon as Keats had finished *Otho the great*, I pointed out to him a subject for an english historical tragedy in the reign of Stephen, beginning with his defeat by the Empress Maud, and ending with the death of his son Eustace, when Stephen yielded the succession to the crown to the young Henry. He was struck with the variety of events and characters which must necessarily be introduced; and I offered to give, as before, their dramatic conduct. "The play must open", I began, "with the field of battle, when Stephen's forces are retreating—" "Stop!" he said, "stop! I have been already too long in leading-strings. I will do all this myself." He immediately set about it, and wrote two or three scenes, about 130 lines.
>
> This second tragedy, never to be resumed, gave place to "Lamia", a poem which had been on hand for some months. He wrote it with great care, after much study of Dryden's versification.

Unfortunately, when Brown copied the fragment in the following November, he dated it, as so often, not with the date of composition but with the date of his copying, thus confusing some biographers[16] into denying that Keats wrote it at Winchester. Brown's statement that it was written between *Otho* and Part II of *Lamia*, of course, dates it exactly, and there is plenty of evidence on the first page of Keats's manuscript to confirm this.

The very first line of the fragment is a reminiscence of the just-finished *Otho*, where Ludolph raves of

> The purple slaughter-house, where Bacchus' self
> Pricked his own swollen veins!

Stephen opens

> If shame can on a soldier's vein-swollen front
> Spread deeper crimson . . .

Then again the line,

> How like a comet he goes streaming on

is a reminder of the comet Keats had seen in July, and of the use he had made of it in a similar battle-scene in *Otho*, both of which would have been forgotten by November. Only a speech later, Stephen's line,

> What is the monstrous bugbear that can fright
> Baldwin?

is derived from Dryden, whom Keats was still studying for his attack on Part II of *Lamia*. It is an echo of the first line of Lucretius *Against the Fear of Death* in Dryden's translation:

> What has this Bugbear Death to frighten Man?

As Brown says, *King Stephen* was begun directly after *Otho the Great*, shortly after Keats described himself as engrossed in the last act of that tragedy on August 16th. It was evidently written very fast, for the very last speeches of the fragment show the influence of another passage in Burton only a few pages farther on than where Keats had already reached.[17] Still speaking of artificial allurements to love, Burton says:

> And not at feasts, plays, pageants, and such assemblies, but as Chrysostome objects, these tricks are put into practise *at service time in churches, and at the communion itself.* If such dumb shews, signs, and more obscure significations of love can so move, what shall they do that have full liberty to sing, dance, kiss, coll, to use all manner of discourse and dalliance? What shall he do that is beleagred of all sides?
>
>> After whom so many rosie maids enquire,
>> Whom dainty dames and loving wights desire,
>> In every place, still, and at all times sue,
>> Whom gods and gentle goddesses do wooe;
>
> How shall he contain? The very tone of some of their voices, a pretty pleasing speech, an affected tone they use, is able of it self to captivate a yong man; but when a good wit shall concur, art and eloquence, fascinating speech, pleasant discourse, sweet gestures, the Syrens themselves cannot so enchant.

Chester's complaint about the easy terms of Stephen's captivity is based in feeling and words on this passage, the latter part of which Keats himself marked.

Why did he write this very successful fragment, and why, having begun in such a promising way, did he abandon it in mid-scene? He had just finished a five-act tragedy, with which both he and Brown were pleased, and for which he had put aside for over a month the new popular poem he had half written. There was every reason for him to get back to *Lamia*, if he wanted, as he said, a book out by the end of the year; there was no apparent reason for him to embark unaided on another five-act drama. It is clear how the idea came into Brown's mind to suggest the subject. The move to Winchester had itself provided the suggestion. The city was traditionally associated with Stephen, whose brother had been Bishop there; the so-called Round Table, which hung in the Great Hall, was supposed to date from the reign of Stephen. Books of reference were at hand; Keats probably bought in Winchester Selden's *Titles of Honour*, which he began to use as a source-book for the play. Yet all this does not explain why Keats took Brown's hint so readily.

The answer lies in the purpose, from Keats's point of view, of their play-writing. It was not, as it may have been with Brown, solely to make money. It was to provide a worthy part for Keats's great theatrical hero, Edmund Kean. With Kean, whom he actually resembled in appearance and temperament, he felt a particular affinity. At this very moment he felt conscious of his powers to match the tragedian; he wrote that "One of my Ambitions is to make as great a revolution in modern dramatic writing as Kean has done in acting——". Yet as he finished *Otho*, he must have felt misgivings about this tragedy, in which his invention had been, for the most part, in leading-strings to Brown. Brown, though a man of the theatre, might be over-optimistic about their chances. Keats's later remark about Kean confirms the doubt—"*If* he smokes the hotblooded character of Ludolph"—what if the actor did not see himself in the part? Yet Keats felt himself capable of writing such a part. Stephen was to be his way of making sure.

This is evident from his whole conception of the main

acting part. For Stephen is conceived in terms of Kean's greatest role—Richard III, in which Keats had seen him in December, 1817. The tremendous sense of physical action, the manly defiance, echoes of Shakespeare's play—the famous "A horse, a horse" becomes "O, for a sword"—make it at once a role much more suited to Kean's special powers than the rather morbid Ludolph. It really is full of "hotblooded character". If Keats had gone on with it, he might have given the actor a part not to be lightly rejected.

Why he started it and why he gave it up are part and parcel of the same reason. Sometime just after August 24th, when nearly two hundred lines had been written, in growing confidence of style, the blow fell. Keats and Brown read in the journals that Kean was going on an American tour.[18] It meant that he was not likely to consider even the finished *Otho* until next season; there was less than no point in going on with *King Stephen*. Keats awoke to sharpest reality. He had been borrowing money from Brown for the last three months; now the latter's supplies were running dry, and they had both just had to write a joint letter to Taylor, asking the publisher for an advance for Keats. The dream of making a revolution in the drama was over almost before it had begun, with only the fragment to show for it. A book of poems which would take the public fancy was now the only hope. Everything must be concentrated on that, in spite of a dislike of writing for the public which, even at this moment, he could not hide. With necessity at his elbow, he began the second part of *Lamia*.

(King Stephen: A Fragment of a Tragedy)

18

THE FEAST AND THE LADY

K EATS wrote Part II of *Lamia* in the last week of August and the first days of September, at his usual 1819 rate of about 30 lines a day. Brown went on with the elegant fair-copy of *Otho*, with which they had hoped to impress Kean and the management at Drury Lane. He was always an optimist; but Keats showed the shock of their disappointment in the first lines he wrote:

> Love in a hut, with water and a crust,
> Is—Love, forgive us!—cinders, ashes, dust;

In these opening lines, as in the lines about "a real woman" in Part I, he has been accused of cynicism. It is interesting that here, just as in the former lines, the thought is taken straight from Burton. He had read and marked, both with a tick and a line down the margin, the passage where Burton breaks off his discourse on *Artificial allurements*:

> But I am over tedious, I confess, and whilst I stand gaping after fine clothes, there is another great allurement (in the worlds eye at least) which had like to have stoln out of sight, and that is mony; *veniunt a dote sagittae*, mony makes the match;

Burton develops the worldly-wise contention that marriage is nothing without money, "not amongst your dust-worms alone", but also in the reckoning of the good and great. Yet also—and here Keats follows his thought exactly—such marriages made for money end in even greater disasters, "and instead of love comes hate; for joy, repentance and desperation it self".[1] There is nothing Byronic here; Keats is only repeating the onlooker's wisdom of the old Oxford don.

Yet Keats's reading at this time was by no means confined to Burton. He had come to Winchester, he said, for books; the lack of books explains the long gap between Parts I and II of *Lamia*. He needed a background, some source-book to which he could apply his usual careful study. He found it in the *Archæologia Græca* by John Potter.[2] Like Selden's *Titles of Honour*, he probably bought this in Winchester; from the use he made of it, it is clear how much the lack of a library in the Isle of Wight had irked him. He knew from Burton that an essential part of his story would be to describe a marriage-feast in classical Corinth; as he knew no Greek, he had very little idea how the Greeks behaved in everyday life. Potter gave him all he wanted, and more. In Keats's walk under the elms by the Cathedral, he must have stopped often to finger the volumes in the bow-fronted shops that abut on the Close; turning over the pages, he saw them clustered with information which he could weld into the poem. Between lines 106 and 220 of *Lamia* Part II, the marriage-feast, Potter's work is used about two dozen times to describe the different details and customs—the bride's coming, the banquet room, the perfuming of the room with myrrh, the round tables with leopard's-paw feet, the washing of the guests, and the way they were disposed at the tables, garlanded "with flowers and greens", as Potter says.

Nothing shows more clearly Keats's determination to make a real popular success of this poem than the care he took over its composition, and the concentration with which he used this source; most of his deliberate borrowings come from a bare thirty or forty pages of Potter's large work, and all are perfectly assimilated to the style he had adopted for *Lamia*. The dramatic climax of the poem is supremely successful and completely his own; he not only left all sources behind, but he used the dramatic skill he had acquired in the hard apprenticeship of *Otho* to produce a scene of horror far more gripping than the similar last scene of the play. He had now achieved the key poem which he wanted in order to make his new volume a success.

Meanwhile, at this exact time, a curious minor drama was being played behind his back by Keats's publishers. Seconded by Brown, Keats had written on August 23rd to ask Taylor for an advance of money, offering as security their prospects of profit from *Otho*. He had added to this one of his typical harangues against writing for the public, adding significantly, "I equally dislike the favour of the public with the love of a woman". A week passed, and Taylor did not answer. Keats wrote again, this time uneasily. He had anticipated that Taylor's reaction to his first letter might be, in his own words, "How a solitary life engenders pride and egotism!" Now he wrote in a more subdued tone; he surmised politely that Taylor might not have answered because he was out of Town.

Keats had guessed right in both instances. At the same time as he wrote the second letter, on the last day of August, Richard Woodhouse in London was writing a letter of special pleading on his behalf to Taylor.[3] The publisher had indeed gone on holiday, and because of illness was making a long stay out of Town. Keats's letter had been forwarded to him at his family home in Nottinghamshire. He in his turn had sent it back to Woodhouse in London with just the remarks about pride which Keats had anticipated. The loyal Woodhouse put himself out to absolve the poet to Taylor—"It is not in my opinion personal pride but literary pride which his letter shows"—and to justify Keats for showing this. He then offered to scrape together £50 of his own money to help Keats, in words which deserve to make him remembered as the best friend a young poet could have:

> Whatever People regret that they could not do for Shakespeare or Chatterton, because he did not live in their time, that I would embody into a Rational principle, and (with due regard to certain expediencies) do for Keats.

The result was that on September 5th, just after finishing *Lamia*, Keats received a much kinder letter from Taylor than he might otherwise have done. By the same post, from Hessey, arrived thirty of the fifty pounds which Woodhouse had arranged to lend the firm of Taylor & Hessey for this purpose. At exactly the same time, news came that one of the friends to whom Keats had lent money had repaid it.[4] Keats, with his usual quick reaction to circumstances, bubbled up into a burst of optimism; it only needed someone to send him a pair of asses' ears, he said, to make him a complete Midas. From being at his last shilling, he was now temporarily in funds; he wrote off in high spirits, not, of course, to his real and unknown benefactor, Woodhouse, but to both Hessey and Taylor.

The news about Kean had made him less confident about *Otho*, and he plays it down in his letter to Taylor. Brown, he said, liked their tragedy very much, but "of course he will be fond of his own child". He would not give Taylor any extracts, and only hoped that when the publisher came to read it as a whole, he would not think Keats's labour mis-spent. This was very unlike his former tone about the play. His trump card was now the enthusiasm of the moment, *Lamia*, and he did not hesitate to send Taylor a long extract from the Second Part. Unfortunately he also was over-fond of his brain-child, and was too close to it to be properly critical. In the banquet-scene, which he chose to quote, he included some lines which he later had the good taste to cut; now he accompanied them with the comment, both unfortunate and untrue—"This is a good sample of the Story." It was not; nor was it even a sample of the style of the poem. Keats, in an off moment, had reverted to Dryden's translation of the Latin satires of Juvenal and Aulus Persius Flaccus, which abound in crudely-described drunken feasts.[5] For once Keats's reading led him astray.

There is another and more fruitful source that appears from this letter to Taylor. The main part of the letter is taken up with a typical "rhodomontade" by Keats on the subject of Taylor's health. Ignoring the fact that Taylor was a Notting-ham man, and might be supposed to have some knowledge of the geology and geography of his own shire, Keats developed a series of grave doubts whether Taylor was taking his holiday in the right place. His thesis was that climate has a great effect on the constitution and character of people. "This", he con-cluded triumphantly, in spite of evidently knowing less about China than about Nottingham, "This appears a great cause of the imbecillity of the Chinese." It was a strange though well-meant harangue; but it shows that Keats was still reading his school-prize, Robertson's *History of America*. Robertson was one of the first historians to emphasise the effect of climate upon character, and his handling of such themes later drew praise from the great exponent of that theory, Buckle. Keats's dissertation to Taylor might have come straight out of Robertson's pages, and there is a part of *Lamia*, also quoted by Keats in this letter, which is curiously related to Robertson. Lamia, in preparing her magic banqueting hall, makes exotic trees part of the architecture:

> Fresh carved cedar, mimicking a glade
> Of Palm and Plantain, met, from either side, . . .
> Between the Tree stems, wainscoated at first
> Came jasper pannels; then, anon, there burst
> Forth creeping imagery of slighter trees. . . .

Keats, quite unconsciously, was reproducing the frontispiece of his two-volume edition of Robertson, where a classical design is engraved to do honour to the author and his subject. Out of a building with Ionic capitals there springs on the one side a palm and on the other a plantain or bread-fruit; lower down, out of the panelled structure, burst some creeping bushes, also native to America, transported thence by Keats for his heroine's feast.

Quite apart from this odd transference, there are curious things about this feast passage. It is part of a larger problem. All through this year, every work which Keats had completed, with the exception of odes and sonnets, had been built on a common pattern. There is always a luxurious feast, a banquet, or eating and drinking, accompanied by music; this is always followed by some sort of shock or revelation concerning a woman. In *The Eve of St. Agnes*, the surprise is a pleasant one. Madeline reveals her love to Porphyro, and though there are "sleeping dragons all around", the lovers escape together. In *La Belle Dame Sans Merci* the knight at arms is fed by the heroine on ethereal food, "roots of relish sweet, And honey wild and manna dew". He sleeps, has a ghastly vision, and wakes alone. The last scene of *Otho the Great* opens in a banqueting hall of great magnificence with gold and silver plate. Ludolph enters and raves first of the luxurious setting, half-seen, half-imagined, and then of the drinking of various potent wines. At the critical moment the door leading out of the banqueting hall is opened, and the heroine is revealed. She has committed suicide; Ludolph himself falls dead. In *Lamia* Part II, the wedding-feast is described in a detail never contemplated in the original story; the feast is interrupted by the philosopher, a terrible sense of horror fills the room, the bride withers before everyone's eyes. She vanishes with a shriek, and Lycius collapses and dies.

Poets should not be strictly called to account for the images they use; but when the same theme occurs over and over again in such a short space of time, it must mean something. The experience connected with a woman, whatever it may be, grows worse every time he writes about it. For Porphyro, although beset with dangers, it is a joyful experience; for the knight at arms it is the path to deepest melancholy. The horror increases from *Otho* to *Lamia*. At the same time, the banquet remains a constant part of the story. So does the music—Porphyro's lute, La Belle Dame's song, the soothing music for Ludolph, and the unseen mysterious orchestra which accompanies Lamia's feast. The pattern is consistent, and, in fact, it is seen fully developed in the poem which Keats wrote directly after he finished *Lamia*. Before turning to that, it is worth asking what this image might mean to him.

Probably no single solution will fit the exact meaning of this set of images in Keats's mind this year. A psycho-analyst, searching back into Keats's childhood, might put it down to his being an orphan, a child who had lost his mother, of whom he was passionately fond, at the time of puberty. The food and drink would be a symbol of the lost mother, the terror-filled experience his failure to find that love and security again in his relationships with other women. A purely literary solution would be to look at Keats's early reading, and see if he acquired these dominant images there. It has been found that the image and something like the incident occurs in a poem which he undoubtedly read in his student days, Sotheby's translation of Wieland's verse-romance, *Oberon*.[6]

Either of these elements might have something to do with this often-repeated vision, but there is a serious objection to both. If the image is drawn from a deep and distant experience in Keats's life, whether psychological or literary, it is strange that he never uses it before this year. In all the elaborate and semi-allegorical wanderings of *Endymion*, this set of circumstances never once occurs. Nor is there any hint of it in *Isabella*, which he had written in the spring of 1818, nor in the early stages of the first *Hyperion*, written that autumn. It is at least possible that it had something to do with the actual experiences of his life in 1819.

Late in October, 1818, he had first visited Isabella Jones in her room. Its commonplaces of furniture, food, wine, and music, he had at once translated into sublime terms, "the food Manna, the Wine beyond Claret", in his prose letter. It is only after this experience that the same description occurs in the poetry of some of his greatest work. His visits to Isabella showed signs of a happy consummation at about the time when he wrote *The Eve of St. Agnes* at her suggestion. Then something in their relationship failed. He entered into his days of darkness, became restless, torn, uneasy, cynical. She dropped out of his life. He turned to the more simple though ultimately just as agonising relationship with Fanny Brawne.

This is not a whole interpretation. We can never know exactly why and how this image gripped him. Yet we do know, from a hundred other instances, how actual events and symbols in his life and reading entered into all his poetry during this year. This literal and factual explanation cannot be omitted. At the same time, there is always the warning uttered by Keats himself when he was entering into his March crisis[7]—"they are very shallow people who take everything literally. A Man's life of any worth is a continual allegory——". In the next work he wrote, he once again took up this strange, personal set of images, and turned them into the most profound allegory of his whole poetic life.

(*Lamia*, Part II)

19

A DREAM AND AN AWAKENING

EVERYTHING for once was favourable to poetry. First, he was just beginning to feel the benefit to his health of the move to Winchester. The dry chalky air of the downs was, he said, worth sixpence a pint. He and Brown lodged in a back road somewhere between the Cathedral and the High Street. The room was large and looked out on a blank wall; he was not distracted as he had been at Shanklin. Keats's usual ill-luck about small boys had followed him, for the land-lady's son played the violin, but in general there was no noise except the genteel tapping of door-knockers and walking sticks "of the good old Dowager breed". Keats was back in a setting like that of the Lacy's and the Mullins's, which had proved so fruitful at Chichester.[1]

Soon his quiet was complete. On Monday, September 6th, Brown left him and went off by himself on a mysterious three weeks' errand. The likelihood seems to be that, without telling Keats, Brown slipped over to Ireland to contract a Roman Catholic marriage with Abigail Donaghue, their Irish servant at Wentworth Place.[2] Keats too had had his reasons for keeping quiet about women, so perhaps he did not enquire too closely; he himself stood to gain by Brown's absence. When he was engaged on anything of a serious or philosophic nature, he found that Brown's joviality burst in on him "like a thunder-bolt". Yet, equally, contact with Brown and the collaboration in dramatic work had loosened and improved his poetic technique. Now he was alone with poetry, and with books to hand. To buy books, and some of the minor amenities of life, he now had money; that worry was over for the time. After money, the next enemy to his peace of mind, Love, had also been temporarily defeated. His "flint-worded" letter to Fanny Brawne had apparently cut off their correspondence. Neither had written to the other for three weeks. He had shut her out, and all the complications that might go with her. Finally, he had heard nothing for two months from George; he had fretted at this in the spring, but under the new circumstances, no news might be good news. For a small poised space, Keats's poetry lay undisturbed like his own dead leaf in *Hyperion*. He rewarded the respite with the unearthly, calm, compassionate and humble beauty of the beginning of a great new poem. Many arguments have been raised about its philosophy; it does not seem that any interpretation can give us the truth. Keats was still "straining at particles of light in the midst of a great darkness", as he had described himself earlier in the year.[3] Though unformed, it is, however, a real attempt at a philosophy of his own. He discards, for a time at any rate, the 17th-century aphorisms and wise saws of Burton. He had begun to create, in this magical period of calm, a new poetry.

> Fanatics have their dreams wherewith they weave
> A Paradise for a Sect; the savage too
> From forth the loftiest fashion of his sleep
> Guesses at Heaven: pity these have not
> Trac'd upon vellum or wild indian leaf
> The shadows of melodious utterance:
> But bare of laurel they live, dream, and die,
> For Poesy alone can tell her dreams,
> With the fine spell of words alone can save
> Imagination from the sable charm
> And dumb enchantment.

This was the beginning of his new and second version of *Hyperion—The Fall of Hyperion, a Dream*, as he called it. He had been tinkering with the first *Hyperion* at Shanklin; he called his life then "a history of sensations, and day-night-mares". It was upon these sensations that the unearthly, nightmare quality of the new *Hyperion* was founded. The first 180 lines were written in these few days of quiet, between the 6th and the 10th of September. Some of their strange quality derives from the fact that Keats, at this time, was preparing for the press the poems he had written in the past year, and which he had ready to offer his publishers by September 11th. The first few pages of the new poem are full of echoes of all the great poems he had just written, and which he was to publish

next year. It begins with a feast once more, of which many of
the details are taken from *The Eve of St. Agnes*, and most of the
rest from *Lamia*. This feast, unlike all the others except that
of *La Belle Dame*, is set out of doors in a floral arbour. Keats
borrowed the scenery of this retreat from another poem to be
published, the *Ode to Psyche*, where

> A rosy sanctuary will I dress
> With the wreath'd trellis of a working brain,
> With buds, and bells, and stars without a name,

provided him with the vision of the new poem, in which

> I saw an arbour with a drooping roof
> And trellis vines, and bells, and larger blooms,

The "full draught" from a "cool vessel" in the new poem, he
took from the *Ode to a Nightingale*, and the poet's swoon,

> Like a Silenus on an antique vase

from the *Ode on a Grecian Urn*.

Yet of all the odes, it is the *Ode on Melancholy* which pervades,
in words and thought and atmosphere, the early stages of
what Keats was now writing. The liquor "Sipp'd by the
wander'd bee", which affects his senses as if they had been
overcome by poison, is like the Pleasure

> Turning to poison while the bee-mouth sips

of the last stanza of the *Ode on Melancholy*. The beautiful image
which Keats used to describe the mysterious altar flame of his
new poem

> When in mid-May the sickening East Wind
> Shifts sudden to the South, the small warm rain
> Melts out the frozen incense from all flowers,
> And fills the air with so much pleasant health
> That even the dying man forgets his shroud;

has the exact expression and cadence of stanza two of the ode:

> But when the melancholy fit shall fall
> Sudden from heaven like a weeping cloud,
> That fosters the droop-headed flowers all,
> And hides the green hill in an April shroud;

The whole thought and imagery is that of the *Ode on Melancholy*—

> Ay, in the very temple of delight
> Veil'd Melancholy has her sovran shrine,

A mysterious veiled figure presides over this new shrine, just as the Goddess of Melancholy had presided in the ode:

> Though seen of none save him whose strenuous tongue
> Can burst Joy's grape against his palate fine.

In the new *Hyperion*, however, the test is more severe, and there enters that element of horror, which had haunted Keats's poems and thoughts for months past. He has to feel

> What 'tis to die and live again before
> Thy fated hour.

The poet of the new *Fall of Hyperion* has to undergo the test of experience. This experience is expressed in the imagery which Keats had made familiar through his year's work—the feast and the awakening, the terror, this time in performing the command of the veiled priestess. Yet though much of the expression recalls his own earlier poems, there is a deeper source, and one which gives the whole experience a much more profound tone. Keats had begun to read again the *Divine Comedy* of Dante, this time the Purgatorio.[4] Until this time, like so many people, he had never got any further than the Inferno, which he had read, on and off, for the last year or so in Cary's translation. Now he had begun to study Italian itself; a laconic remark reveals that he found the reading of Dante "well worth the while".[5] He was not, of course, reading it in the original. It is too much to suppose that he could master the complexities of Dante after only a few days' study;

a fortnight later, he was only managing with difficulty half a dozen or so stanzas of Ariosto at a time, a much easier business. He turned to Cary. Here, even more than when he was writing the original *Hyperion* a year before, he borrowed the translator's style. Cary himself had translated the Inferno and the Purgatorio at different times in his life, and, quite apart from the requirements of their subjects, he produced a very different result. The change in poetic tone between *Hyperion* and *The Fall of Hyperion* is the change in the verse of Cary between the Inferno and the Purgatorio.

It was in Dante speaking through Cary that Keats found the conflict and distinction he was trying to make all through the new poem, the antithesis between the true poet and the mere dreamer. When at last Dante stands at the side of Beatrice in the last canto of the Purgatorio, her first words to him are

> Of fearfulness and shame, I will, that thou
> Henceforth do rid thee: that thou speak no more,
> As one who dreams.

Keats's priestess, white-veiled like Beatrice, speaks in like terms to him:

> Every sole man hath days of joy or pain,
> Whether his labours be sublime or low—
> The pain alone; the joy alone; distinct:
> Only the dreamer venoms all his days,
> Bearing more woe than all his sins deserve.

It seems as though the terrifying female figure, the symbol of so many poems, is probing at the root-cause of Keats's dilemma, that horrid morbidity of temperament which, in his own words, made the difficulties of the imagination so much more than the difficulties of life. Not until he banishes these from his system, she seems to say, can he be a true poet. Yet in writing this very passage, he became one. The poetry and philosophy of these 180 lines are specially his, and mark a new strong development in his technique and thought. They reflect too the fact that these few days were the only time in this whole hectic creative year in which he was allowed to be, as he wished, solely and exclusively a poet; they show what he might have been, had fate always allowed him this scope.

It did not last. Perhaps it could not. We can only regret that the weakest link in this delicate web of circumstances should have snapped so soon. It was George who shattered the spell. Obstinacy and self-centredness was a family trait. In Keats, genius redeemed it; in George it seems less attractive. Yet he can hardly be blamed, for the disaster he had run himself into was real and complete. On Friday, September 10th, his news arrived; it was as bad as could be. He had first settled at Hendersonville on the suggestion of the famous naturalist and pioneer Audubon. Now—the truth of the transaction will probably never be known—Audubon had tempted him into unwise speculation.[6] His prospects, contained in a trading vessel, were literally a wreck, at the bottom of the Mississippi River. He was ruined unless capital came quickly. Keats laid down his poem and took the night coach to London.

His first thought, he said, was to get a substantial advance for a poem from Murray, Byron's publisher. It was an idea he must have rejected on his way to London. He had no complete poem of any length to make a book by itself. There was no guarantee that Murray would be impressed by the fragmentary *Hyperion*, much less by the mystical promise of the new *Fall of Hyperion*. He burst into Taylor & Hessey's office on the Saturday with a new plan.[7] They must print *The Eve of St. Agnes* and *Lamia*, together with other poems to make up a book, before Christmas. Publishers are used to withstanding the impetuous demands of authors. Taylor was still in the country, and Hessey was a cautious man. Indeed, if Keats had thought, a week-end during the summer holidays was not the best time to come and do business in London. Everyone was out. Abbey could not see him till Monday evening. The wave of his impetuous resolve broke on a stony shore.

He had one piece of real luck. When he arrived at the Fleet Street office, he found Woodhouse there. The lawyer was due to leave London on the next afternoon, but he invited Keats to spend all Sunday morning in his chambers in the Temple. Keats came to breakfast, and stayed to see Woodhouse off on the Weymouth coach at 3 p.m. They talked all this time of

Keats's poems. Keats read *Lamia* aloud, very badly, as, according to Woodhouse, he always did. All the same, Woodhouse was impressed. They then fell into argument about the other poems for the book. Keats was now violently against printing *Isabella*. Woodhouse demurred, but Keats condemned the poem as mawkish and sentimental. When we recollect— as even Woodhouse could not—what a year of experience Keats had passed through, with death, divided love, dissipation, and intense creation making up the pattern, we can sympathize with Keats's feeling that a poem written before that time lacked experience of life.

Their other controversy, lasting a full hour, was over the alterations to *The Eve of St. Agnes,* upon which Keats had such a strong prejudice. These only concerned three stanzas. One was the new early stanza, with its hint that the pleasures of the hero and heroine were to be "a dizzy stream, Palpable almost". The other two comprised the last couplet of stanza xxxv, where Keats made his hero's arms, "encroaching slow", "zone" the heroine "heart to heart". His alterations to the next stanza did not amount to much more than using the word "Marryeth" instead of "Blendeth" to describe the embrace of Porphyro and Madeline, but it was all enough for Woodhouse. With the quick eye of the publisher's reader he saw, or thought he saw, that the general public, especially ladies, would be offended by what was implied. His doubts touched off the scorn of public taste which Keats had shown in the letter to Taylor, and the poet went off into a characteristic harangue. However, they knew each other well enough for no harm to be done. Keats's last words, as Woodhouse leant from the coach, were perhaps a little contrite. He promised to drop Woodhouse a line, "and if it should be in verse, I daresay you will forgive me." He meant the new *Fall of Hyperion,* and Woodhouse received a long extract just ten days later.

(*The Fall of Hyperion,* Canto I, 1–181)

20

THE RETURN TO WINCHESTER AND THE *ODE TO AUTUMN*

K EATS'S heart sank as his friend's coach clattered off to the West country. His next appointment was to dine with George's mother-in-law. He would have to play a part, for he could hardly show her George's disastrous letter, revealing what straits her daughter and tiny grandchild were in. He got through the evening with "quizzing" and gossip. Next morning—he was staying as usual in Fleet Street—he went over to see Fanny Keats at Walthamstow. That evening at seven, he sat down to tea with Abbey in the City. The merchant was in a good humour. The privilege of being able to say, "I told you so", had perhaps flattered him into being helpful. He undertook to get the Chancery suit settled and release some of Tom's money. As the result of this interview Keats eventually got an advance of £100 for George and £100 for himself. As a price, he had to endure Abbey's well-meant but ponderous humour. That John should be a poet was still inexplicable to his former guardian. He had a magazine with him which, like every periodical at that time, contained a review of Byron's *Don Juan* with quotations. Abbey did not approve of *Don Juan*, of course; his opinion was probably that of *The St. James's Chronicle*, which greeted the first two cantos as the most licentious poem which had for many years issued from the English press. "However," he remarked, "the fellow says true things now and then", and with heavy slyness he read out[1]

> What is the end of Fame? 'tis but to fill
> A certain portion of uncertain paper:
> Some liken it to climbing up a hill,
> Whose summit, like all hills, is lost in vapour:
> For this men write, speak, preach, and heroes kill,
> And bards burn what they call their "midnight taper",
> To have, when the original is dust,
> A name, a wretched picture, and worse bust.

Abbey's humorous attempt to score off him is the origin of the curious lines which Keats scribbled into *The Fall of Hyperion* the next day or soon after. Woodhouse noted against these lines (187–210) that "Keats seems to have intended to erase this". There seems no doubt that the lines which follow are a revision of this unhappy outburst; but, standing as it does in most modern editions, it is at least evidence of his state of mind. If *Don Juan* was poetry, then he was no poet; but it could not be, this mocking, careless hectoring "in proud bad verse". All his bitterness with Byron welled up. Keats had just been reading Dante's address to Apollo, which begins Canto One of the Paradiso; there was precedent there for a rebuke to unworthy poets—"more shame to human wills Depraved". He dashed off the lines perhaps with some memory of Byron's own stanza in them; his "misty pestilence" may be a reminder from Byron's satire on the pursuit of literary fame, "lost in vapour". Abbey's well-meaning but ill-timed joke had produced a nervous blot on the pages of Keats's own poem.

There was another reason for Keats's nerve to be shaken. After leaving Abbey, he began to walk up Cheapside, then turned back toward the General Post Office in Lombard Street. He had to post a letter to Fanny which had been burning a hole in his pocket all day. Perhaps deliberately, he had kept it by him until he had missed that night's post. It told its own story.[2]

Am I mad or not? I came by the Friday night coach and have not yet been to Hampstead. Upon my soul it is not my fault. I cannot resolve to mix any pleasure with my days: they go like one another undistinguishable. If I were to see you to day it would destroy the half comfortable sullenness I enjoy at present into downright perplexities. I love you too much to venture into Hampstead, I feel it is not paying a visit, but venturing into a fire. Que feraije? as the french novel writers say in fun, and I in earnest: really what can I do? Knowing well that my life must be passed in fatigue and trouble, I have been endeavouring to wean myself from you: for to myself alone what can be much of a misery? As far as they regard myself I can despise all events: but I cannot cease to love you. . . I am a Coward, I cannot bear the pain of being

happy: 'tis out of the question: I must admit no thought
of it.

Yours ever affectionately

John Keats

"Really what can I do?"—there was not much more that he
could say. All his dilemmas had revived—Love, Money, the
bitterness of Ambition; the circle had started to revolve again.
Just at the moment, life played one of its familiar cards of
unconscious comedy. Hardly had Keats posted this letter than
Abbey again appeared, rotund and old-fashioned, walking
towards the Poultry. As Keats fell into step beside him, Abbey
returned to a subject he had mentioned some months before;
he hinted that Keats might be interested in a career in a hat-
making firm. For one moment the prospect of Keats as a
successful hat-manufacturer flashes in among the other possi-
bilities of his life, and then disappears. Keats hurried toward
the West End, to get in half-price for the second half of the
programme at Covent Garden before tumbling into bed.

He did not, as he had intended, return to Winchester the
the next day; in fact, what he did on this Tuesday is a mystery.
He had finished his business, resisted the temptation to visit
Hampstead, and had no inducement to stay in Town. The
answer may be simple. He may have overslept after his
exhausting day, or he may have been detained by curiosity.
The streets of London were in a ferment. Henry Hunt the
Radical, released on bail after the riot in Manchester at St.
Peter's Fields, had entered London on the Monday; 200,000
people had watched his triumphal progress from Islington to
the Strand. To anyone with Liberal sympathies, it was an
exciting moment. Wednesday, the 15th, certainly found Keats
back in Winchester. After a day to collect his thoughts, he
began on Friday a long letter to George.

From this letter it is clear how he resumed the routine of
reading and work after this unsettling week. Although he
went on with *The Fall of Hyperion*, it was not to the same background as in the five previous unclouded days. Though there
are two passages in it which correspond exactly with two
sections in Canto One of the Paradiso, it looks as though he
dropped his reading of Cary, and did not get beyond that

canto. In his perturbed state of mind, he fell back on Burton and his comfortable worldly-wise philosophy. At no time is his thought and style so full of direct quotation from the *Anatomy*. He plunged back into the long subsection where he had left off, on the symptoms of love-melancholy. He was delighted with one page, on the significant theme that "Love is like a false glass, which represents every thing fairer than it is". He underlined this whole page, put an appreciative comment in the margin, and then copied the whole passage, comment and all, into his letter to George.[3] He echoed Burton in a reference to Abelard, who is mentioned three times in this part of the book.[4] More than this, he described his own doings and character in terms used by Burton. He remarked

> Whenever I find myself growing vapourish, I rouse myself, wash and put on a clean shirt brush my hair and clothes, tie my shoestrings neatly and in fact adonize as I were going out—then all clean and comfortable I sit down to write.

Burton makes great play with the habits of the lover:[5]

> And then he did begin to prank himself,
> And pleate and combe his head, and beard to shave,
> And look his face ith' water as a glass,
> And to compose himself for to be brave.

On the next page, he adds, in a passage which Keats underlined,[6]

> *He must be in league with an excellent taylor, barber, have neat shooe-ties, points, garters, speak in print, walk in print, eat and drink in print, and that which is all in all, he must be mad in print.*

Keats, in spite of such borrowings from Burton, was not yet mad in print; yet he did take another borrowed idea, Burton's scheme for a city or an army consisting entirely of lovers,[7] and make it into a series of cynical couplets about the absurdity of lovers *en masse*. Once again, this has been pounced on as showing how he was concealing the real feelings of his heart,

H

and once again he is only taking refuge in a borrowed and easy philosophy, ready-made in his bedside reading.

His life, overstrained at every point, needed ease and calm. He found it in reading but even more in his earliest and best love—nature. His daily walk after a morning's intense composition, reading or writing, was the consolidation of Keats's day. He turned to it again and again for relief and meditation, pacing down by the West front of the Cathedral, past the clergy buildings, down College Street, along "a country alley of gardens" to the monastery of St. Cross and its beautiful water-meadows. The clear unbroken autumn weather and the familiar shapes of field and tree restored day by day the shattered calm of his former solitude here. On Sunday, September 19th, the mood was complete again. On his walk he composed the most serene poem in the English language, the *Ode to Autumn*.

Season of mists and mellow fruitfulness,
    Close bosom-friend of the maturing sun;
Conspiring with him how to load and bless
    With fruit the vines that round the thatch-eves run;
To bend with apples the moss'd cottage-trees,
    And fill all fruit with ripeness to the core;
To swell the gourd and plump the hazel shells
    With a sweet kernel; to set budding more,
And still more, later flowers for the bees,
    Until they think warm days will never cease,
For Summer has o'er-brimm'd their clammy cells.

Who hath not seen thee oft amid thy store?
    Sometimes whoever seeks abroad may find
Thee sitting careless on a granary floor,
    Thy hair soft-lifted by the winnowing wind;
Or on a half-reap'd furrow sound asleep,
    Drowsed with the fume of poppies, while thy hook
Spares the next swath and all its twined flowers:
    And sometimes like a gleaner thou dost keep
Steady thy laden head across a brook;
    Or by a cyder-press, with patient look,
Thou watchest the last oozings hours by hours.

Where are the songs of Spring? Ay, where are they?
    Think not of them, thou hast thy music too—

> While barred clouds bloom the soft-dying day,
>   And touch the stubble-plains with rosy hue;
> Then in a wailful choir the small gnats mourn
>   Among the river sallows, borne aloft
> Or sinking as the light wind lives or dies;
>   And full-grown lambs loud bleat from hilly bourn;
> Hedge-crickets sing; and now with treble soft
>   The red-breast whistles from a garden-croft;
> And gathering swallows twitter in the skies.

This poem is so much of its own time and place, and echoes so much his own description of his walk, that it might seem unnecessary to seek any literary source as well. Yet such there was,[8] recognized quite consciously by Keats in the words "I somehow always associate Chatterton with autumn." The full impact of this can best be seen in stanzas i and iii of the ode. Keats first wrote "With a *white* kernel" in the first stanza, and line 3 of the third stanza at first read

> While a gold cloud gilds the soft-dying day

These add to the resemblance between the ode and the song of the third minstrel in Chatterton's *Aella*:

> When Autumn bleak and sunburnt do appear,
> With his gold hand gilding the falling leaf,
> Bringing up Winter to fulfil the year,
> Bearing upon his back the riped sheaf,
> When all the hills with woody seed is white,
> When lightning-fires and lemes do meet from far the
>   sight;
> When the fair apple, red as even sky,
> Do bend the tree unto the fruitful ground,
> When juicy pears, and berries of black dye,
> Do dance in air, and call the eyes around:
> Then, be the even foul, or even fair,
> Methinks my hartys joy is steynced with some care.

Less obvious, but none the less clear, is the way in which the second stanza echoes some earlier lines from *Aella* spoken by Bertha herself—

> Oft have I seen thee at the noon-day feast,
> When daised by thyself, for want of peers,

while as the stanza goes on with its beautiful personification
of the female figure of Autumn, there is a striking resemblance
to a passage marked by Keats only a page or two later in his
reading of Burton. This is the story of Cymon and Iphigenia,
which he knew already in Dryden's translation, and in which
Burton describes[9] how Cymon on a country walk

> espied a gallant yong gentlewoman named Iphigenia,
> a burgomaster's daughter of Cyprus, with her maid, by
> a brook side, in a little thicket, fast asleep . . .

Yet these, though strong, are only immediate and verbal
influences. The real source remains the deep-seated calm
which had returned to him, the joyful peace which the country-
side always brought him, if the pressure of the world did not
intrude.

For a day or two, it still hung in the balance. He went on
with his daily routine, writing to George, walking, revising, and
composing. It is impossible to say exactly what he was doing
in *The Fall of Hyperion*, apart from two passages which derive
from the Paradiso. The greatest passage, perhaps the finest
single piece of poetry that Keats ever wrote, does not derive
from Dante, nor indeed from anything except Keats's own
growing mastery of his own new manner. It consists of the
thirty lines which describe the parting of the priestess's veils,
and it was like nothing that Keats had yet written in his life.
It is something like his own summary of himself, or rather of
what he hoped to be, at which his meditations had arrived by
Tuesday, September 21st.[10]—"Quieter in my pulse . . . , exert-
ing myself against vexing speculations—scarcely content to
write the best verses for the fever they leave behind. I want to
compose without this fever." If, as we may guess, the parting
of the veils was the first-fruits of this resolve, then indeed Keats
was on the threshold of a new era in his poetry.

Yet on this very day, he was turning his back on poetry.
It was the exact anniversary of his starting *Hyperion*; by some
unconscious instinct, he began to sum up his last year in his
mind. He wrote that morning, in his letter to George, "From
the time you left me, our friends say I have altered completely
—am not the same person——" He ended his morning's

writing to George with a criticism of the language of *Paradise Lost*—"A northern dialect accomodating itself to greek and latin inversions and intonations". He mentions Chatterton in the same breath, for in fact he had borrowed the terms of this criticism from the prologue to Chatterton's *Aella*, where Chatterton wrote of "Sir John", i.e. Milton, for whom

> The English, him to please, must first be Latinized.

Latin, Keats continued, was useful for his own private reading, especially of Renaissance authors; he mentions three from whom he was now reading copious quotations in Burton. As Hessey said, a year back, he was "recovering his Latin". Latinate English, however, such as Milton used, must be harmful for the type of poetry he now wishes to write. At this point he breaks off. He had heard from Reynolds and Wood-house, who were staying at the latter's family home in Bath. Beginning to write to Reynolds, he continued his theme, and the decision underlying it. He has just decided to give up *Hyperion*—both versions. With this news, he puts down his pen and goes for his daily walk.

He walked, thinking. Among his reflections he included his own obstinacy. He stooped under a fence in the meadows. Why not get over, he asked? Because no one tried to make you get under, he told himself. The weather was colder, and he lingered by a blacksmith's fire. The first chill of the failing year increased his mood of remembrance and stocktaking. That evening he wrote on to Reynolds and Woodhouse.[11]

> To-night I am all in a mist; I scarcely know what's what. But you knowing my unsteady and vagarish disposition, will guess that all this turmoil will be settled by tomorrow morning. It strikes me to-night that I have led a very odd sort of life for the two or three last years—Here & there—No anchor—

"I am glad of it", he added, joking; but already another serious decision faced him. He had decided to give up *Hyperion*; what was he to do with his life now? His hopes for his new collection of poems were not high. He must reason his course out, without prejudice or false starts, all contrary to his own essential nature. "I would give a guinea to be a reasonable man—good sound sense—a say what he thinks, and does what he says man——." In other words, he must be the opposite of all he had been in the past year. He finished the letter to Reynolds before coming to any decision, and embarked, without stopping, on a companion piece for Woodhouse. He gave him the poetry he had promised, three extracts from *The Fall of Hyperion* with the whole of the *Ode to Autumn* thrown in for good measure.

The first extract was probably the last he had written, the opening to what he now called Canto II of the new poem. The accumulated Miltonisms of what followed it, the description of Hyperion's palace, had apparently brought him to his decision. Behind this apparent reason, one must feel a stronger power. The real reason was the accumulated strain and exhaustion of the whole complete and prodigious year, a year on which he looked back for ever after with a sort of horror. "Nothing could have in all its circumstances fallen out worse for me than the last year has done"—that was his own verdict.[12]

Remembering the great work of the year, it is difficult for us to agree with this. It is the supreme paradox that, in his own eyes, this year of triumph had been a year of catastrophe. It is very natural. Tom's death, his strange relationship with Isabella, the failure of *Endymion*, the interlude of darkness, the torment of a new attachment to Fanny, money difficulty, clouded health, the horrors of morbid imagination, George's disaster, and the final break-up of his second attempt on his great epic poem—such must have seemed to him the pattern of these twelve months. Moreover, his summing-up was written in November, after he had experienced for some weeks the bitterness and confusion following this year which, to us but not to him, had been one of triumphant creation. He judged this year by its epilogue; and in the epilogue, which we too must consider, nothing could have seemed worse than the sudden decline which attacked every aspect of his life and work.

(*The Fall of Hyperion*, Canto I, 182–318,
Canto II, 1–6. *Ode to Autumn*)

EPILOGUE:
FANNY AND THE AFTERMATH

I

HE had taken a decision on September 21st, 1819, against
the whole run of the previous year; from the moment he
took it, he hardly wrote a line of poetry which he can have
wished to keep. The decision, which he came to on the night
of September 21st-22nd, does not at first sight seem such a
fateful one. He resolved not to depend any longer on the uncertain hopes of plays or poetry, but to earn his living by literary
journalism. He announced this to Dilke, Woodhouse, and
Brown on the same day. Only to Brown did he reveal his
real reason for another decision, to live in some other part of
London than Hampstead. He felt, as he had told Fanny, that
returning to Hampstead would be like venturing into a fire.
"On that account", he wrote to Brown, "I had better not live
there."[1] Brown had returned to Bedhampton after his Irish
adventure; he now came back to Winchester in some alarm at
this news. Both self-interest and genuine affection for Keats
were mingled in his concern. After a week spent in discussion,
Keats was still at least firm on one part of his decision. He asked
Dilke to get him lodgings in Westminster—"for myself alone",
he added hastily, in case Dilke, hearing of his intense feelings,
might think he planned an elopement.[2] He only stayed in
these lodgings for two or three days. On Sunday, October 10th,
he did exactly what he said he would not do. He visited
Hampstead with Brown. The result fulfilled his own prophecy.
He met Fanny again and was overwhelmed by her.

The verses and letters he wrote in the next week or so show
him struck down by violent physical passion. Even his reading
is filled by it. He was now nearing the end of Burton's great
third treatise on Love-Melancholy, and studying, perhaps
unhappily for himself, the chapters on *Prognosticks of Love-
Melancholy* and on *The Cure of Love-Melancholy*. Until now, with
one or two sudden exceptions, he had marked the pages of

Burton largely for literary or philosophic interest, for an appropriate turn of phrase or thought. Now he began to apply Burton's remarks in a personal and almost morbid way to his own situation, to interject comments such as, "Aye, aye" or "Good", when he agreed, and "Query" or even ·"Pshaw!", when he disagreed. Everything is absorbed in his own situation. The verses he wrote to Fanny follow the same sequence as his fevered reading. The first *Lines to Fanny*, written only an hour after meeting her, do indeed share another fever and another source. His terrible anxiety over George and Georgiana is present as well as his devouring love. Ever since he received George's letter, some lines which he had then been reading in Dryden, from the Sixth Satire of Aulus Persius Flaccus, had been beating in his brain:

> My Friend is Shipwreck'd on the *Brutian* Strand,
> His Riches in th'Ionian Main are lost;
> And he himself stands shiv'ring on the Coast;
> Where, destitute of help, forlorn, and bare,
> He wearies the Deaf Gods with Fruitless Pray'r.

This allied with his reading in Burton[3] and in Robertson's *History of America* to paint the dismal scene which breaks into the middle of the *Lines to Fanny*:

> Where shall I learn to get my peace again?
> To banish thoughts of that most hateful land,
> Dungeoner of my friends, that wicked strand
> Where they were wreck'd and live a wrecked life;
> That monstrous region, whose dull rivers pour,
> Ever from their sordid urns unto the shore,
> Unown'd of any weedy-haired gods;

That evening he wrote a sonnet of comparative calm:

> The day is gone, and all its sweets are gone!
> Sweet voice, sweet lips, soft hand, and softer breast,
> Warm breath, light whisper, tender semi-tone,
> Bright eyes, accomplish'd shape, and lang'rous waist!
> Faded the flower and all its budded charms,
> Faded the sight of beauty from my eyes,

Faded the shape of beauty from my arms,
Faded the voice, warmth, whiteness, paradise—
Vanish'd unseasonably at shut of eve,
When the dusk holiday—or holinight
Of fragrant-curtain'd love begins to weave
The woof of darkness thick, for hid delight;
But, as I've read love's missal through to-day,
He'll let me sleep, seeing I fast and pray.

It is at least a respite, some attempt on his part to reconcile
the daemon of his awakened passion with poetry. This sonnet
too echoes his reading to a remarkable degree. The second
quatrain, with its fourfold opening repetition of the word
"Faded", is an exact replica in form of the beautiful Latin
lines which Burton quotes:[4]

> Frustra blanditiae appulistis ad has,
> Frustra nequitiae venistis ad has,
> Frustra deliciae obsidebitis has,
> Frustra has illecebrae, et procacitates,

while on the next page Burton recommends reading and study
to conquer physical passion, and adds that, in extreme cases,
This kinde of divel is not cast out but by fasting and prayer. Keats's
final couplet is based on this advice. More than that, he was
taking Burton's prescription literally. By October 20th, when
he had returned to live with Brown at Wentworth Place, he
spoke of putting himself on a vegetarian diet. There is no
evidence that he did this on doctor's orders, nor that he was
aware to that extent of his latent illness. On the other hand,
Burton, in these very pages which Keats was reading, recommends this course to overcome physical passion—[5]

> And all lascivious meats must be forsaken.

This was no coincidence. When he read, later in the year, a
passage where Burton repeated this advice, he marked it
heavily down the margin, and commented, "Good".[6] This
diet was one of the chains, which, he told Fanny, he must
impose upon himself now that he had come to live next door
to her again.

The next poem he wrote to her in this situation itself begins with a medical metaphor—

Physician Nature! let my spirit blood!

which is taken straight from Burton, who, on the next page that Keats read, recommended[7]

bloud-letting above the rest which makes amantes ne sint amentes, lovers come to themselves, and keep in their right mind.

Keats's description of his own unhappy condition is physical and actual.

My temples with hot jealous pulses beat

was his cancelled beginning for stanza ii, while in stanza iii the jealous description of Fanny's partner at a dance comes from Burton's[8]

and shall perceive his eyes, with a kind of greediness, to pull unto them this image of beauty, and carry it to the heart;

Jealousy, in fact, as wild and violent as any described in Burton's pages, now invades his whole being. Another cancelled line in this Ode to Fanny was used at once for the opening of the distracted final sonnet, written at this same time and in a state approaching frenzy.

I cry your mercy—pity—love!—aye, love!

II

He had reached this state in a bare month from his moment of calm decision at Winchester. It is true that incipient disease was growing on him, and warping his judgment. Yet the contrast is striking and rapid. He had inherited from his mother a strong and passionate nature. Now it swallowed up his life.

Much must depend upon something which still, because of her own reserve, remains uncertain, the character of Fanny Brawne. For many years after Keats's death, she was thought to have been trivial, shallow, thoughtless; in recent times, particularly since the publication of her letters to Fanny Keats, opinion has swung the other way. She is now often represented as a true mate for Keats, understanding, stimulating, thoughtful, patient. In the light of what actually happened, there must be some unreality in either view. What does fit the facts is that both are partly true, but of different times in her life. Her character developed and deepened as the result of the stress and later the suffering of Keats's own life. The girl Keats himself wrote about in December, 1818, is a fashionable, heartless, rather silly flirt; the girl who wrote to Fanny Keats in September, 1820, is an understanding and sensitive young woman.

Nothing shows this more clearly than the only direct evidence that remains of her at this time, her handwriting.[9] The handwriting in which, early in 1819, she copied the *Hush, hush* lyric, wrote her own birthday and that of a cousin, and scribbled a couplet in French, is not that of a mature woman. Unformed, careless, casual, uncertain in spelling and punctuation, it is that of a schoolgirl. The strokes are short, stubby, indecisive, and the way in which letters are carried above and below the line is experimental and variable. It is a very different hand from that in which she wrote to Keats's sister during his last illness, and in which, after he had gone abroad, she noted down dressmaking work finished or to be done, and lists of books to be bought or read. This is the hand of a woman whose character has at least begun to form. It is assured and all of a piece. The same characteristic formations are still there, especially the capital letters, but they are now all in harmony. The strokes are long and firm and uniform above and below the line. Though it cannot be made a scientific proof, these two examples of her handwriting, as they actually exist side by side, can at least be treated as a symbol of the change in her nature that had taken place between the winters of 1818 and 1820.

In this October of 1819, she was in a state somewhere between the two, exactly halfway in this process of change. The younger coquettish habits were allied with a new maturity. It is ironic that this maturity, which accounts for Keats's sudden access of passion, was also the result of his own conduct during the past summer. Assuming that there was an "understanding" between them when he left for the Isle of Wight, he had, by any ordinary standards, behaved badly. He had promised to see her within a month, and she had had to wait for over three; he had said he would see her if he came to London, and he had not kept the promise. He had answered her flirtatious letter, with its news of dances and parties, by his "flint-worded" one. This was an experience she had probably never had before, and it matured her. On the other hand, she was still young enough to take revenge. All Keats's October letters speak of her threatening to be cruel to him; the *Ode to Fanny* shows that she had no intention of giving up the dances nor the dancing-partners she had acquired in the summer. This was a natural reply to his season of apparent indifference, an indifference which had really hurt her, and to which she harked back later in their life.[10]

No one can anticipate the extent and the nature of sexual jealousy. Fanny cannot have known what she was arousing. Yet there was something in Keats's dilemma equally tormenting and equally unknown to her. This was the mere fact that they had at last become officially engaged, and that he was now contemplating, or being forced to contemplate, marriage according to the rites of the Christian Church. The proof is in his verses and letters at this time. Their images are drawn, for the first time in his life, from a source generally foreign to him, the language of the Church itself—in the poems "a heresy, and a schism", "the canon law of love", "love's missal", "the Holy See of Love", "the sacramental cake"; in the letters, "My Creed is Love and you are its only tenet." All these terms mean engagement and a serious contemplation of the sacrament of marriage, however far away his material circumstances might place it.

This was a dilemma of a higher order than any other. Fanny was an orthodox Christian believer; Keats was strongly anti-clerical. His bitterness with what he called "the pious frauds of religion" was abnormal. He loathed the Church. Every anti-clerical remark in reading or conversation drew from him a mark of approval. Yet now he was proposing to bind himself by one of the sacraments of the Church. The violence of the conflict can be seen by two quotations. To Fanny he wrote:[11]

> I have been astonished that Men could die Martyrs for religion—I have shudder'd at it. I shudder no more— I could be martyr'd for my Religion—Love is my religion— I could die for that.

Yet his real feeling burst out when against the word "martyrs" in the pages of Burton, he wrote,[12] "The most bigotted word ever met with". It is clear from all his comments that his whole being was in revolt against the idea of marriage.[13] To him it was only a part of a greater hypocrisy, and to accept it would be to desert his principles. Yet the plain fact was that to get Fanny he would have to accept this and much more. He would have to condone something which he believed was absolutely wrong in order to obtain his physical desire. "Cogliam la rosa d'amore" he wrote with longing in his Burton,[14] and then, bitterly underlined, "ubique". That is what he would have wished to do. He was being made to accept a line of conduct which he knew to be false to his nature and belief. The torment for him was spiritual as well as physical. There is small wonder that he virtually ceased to be a poet, that he could do nothing but

> Forget, in the mist of idle misery,
> Life's purposes—the palate of my mind
> Losing its gust, and my ambition blind!

III

After October, poetry is at an end. There were some unavailing attempts to go on revising *Hyperion*, and a proposal to write a new poem about Elizabeth's Earl of Leicester, of which possibly a few lines survive.[15] Otherwise there was nothing except the long comic poem with which Brown persuaded him to occupy his mind. The title Brown selected was *The Cap and Bells*; Keats significantly preferred to call it *The Jealousies*. It was never finished. In January, 1820, George made a brief appearance to extract his money, and some of Keats's share, from Abbey. In February, 1820, Keats had the hæmorrhage which announced the fatal onset of his disease. A year later, without having written a word of poetry more, he was dead.

The stress of his love, disease, money worry over George, all took their part in this sudden and tragic finale. Yet more than these are needed to account for the complete blotting-out of poetry from his system. It is often asked what he might have written had he survived; it is more pertinent to see the state in which his life had arrived before his last illness. By this winter of 1819, he was by all signs close to a physical and nervous breakdown. Brown says he was attacked by melancholia in which he began secretly taking laudanum.[16] According to Brown, he promised to give it up, and kept his promise; but on the journey to Italy a year later he harassed Severn by asking to be allowed to end his life with laudanum.

For this state, most accounts dwell on the year of illness which followed the winter of 1819; the real clue lies in the year of supreme activity which preceded it, and the elements which made up that year. First, there was the illness and death of Tom. When everything else is considered, this still remains the deepest event in Keats's story. To spend over two months watching the slow death of his brother was something which altered the whole colour of Keats's life, and was at the back of his mind for all the rest of his working days. The reality and horror of the experience—"The last days of poor Tom were of the most distressing nature"[17]—brought a profundity into his own life. Then there is his association with Isabella Jones. He kept his secret well enough; but there emerges the picture of an attachment both passionate and intellectual which lasted through the first six months of this year, was connected with several of his greatest poems, and haunted him with recurring and symbolic images. It is noteworthy that when we last hear of Isabella, she writes on delicately black-edged paper on the subject of his recent death,[18] and that Brown made her one of the legatees of Keats's pathetically brief will[19]—"My Chest of Books divide among my friends."

Again, in this same year, there are the six weeks of dark experience and the flight to dissipation in February and March, which must at the least have left a weakness and a temptation which was liable to return under similar stress. Then there is the slow falling in love with Fanny Brawne, the strain of which was all the greater for being slow, as it undoubtedly was. It brought its happiness, but also its conflicts and torments much more surely by being of such gradual growth; for this reason it fastened so deeply on his heart in the last year of his life. Lastly we cannot forget the intense reading with which he filled almost every waking hour of this year—*King Lear, Troilus and Cressida*, the whole of Burton's great work, closely noted, all of Dryden's fables and translations, down to the minutest cadence of individual lines, to say nothing of his day-to-day study of other books, plays, contemporary works, and periodicals.

Keats all this year had been living on spiritual capital. He had used and spent every experience almost as soon as it had come into his possession. Every sight, person, book, emotion, or thought had been converted instantaneously into poetry. Could he or any other poet have lasted at such a rate? The reason for his sudden collapse is simply that he could write no more by these methods. He realised this himself, when he wished to compose, as he said, without fever; he could not keep this high pulse beating and endure. In November, after this feverous year, he wrote of his ambition to produce two or three fine poems in the next half-dozen years. Two or three in six years—when in one year only he had written some dozen major poems, a whole play, and much incidental verse. He knew he could not exist any more at that rate; yet no one will ever know whether he could have altered his self-consuming nature. Some tremendous change, perhaps even a breakdown in his personality, would have to have taken place. "How he can be Keats again from all this I have very little hope", wrote Severn from Rome, after his friend's last and fatal relapse. The final truth perhaps is that, even if illness had not intervened, he could never have been the old Keats and survived. "New Phoenix wings", in the words of his own sonnet, he might have achieved; but all of Keats that the world can know died, seventeen months before his death, at the moment when his living year was ended.

(*Lines to Fanny. Sonnet:* The day is gone.
Ode to Fanny. Sonnet: I cry your mercy.)

NOTES

The following general abbreviations are used in the notes:

1. LETTER. *The Letters of John Keats*, edited by Maurice Buxton Forman. Fourth edition. Oxford University Press, 1952. These letters are referred to by their numbers, which are the same in most editions. The page references are those of the fourth edition. These are added for longer letters.
2. ROLLINS. *The Keats Circle. Letters and Papers 1816–78*, edited by Hyder Edward Rollins. Harvard University Press, Cambridge, Mass., 1948. These documents are referred to by their numbers, not by pages.
3. BURTON. *The Anatomy of Melancholy* . . . by Democritus Junior (Robert Burton). Eleventh edition, 2 vols. London, 1813. The numbers of the pages are given from this edition, which Keats possessed. The numbers of the various Sections, Members, and Subsections are also given, so that the quotations can be traced in any edition of the work. *Keats House volume* refers to Keats's copy of vol. II, now in the Museum, Keats House, Hampstead.

PROLOGUE: *HYPERION* TO *HYPERION*

[1] Manuscript letter, Hessey to Taylor, September 16th, 1818; quoted by Blunden, *Keats's Publisher*, p. 56.

[2] J. Middleton Murry, *Keats and Shakespeare*; also C. L. Finney, *The Evolution of Keats's Poetry*.

[3] Hale-White, *Keats as Doctor and Patient*.

[4] Middleton Murry, "Fanny Brawne", in *The Mystery of Keats* has clearly demonstrated this point, using Fanny's own words in her letter of May 23rd, 1821, to Fanny Keats. Even more significant is Fanny Brawne's statement in her draft letter to Charles Brown, dated December 29th, 1829.

> I was more generous ten years ago, I should not now endure the odium of being connected with one who was working up his way against poverty and every sort of abuse.

She repeats the term "ten years ago" later in the letter. It is clear that by "being connected" she can only mean "formally engaged" and that she associates this with ten years ago, i.e., in 1819. Nor could Keats, though sometimes in money difficulties, ever be said to be in poverty till late in that year; certainly at no time in 1818.

[5] Letter 14 note.

[6] Letter 123, pp. 295–341.

[7] Appendix A.

[8] Mabel A. E. Steele, *The Woodhouse Transcripts of the Poems of Keats*, Harvard Library Bulletin, Vol. III, No. 2, p. 244.

1. CHARMIAN AND POOR TOM

[1] Burton II, p. 340. Part 3, Sec. 2, Mem. 4, Subs. 1.

[2] Letter 86.

[3] Letter 87.

[4] Letter 94, pp. 231–232.

[5] Helen Darbishire, *Keats and Egypt*, The Review of English Studies, Vol. III, No. 9, January, 1927.

[6] Rollins 20.

[7] Some likenesses between *Hyperion* Book I and *King Lear* have been noted: see C. L. Finney, *Shakespeare and Keats's Hyperion: a Study in the Processes of Poetical Composition*. It has not been sufficiently appreciated that Keats was writing at the actual time of re-reading the folio, nor how extensively he echoed the play.

[8] These lines include a memory of one of the most famous speeches in *King Lear*:

> Men must endure
> Their going hence even as their coming hither:
> Ripeness is all.

Saturn's words

> it must—it must
> Be of ripe progress

were first written

> it must—it must
> Be going on

Both versions echo Shakespeare's words.

[9] Letter 89.

[10] Letter 77.

[11] Letter 81.

[12] Rollins (17 note 6) says that it was Tom who turned these letters over to Haydon, but there seems no evidence for this. Tom only mentions sending them to Reynolds (Rollins 14) while Haydon's letter of September 25th (Rollins 17) speaks as if he had received no account of the tour by that date. Keats's visit to Haydon took place before October 14th (Letter 94) and Keats's remark "I believe Haydon has two" (ibid.) does not mean that Keats did not give him the letters himself—only that he was not sure whether Haydon had returned them.

2. A NATIVITY ODE AND THE SCOTCH LETTERS

[1] Letter 90, where it is misdated October 9th. Keats clearly refers in it to "today's" Chronicle, i.e., the issue of October 8th.

[2] Letter 151.

[3] M. R. Ridley, *Keats' Craftsmanship*, p. 80.

[4] Letter 123, pp. 327–328.

[5] Douglas Bush, *Notes on Keats's Reading*, PMLA 50 (1935), pp. 785–806 notes some resemblance between Hyperion's palace and the cloud palaces of the sky at the end of *The Excursion* Book II. The resemblance, however, is very generalized.

⁶ Letter 94, pp. 228–236.

⁷ This stanza of Milton's Ode may also be responsible for some of the Egyptian setting of *Hyperion*; the word "Memphian" occurs in both poems.

⁸ Rollins 19. By "the Tale" Reynolds cannot refer to the already-written *Isabella*, which he always calls "the Poem".

⁹ Letter 94 p. 238.

¹⁰ Letter 71, 73, 75 henceforward referred to in the text by the numbers with which Tom Keats himself appears to have marked them, 1, 2, and 3.

¹¹ "I sent you in my first Packet some of my scotch Letters. I find I have kept one back which was written in the most interesting part of our Tour, and will copy parts of it. . . ." Letter 156, p. 408 (September 18th, 1819) "My first Packet" clearly refers to the letter of October, 1818, which Keats marked A. In this "Packet" he probably sent, as well as the three letters from himself to Tom, the letters he himself had recently received from Reynolds and Wood-house. He called the whole collection, at the time he sent it, a "Parcel"; it must have been a considerable one.

¹² Letter 78.

¹³ *Hyperion* Book II, 5–17 are based on the description of the Ambleside waterfalls (Letter 71); lines 34–38 describe the "Druid temple" of the Vale of St. John (Letter 73); Saturn's ascent in line 85 "with damp and slippery footing" takes its wording from Keats's experience on the same day when he "was damped by slipping one leg into a squashy hole".

3. *BRIGHT STAR* AND THE BEAUTIFUL MRS. JONES

¹ C. W. Dilke said that Keats met Fanny Brawne at his house in October or November. For reasons discussed in the next chapter, the November meeting must be presumed. It is sufficient to say here that there is no word of any meeting with Fanny Brawne in the long, detailed letter from Keats to George (Letter 94), of which the last sheet is dated October 31st.

² Colvin, *John Keats*, p. 335 and p. 494, believed it to have been written in the last week of February, 1819. Lowell, *John Keats* II, pp. 202–206, put forward the theory that it was written about April 15th–16th, 1819, when Keats was re-reading some of the remaining Scotch letters. She did not observe that the relevant letter was out of Keats's possession nearly six months earlier.

³ Letter 71.

⁴
>   There is sad feud among ye, and rebellion
>   Of son against his sire.
>   *Hyperion* I, 321–22.
>   And the rude son should strike his father dead.
>   *Troilus and Cressida* I, iii, 115.
>   My life is but the life of winds and tides.
>   *Hyperion* I, 341.
>   The Seas and Windes (old Wranglers) tooke a Truce.
>   *Troilus and Cressida* II, ii, 75 (underlined by Keats).

The adjective "airy" is specially noted by Keats in T. & C., and used by him in the last line but one of *Hyperion* I; moreover another note in his folio of the play half-quotes his own line in *Hyperion* I, 9.

⁵ Letter 92 and 95.

⁶ Rollins 22.

⁷ Hazlitt was collecting together his *Political Essays*, which he published next year. These included his three *On the Clerical Character*, in the first of which he quotes Milton:

> "Eremites and friars,
> White, black, and grey with all their trumpery."

Keats echoes these essays in his own writings on the clergy. He may have had a sight of them now at Hessey's, or Hazlitt may have recalled their previous magazine publication earlier in the year.

⁸ Appendix D. Joanna Richardson's *Fanny Brawne* conjectures this.

⁹ Rollins 347.

¹⁰ Blunden, *Keats's Publisher*, pp. 96–98.

¹¹ Appendix D.

¹² Appendix D.

¹³ Lowell, *John Keats*, I, pp. 462–63.

¹⁴ *Times*, April 23rd, 1818; Letter 98, p. 248, and Letter 156, p. 405.

¹⁵ Rollins 35.

¹⁶ Islington Land Tax 2118, Middlesex County Record Office; Islington Rate Books, 1811–27, Islington Town Hall; *Alphabetical List of Officers of the Indian Army*, Dodwell and Miles, 1838. Rollins (35 note) says "the British Army Lists of the period give too many Colonel Greens to provide any clue". The Islington records, however, provide the Christian name Thomas, and the East India Company's list confirms that he was the only officer of that name and rank. Lowell, *John Keats*, I, p. 114, supposed him to have been the future father-in-law of Marianne Reynolds, who married H. G. Green, but there seems no support for this conjecture.

¹⁷ It may be argued that since there was no boarding-school in Islington kept by Mrs. Green, according to *The Boarding School and London Masters' Directory of* 1828, she is unlikely to have been Isabella Jones's friend, and that the Islington address is a coincidence. Keats, however, did not say that he visited a boarding-school in Islington, but only "a friend of her's who keeps a Boarding School". Just round the corner from Isabella Jones, at 2 Brunswick Row, Queen Square, there was an establishment known as Miss Green's Boarding School (*Triennial Directory 1817–19*), which had been connected with a Mary Green since 1815.

¹⁸ Her incoherent remarks about "the Book of trifles" may be explained by the fact that at about the same time as *Endymion* a book entitled *Trifles, imitative of the chaster style of Meleager* was published anonymously. Woodhouse, and perhaps others of the Keats set, believed that one of the poems in this book had been written by Keats, i.e., "the other trifle". See H. W. Garrod, *Poems*, vi and lxix. Dr. Garrod, like Mrs. Colonel Green, convicts the author of the poem of "a great *Mistake*"—that is, of introducing a reference to the Garden of Eden in a poem supposed to be from the Greek.

¹⁹ Letter 93.

²⁰ Rollins 24.

4. THE MOURNFUL HOUSE AND FANNY BRAWNE

[1] Letter 95, 97.

[2] Letter 98, p. 257.

[3] Letter 78. Rollins 66, p. 146 note.

[4] Letter 80. Rollins 28.

[5] Rollins 166. Brown's description in after years, "From that moment he was my inmate", was meant to emphasise that he regarded Keats in the then sense of that word as a paying lodger.

[6] The date is conjectural; it was later marked by Fanny in a diary (Appendix E) with the pencilled X she often used for important memoranda.

[7] Rollins lvi.

[8] Letter 87 note.

[9] Letter 139.

[10] Appendix E.

[11] T. Medwin, *Life of Shelley*.

[12] The only evidence to the contrary is this. On September 18th, 1820, Fanny Brawne wrote to Fanny Keats "I have known your brother for two years". There is, however, no reason to suppose that she meant precisely twenty-four months. She was probably referring generally to 1818 as the year when she met Keats, just as she later referred to 1819 as the year in which she became formally engaged. In writing to Fanny Keats, also, she had every reason to make her relationship with John both as vague and as longstanding as possible, so as to make a favourable impression on the Abbeys.

[13] *Letters of Fanny Brawne to Fanny Keats*, No. 4.

[14] Appendix D.

[15] Letter 139.

[16] Letter 111.

5. LEIGH HUNT AND ROBERT BURTON

[1] Letter 98. p. 252.

[2] Letter 98, p. 254.

[3] Hunt, *The Literary Pocket Book* for 1819 (Keats House), Appendix E.

[4] Burton I, xxii.

[5] Burton I, xi.

[6] Burton (Introduction), p. 4. Appendix A.

[7] In our own time, Christopher Fry has taken the title of one of his plays and some of his verbal gusto from the *Anatomy*.

[8] Burton (Introduction), p. 5.

6. *HUSH, HUSH* AND ISABELLA JONES

[1] Letter 98, p. 252.

[2] Letter 100.

[3] Letter 102.

[4] Letter 98, p. 259. H. E. Rollins, *Keats's Misdated Letters*, p. 180.

⁵ Leigh Hunt. *Autobiography*, edited J. E. Morpurgo, p. 341.

⁶ ibid, p. 343.

⁷ Hale-White, *Keats as Doctor and Patient*.

⁸ *Letters of Fanny Brawne to Fanny Keats*, Letter 16, p. 41. For reasons which it is not easy to follow, this chance remark has been taken to mean that she and Keats became engaged on that day. It has been demonstrated, on Fanny Brawne's own evidence, that this cannot possibly be so, (Middleton Murry, *The Mystery of Keats*, "Fanny Brawne", pp. 28–29) but the tradition unaccountably persists.

⁹ Letter 123, p. 301.

¹⁰ He was back in Hampstead, answering a letter which awaited him there on Thursday, February 4th (Letters 112). He told Taylor that he would perhaps stay a fortnight (Letter 103) and Fanny Keats that he did stay a fortnight (Letter 113). He spent only a few days at Chichester before walking over to Bedhampton on Saturday , January 23rd. The odds are that he travelled from London to Chichester on Thursday, January 21st.

¹¹ Charlotte Reynolds told H. Buxton Forman that she sometimes played to Keats for hours, and that he composed the poem to a Spanish air which she played. These reminiscences of Charlotte Reynolds in her old age were, however, extremely hazy, and Keats had been distinctly cold to all the Reynolds girls since their behaviour to Jane Cox three or four months earlier. It is possibly the same tradition which associates the song with an air by Steibelt, who certainly had a Spanish wife (*Athenæum*, October 15th, 1859), but no existing piano study by Steibelt can be made to fit the words.

¹² Lowell, *John Keats*, I, pp. 462, 463.

¹³ *Hastings Guide*, by an inhabitant. Hastings Museum No. 840.

¹⁴ Appendix D.

¹⁵ Appendix D.

¹⁶ Appendix D.

¹⁷ Letter 94, p. 238.

¹⁸ H. M. MacCracken, *The Source of Keats's Eve of St. Agnes*, Modern Philology, Vol. vii. This has been widely questioned, but there is no difficulty in supposing that Keats heard a version of the story by word of mouth from Reynolds.

¹⁹ Rollins 40.

7. ST. AGNES EVE AND CHICHESTER

¹ *Manuscript Reminiscences of William Hoare* (1887).

² West Sussex County Record Office.

³ Letter 111.

⁴ Manuscript work-book of Samuel Peat, 1811–17, Chichester.

⁵ C. L. Finney, *The Evolution of Keats's Poetry*, II, p. 540.

⁶ ibid., p. 541.

⁷ Finney (*op. cit.*, p. 545) actually attributed the *form* of the poem to "Keats's love for Miss Brawne" and to the suppositious engagement at this time.

⁸ Letter 111; *The Faerie Queene*, Book 4, Canto II, 25.

[9] Leigh Hunt, *Autobiography*, p. 343.

[10] Letter 166.

[11] Letter 123, p. 295.

[12] *Land Tax Assessments*, Chichester Archives, County Record Office.

[13] Peat Manuscript.

[14] *Leases of the Priest Vicars Choral*, Diocesan Record Office, Chichester, 80.

[15] James Rouse, *Beauties and Antiquities of the County of Sussex*, 1825, p. 384.

8. ST. AGNES EVE AND STANSTED

[1] The legend of St. Agnes Eve only receives a cursory line in Burton II, p. 341. Part 3, Sec. 2, Mem. 4, Subs. 1, which Keats was reading many months later, and where it is attributed to St. Anne.

[2] Burton I, pp. 55–77, Part I. Sec. 2, Mem. 1, Subs. 2. (Appendix A.)

[3] ibid., pp. 67–70. (Appendix A.)

[4] *Hampshire Telegraph and Sussex Chronicle*, August 2nd, 1819.

[5] ibid., January 18th, 1819.

[6] The Right Hon. the Earl of Bessborough, *Stansted and Its Owners*, The Sussex County Magazine, August, 1952.

[7] T. W. Horsfield, *History, Antiquities, Topography of the County of Sussex* 1835. Vol. ii, p. 78.

[8] A. M. W. Stirling, *The Ways of Yesterday*, p. 119 *passim.*

[9] Why, it has been asked, "knot-grass"? It was only one jump from the acorn motif of the carvings throughout the house, and even in the Chapel, to Lysander's speech, which Keats had marked in his pocket Shakespeare:

> You minimus, of hind'ring knot-grass made;
> You bead, you acorn.

[10] Letter 123, p. 299.

[11] Lowell, *John Keats*, II, pp. 176–77.

[12] Luke Howard, *Climate of London*, Vol. II; also *Hampshire Telegraph and Sussex Chronicle*.

[13] *Hampshire Telegraph and Sussex Chronicle*, February 1st, 1819.

[14] The Book of Office for the Archdeaconry of Chichester (119) 1801–22 contains a detailed account of the ceremony.

[15] Wisdom 5 and Acts 22 to verse 22. The description in the latter of St. Paul's conversion on the road to Damascus may well have something to do with Keats's description of Madeline:

> And on her hair a glory, like a saint;

[16] Fane Lombard, F.S.A., *Sussex Archeological Collections*, Vol. LXXV.

[17] At the most recent service held on the Saint's day, January 25th, 1953, at exactly the same time as the dedication service, "rich amethyst" from these windows could be observed falling on the faces and hands of the congregation in just the way that Keats observed.

[18] Burton I, pp. 98–100. Part 1, Sec. 2, Mem. 2, Subs. 1. (Appendix A.)

[19] *Hampshire Telegraph and Sussex Chronicle*, February 1st, 1819.

9. ST. VALENTINE AND ST. MARK

[1] Letter 112.

[2] Letter 123, p. 296.

[3] Joanna Richardson, *Fanny Brawne*, Appendix II, pp. 163–164. This must have been written in 1819. Brown would not have written it in 1820, when Keats had just been taken seriously ill, nor in 1821 when Keats was dying. By 1822 he had left Wentworth Place.

[4] Letter 141, where he speaks of having received a letter from her "when near a Cathedral".

[5] Letter 123, p. 301. On February 19th Keats wrote, "She made me take home a Pheasant the other day, which I gave to Mrs. Dilke". He refers to his meeting with Woodhouse on the 13th as "the other day" also. Game was generally hung for about a week, and Mrs. Dilke had the pheasant for dinner on the 20th. Everything points to his seeing her on the 13th, and probably again on his next visit to Town on the 17th.

[6] Letter 123, p. 299. Speaking of *St. Mark* and *St. Agnes* he wrote, "you see what fine mother Radcliff names I have—it is not my fault—I did not search for them——" The inference is that someone else did, and we already know that Isabella Jones suggested *St. Agnes*.

[7] It has sometimes been wrongly said to be Canterbury, although there is no resemblance. When Keats later used scraps of the *St. Mark* fragment to bolster up the poetry of his comic poem, *The Cap and Bells*, he revived the name Bertha for one of his characters and placed her in Canterbury, thus causing this confusion.

[8] Colvin, *John Keats*, p. 439.

[9] In spite of an attempt to associate the images with Southwell's Family Bible, which Keats possessed (J. L. Lowes, *Moneta's Temple*, PMLA 51 (1936), pp. 1098–1113), there is no doubt that the Way windows are the real source.

[10] For the suggestion that the contents of these windows were Keats's source for the illuminated manuscript in *St. Mark*, I am very much indebted to Mrs. J. R. H. Moorman, who first communicated these points to me.

[11] Stirling, *The Ways of Yesterday*, p. 146.

[12] Woodhouse noted this on his transcript of the poem. His note may have been written at the same time as his note on *The Eve of St. Agnes* about Mrs. Jones, and both pieces of information may have come from the same source.

[13] Letter 110, where both it and Haydon's reply are misplaced in January. The reference in Haydon's letter to his Exhibition makes it certain that both were written in February.

[14] Letter 123, p. 303.

10. DISSIPATION AND DARKNESS

[1] Rollins 187.

[2] B. R. Haydon, *Journals*, Vol. I, p. 302.

[3] Rollins 264.

⁴ Letter 123, p. 297.
⁵ Letter 123, p. 301.
⁶ Letter 123, pp. 304–317. H. E. Rollins, *Keats's Misdated Letters*, pp. 181–2.
⁷ One of these visits was to a dance organised by Mrs. Wylie on March 9th.
Letter 123 (where Keats wrote "19th" by mistake) 114 and 116. It was for this
dance, and not because Fanny Brawne was going out to dances at this time,
that he wished his sister would teach him some dancing steps (Letter 114).
⁸ Burton I, p. 157. Part 1, Sec. 2, Mem. 3, Subs. 10. (Appendix A.)
⁹ Letter 115.
¹⁰ Rollins 59.
¹¹ Rollins 35.
¹² Letter 128.
¹³ Rollins 136.

11. LIGHT VERSE AND PARODIES

¹ Letter 123, p. 323.
² H. W. Garrod, *Keats*, p. 132.
³ Letter 120.
⁴ Letter 123, p. 318.
⁵ W. Robertson, *The History of America*, 2 vols., 1808. The mule in the
poem is said to come from Otaheite, a name Keats got from Robertson, Vol. I,
Note LI, p. 411, and Note LXXXIII, p. 429.
⁶ Rollins 166.
⁷ There are few evidences that Keats had read much Dryden before this date.
The lyric *In a drear-nighted December* has the metre of a lyric poem in Dryden's
play *The Spanish Friar*. De Selincourt, *Poems*, Addenda--Notes, p. 586.
Keats also makes one reference to *Alexander's Feast* (Letter 21).
⁸ Letter 23.
⁹ C. L. Finney, *The Evolution of Keats's Poetry*, II, pp. 652–653. Finney, not
realising the poem was a parody, assigned it to June, 1819, when Keats was
re-reading Wordsworth.
¹⁰ *The Oxford Companion to Music* says, under *Flute*:

> If any collection of eighteenth or early nineteenth century family
> portraits be examined one or two male members of the family at that
> period are likely to be found pictured with a flute in their hands.

The same authority remarks that whole oratorios and operas were arranged
for this instrument. Prominent among these were the works of Bishop, whose
opera Keats had just seen, and whose *Lo, here the gentle lark*, composed this
year, became a tried war-horse for family playing. There is a postscript to
Sam, in a letter this summer from Keats to Fanny Brawne (Letter 139),
which proposes a violent end for somebody or something called "the Bishop".
It is probable that this was the term for Sam's flute, or his playing, or some
particular work which he never stopped practising.

12. LA BELLE DAME AND THE FALSE FLORIMEL

[1] Letter 123, p. 328.

[2] *The Times*, Monday, April 19th, 1819.

[3] Letter 123, pp. 327–328.

[4] *Times Literary Supplement, Ten Days in the Life of Keats*, March 14th, 1952.

[5] Burton I, pp. 280, 281 and 284. Part 1, Sec. 3, Mem. 1, Subs. 2 & 3. (Appendix A.)

[6] *The Faerie Queene.* Book 3, Canto VII, 17.

[7] *The Thorn*, stanza 3.

[8] Letter 123, p. 318.

[9] First printed by Dorothy Hewlett, *A Life of John Keats*, Appendix II.

[10] *On Receiving a Curious Shell, and a Copy of Verses from the Same Ladies.* 8–12.

[11] "Ratsbane" was a threat borrowed from Dryden's *Prologues and Epilogues*, which Keats was reading, and in which Dryden uses the word several times.

13. SONNETS AND THE FIRST ODE

[1] It is likely that the original version of the *Bright Star* sonnet, which only exists for us in Brown's hand, was among these latter.

[2] Letter 123, pp. 338–339.

[3] Burton I, pp. 206–207. Part 1, Sec. 2, Mem. 3, Subs. 15.

[4] Burton I, p. 432. Part 2, Sec. 2, Mem. 5. (Appendix A.)

[5] ibid., p. 434.   (Appendix A.)

[6] ibid., p. 435.   (Appendix A.)

[7] Burton II, pp. 63–66. Part 2, Sec. 3, Mem. 6. (Appendix A.)

[8] E. H. W. Meyerstein. *Times Literary Supplement.* March 22nd, 1923.

[9] Burton II, pp. 82–83. Part 2, Sec. 3, Mem. 7.

[10] Letter 123, p. 325.

14. MAY AND THE TWO GREAT ODES

[1] Letter 123, p. 335.

[2] Rollins 166; Letter 123, p. 336.

[3] Letter 122. This should be dated May 1st, not April 17th. An ultra-violet photograph of the date-stamp shows the word May.

[4] A. W. Crawford, *The Genius of Keats*, p. 103 *et seq.*

[5] H. W. Garrod, *The Profession of Poetry and other Lectures*: "The Nightingale in Poetry", p. 144, traces some of Keats's debt to the Chaucerian original; but there is only one place where Keats seems to have remembered this:

> The nightingale with so mery a note
> Answered him, that all the wode rong
> So sodainly, that, as it were a sot
> I stood astonied.

lines 99–102.

may have suggested the ending of stanza vi. On the other hand, lines 43–45 of the original

> And at the last a path of litel brede
> I found, that gretly had not used be,
> For it forgrowen was with gras and weede

certainly seem to have suggested the opening of the last stanza of the *Ode on a Grecian Urn*.

⁶ Burton II, p. 126. Part 2, Sec. 5, Mem. 1, Subs. 5. (Appendix A.)

⁷ ibid., p. 127. (Appendix A.)

⁸ Burton II, p. 170. Part 3, Sec. 1, Mem. 2, Subs. 2.   (Appendix A.)

⁹ Burton II, p. 177. Part 3, Sec. 1, Mem. 2, Subs. 3.   (Appendix A.)

¹⁰ Keats's known enjoyment of Claude's picture *The Sacrifice to Apollo* obviously contributed to stanza 4.

¹¹ *Letters of Fanny Brawne to Fanny Keats:* No. 9. See also Murry, *The Mystery of Keats*, "Fanny Brawne".

¹² Letter 156, p. 429.

¹³ Letter 127.

¹⁴ Blunden, *Keats's Publisher*, pp. 96–97.

¹⁵ See Note 11 above.

¹⁶ Letter 134.

¹⁷ ibid.

¹⁸ Burton II, pp. 152–53 (Keats House volume).

¹⁹ Burton II, pp. 166–67 (ibid.).

²⁰ The expression "Goatish lust" occurs frequently in Massinger's plays, which Keats was reading. Letter 134.

15. TWO LESSER ODES AND *LAMIA*

¹ Burton I, p. 320. Part 1, Sec. 4, Mem. 1. (Appendix A.)

² Burton II, pp. 83–85. Part 2, Sec. 3, Mem. 8. (Appendix A.)

³ Letter 127.

⁴ Letter 128.

⁵ Burton II, p. 181. Part 3, Sec. 1, Mem. 3. (Appendix A.)

⁶ Letter 136.

⁷ By the terms of his grandfather's will, so Keats understood, Tom's money should have been divided equally between himself, George, and Fanny. Soon after Tom's death, Abbey produced the strange theory that the shares of John and George would not be free for them until Fanny became of age—a matter of six more years. Keats wrote of this in February that he considered it "all a Bam", i.e., a hoax on Abbey's part; but he had not proceeded further.   Letter 110.

⁸ Letter 144.

⁹ Burton II, pp. 196–97. Part 3, Sec. 2, Mem. 1, Subs. 1. (Appendix A.)

¹⁰ Letter 156, p. 402.

¹¹ Burton II, p. 218. Part 3, Sec. 2, Mem. 2, Subs. 2. (Appendix A.)

¹² Letter 134.

16. *LAMIA* AND A SONNET REVISED

[1] Letter 134.
[2] Letter 136.
[3] Letter 137.
[4] Burton II, p. 233. Part 3, Sec. 2, Mem. 2, Subs. 2. (Appendix A.)
[5] ibid. pp. 239–40.
[6] ibid. p. 240. Part 3, Sec. 2, Mem. 2, Subs. 2. (Appendix A.)
[7] Letter 136.
[8] Letter 140.
[9] Letter 138A.
[10] Letter 139.

17. DRAMA AND THE MOVE TO WINCHESTER

[1] Letter 142.

[2] J. H. Roberts, *The Significance of Lamia*, PMLA 50 (1925), pp. 550–61, argues that *The Fall of Hyperion* was actually written at this time, as its thought is reproduced in Keats's letters at this period. This is probably true of much of the thought, but not of the writing, which is associated by many signs with a later period. See Chapter 19.

[3] He had been reading Massinger just before going to the Isle of Wight (Letter 134 note). Later in the year he marked several parallels to Massinger in the *Anatomy of Melancholy* (Keats House volume).

[4] Burton II, p. 234. Part 3, Sec. 2, Mem. 2, Subs. 2.

[5] Letter 183.

[6] Letter 143.

[7] B. R. Haydon, *Journals* I, p. 301.

[8] Alfred H. Burne, *History of the Royal Artillery Mess, Woolwich*, pp. 35, 40.

[9] Colvin, *Life of Keats*, pp. 330–31 note.

[10] Letter 143.

[11] Middleton Murry, *Poems and Verses of John Keats*, edited and arranged in chronological order. Second edition, revised, 1949. Notes (on *Otho the Great*), p. 548.

[12] Burton II, p. 242. Part 3, Sec. 2, Mem. 3, Subs. 3. (Appendix A.)

[13] Burton II, p. 224 (Keats House volume).

[14] Letter 145.

[15] Rollins 166.

[16] For example, C. L. Finney II, pp. 728–30, who tries to connect it with Keats's reading of Holinshed in November, but has to admit that some of Keats's plot does not follow Holinshed's story.

[17] Burton II, p. 261. Part 3, Sec. 2, Mem. 3, Subs. 4.

[18] Letter 146.

18. THE FEAST AND THE LADY

[1] Burton II, pp. 254–56. Part 3, Sec. 2, Mem. 3, Subs. 3. (Appendix A.)

[2] Douglas Bush, *Notes on Keats's Reading*, PMLA 50 (1935), pp. 785–806. Bush also finds one parallel with *Lamia*, Part I and one with *Endymion*, but these contain no verbal echo of Potter, and nothing that Keats could not have known from his ordinary reading.

[3] Rollins 38.

[4] —but to the post office at Chichester instead of Winchester. This was probably Haslam. Though usually a responsible person, he was at this time, in Keats's words, "very much occupied with love and business", and was apt to make unaccountable mistakes about letters. See Letter 126, 146.

[5] Appendix B.

[6] Werner Beyer, *Keats and the Daemon King*. This is convincing in tracing the influence of *Oberon* on Keats's juvenile work, but considerably less so in considering the poems of his maturity.

[7] Letter 123, p. 303.

19. A DREAM AND AN AWAKENING

[1] Letter 156, pp. 413–414.

[2] Hewlett, *A Life of John Keats*, pp. 276–77, though there is some doubt whether Brown would have had time to get as far as Ireland.

[3] Letter 123, p. 316.

[4] Hewlett, p. 274 and J. L. Lowes.

[5] Letter 156, p. 424.

[6] Letter 156, p. 399 and note.

[7] Rollins 40.

20. THE RETURN TO WINCHESTER AND THE *ODE TO AUTUMN*

[1] Letter 156, p. 405. This is the only stanza in the first two cantos of *Don Juan* which can be said to be on literary ambition.

[2] Letter 150.

[3] Burton II, p. 314. Part 3, Sec. 2, Mem. 4, Subs. 1.

[4] ibid., pp. 311, 317, 324. (Appendix A.)

[5] ibid., p. 336. (Appendix A.)

[6] ibid., p. 337. (Appendix A.)

[7] ibid., p. 333. (Appendix A.)

[8] C. L. Finney, *The Evolution of Keats's Poetry*, II, pp. 707–8.

[9] Burton II, p. 334. Part 3, Sec. 2, Mem. 4, Subs. 1.

[10] Letter 156, p. 421.

[11] Letter 151.

[12] Letter 167.

EPILOGUE: FANNY AND THE AFTERMATH

[1] Letter 154.

[2] Letter 157.

[3] Burton II, p. 346. Part 3, Sec. 2, Mem. 5, Subs. 1. (Appendix A.)

[4] Burton II, p. 351. Part 3, Sec. 2, Mem. 6, Subs. 1. (Appendix A.)

[5] ibid., p. 354. (Appendix A.)

[6] Burton II, p. 510 (Keats House volume).

[7] Burton II, p. 355. Part 3, Sec. 2, Mem. 6, Subs. 1. (Appendix A.)

[8] Burton II, p. 357. Part 3, Sec. 2, Mem. 6, Subs. 2.

[9] Appendix E.

[10] Letter 197.

[11] Letter 160.

[12] Burton II, p. 510 (Keats House volume).

[13] Burton II, p. 416 (Keats House volume). On this page Keats puts a query against nine out of the "twelve motions to mitigate the miseries of marriage" quoted by Burton. He is particularly sarcastic about relatives-in-law. On the following page he underlines "The band of marriage is adamantine; no hope of loosing it; thou art undone."

[14] Burton II, p. 402 (Keats House volume).

[15] The lines beginning:

> This living hand, now warm and capable.

[16] Rollins 166.

[17] Letter 94.

[18] Appendix D.

[19] Rollins 122. She was numbered 11 among the eighteen recipients of Keats's books listed by Brown. Since—as I am informed by Dr. Rollins—the number 11 is pencilled in this list (and in a copy of it) against the two volumes of Cary's translation of Dante's *Inferno* (published by J. Carpenter in 1805), it is tolerably certain that she received one or both of these volumes. Thus, by a strange coincidence, or by Brown's deliberate intent, both Fanny Brawne and Isabella Jones eventually seem to have possessed a Dante which had belonged to Keats.

APPENDIX A

PARALLELS BETWEEN BURTON'S *ANATOMY OF MELANCHOLY* AND KEATS'S POEMS AND LETTERS

1. *not to be a slave of one science, or dwell altogether in one subject,* . . . *but to rove abroad,* centum puer artium, *to have an oar in every mans boat, to taste of every dish, and to sip of every cup.*
Burton, Democritus to the Reader (Introduction), p. 4.

> Sit thee there, and send abroad,
> With a mind self-overaw'd,
> Fancy . . .
> She will mix these pleasures up
> Like three fit wines in a cup,
> And thou shalt quaff it:
> *Fancy,* lines 25–27, 37–39.

2. Macbeth and Banco, two Scotish lords, that, as they were wandering in woods, had their fortunes told them by three strange women. To these heretofore they did use to sacrifice, by that ὑδρομαντεια, or divination by waters.
Burton I, p. 67. Part 1, Sec. 2, Mem. 1, Subs. 2.

> 'Thou must hold water in a witch's sieve,
> 'And be liege-lord of all the Elves and Fays,
> *The Eve of St. Agnes,* lines 120–21.

3. They are sometimes seen by old women and children. Hieron. Pauli, in his description of the city of Bereino in Spain, relates how they have been familiarly seen near that town, after fountains and hills: *nonnunquam* (saith Trithemius) *in sua latibula montium simpliciores homines ducunt, stupenda mirantibus ostendentes miracula, nolarum sonitus, spectacula,* etc.
Burton I, p. 68. Part 1, Sec. 2, Mem. 1, Subs. 2.

> While Porphyro upon her face doth look,
> Like puzzled urchin on an aged crone
> Who keepeth clos'd a wondrous riddle-book,
> As spectacled she sits in chimney nook.
> *The Eve of St. Agnes,* lines 128–31.

4. These kind of devils many times appear to men, and affright them out of their wits . . . Such sights are frequently seen . . .

215

in monasteries and about church-yards . . . These spirits often
foretell mens deaths.

> Burton I, p. 69. Part 1, Sec. 2, Mem. 1, Subs. 2.

'Ah! why wilt thou affright a feeble soul?
'A poor, weak, palsy-stricken, churchyard thing,
'Whose passing-bell may ere the midnight toll;

> *The Eve of St. Agnes*, lines 154–56.

5. A little before Tullies death, (saith Plutarch) the crows made a
mighty noise about him; *tumultuose perstrepentes*, they pulled the
pillow from under his head . . . illusions of walking spirits are often
perceived . . .

> Burton I, p. 70. Part 1, Sec. 2, Mem. 1, Subs. 2.

While legion'd fairies round her pillow flew,
> *later altered to*
While legion'd fairies pac'd the coverlet,

> *The Eve of St. Agnes*, line 168.

6. Cardan makes that a cause of their continual sickness at
Fessa in Africk, *because they live so much on fruits, eating them
thrice a day.*

> Burton I, p. 99. Part 1, Sec. 2, Mem. 2, Subs. 1.

Manna and dates, in argosy transferr'd
From Fez;

> *The Eve of St. Agnes*, lines 268–69.

7. Yet these are brave men; Silenus ebrius was no braver.

> Burton I, p. 105. Part 1, Sec. 2, Mem. 2, Subs. 2.

Other wines of a heavy and spirituous nature transform a
Man to a Silenus.

> Letter 123, p. 301.

8. a chicken, a rabbet, rib of a rack of mutton, wing of a capon,
the merry-thought of a hen, etc.

> Burton I, p. 108. Part 1, Sec. 2, Mem. 2, Subs. 2.

I must plead guilty to the breast of a Partridge, the back of a
hare, the backbone of a grouse, the wing and side of a Pheasant and
a Woodcock passim.

> Letter 123, p. 301.

9. Even in the midst of all our mirth, jollity, and laughter, is
sorrow and grief; or, if there be true happiness amongst us, 'tis but
for a time: . . . a fair morning turns to a lowring afternoon.

> Burton I, p. 159. Part 1, Sec. 2, Mem. 3, Subs. 10.

This is the world—thus we cannot expect to give way many hours to pleasure—Circumstances are like Clouds continually gathering and bursting—While we are laughing the seed of some trouble is put into the wide arable land of events.

Letter 123, p. 314.

10. preying upon, and devouring, as so many ravenous birds . . .
Burton I, p. 160. Part 1, Sec. 2, Mem. 3, Subs. 10.

For in wild nature the Hawk would lose his Breakfast of Robins——

Letter 123, p. 315.

11. Our towns, our cities . . . our villages are like mole-hills, and men as so many emmets, busie, busie still, going to and fro, in and out, and crossing one anothers projects . . .
Burton I, p. 157. Part 1, Sec. 2, Mem. 3, Subs. 10.

I go amongst the buildings of a city and I see a Man hurrying along—to what? the Creature has a purpose and his eyes are bright with it.

Letter 123, p. 315.

12. As Bellerophon in Homer

> That wandered in the woods sad all alone,
> Forsaking mens society, making great moan

they delight in floods and waters, desert places, to walk alone in orchards, gardens, private walks, back-lanes:
Burton I, p. 280. Part 1, Sec. 3, Mem. 1, Subs. 2.

> O what can ail thee, knight-at-arms,
> Alone and palely loitering?
> The sedge has wither'd from the lake,
> And no birds sing.

La Belle Dame Sans Merci, lines 1–4.

> And made sweet moan.

ibid., line 20.

13. He forsook the city, and lived in groves and hollow trees, upon a green bank by a brook side, or confluence of waters, all day long, and all night . . .
Burton I, p. 281. Part 1, Sec. 3, Mem. 1, Subs. 2.

> And nothing else saw all day long,

La Belle Dame, line 22.

I

14. They are much given to weeping, and delight in waters, ponds pools, rivers, fishing, fowling . . . they are pale of colour, slothful, apt to sleep, much troubled with the head-ach . . .

> Burton I, p. 284. Part 1, Sec. 3, Mem. 1, Subs. 3

And there she wept and sigh'd full sore,
> *La Belle Dame*, line 30.

And there she lulled me asleep,
> ibid., line 33.

And this is why I sojourn here,
Alone and palely loitering,
> ibid., lines 45–46.

15. this sweet moistning sleep . . .
> Burton I, p. 432. Part 2, Sec. 2, Mem. 5.

Its sweet-death dews o'er every pulse and limb——
> *Sonnet to Sleep*, line 8 *cancelled*.

16. for the most part our speeches in the day time cause our phantasy to work upon the like in our sleep . . .
> Burton I, p. 434. Part 2, Sec. 2, Mem. 5.

Then save me, or the passed day will shine
Upon my pillow, breeding many woes;
> *Sonnet to Sleep*, lines 9–10.

17. God Morpheus . . . with a horn and ivory box . . .
> Burton I, p. 435. Part 2, Sec. 2, Mem. 5.

And seal the hushed casket of my soul.
> *Sonnet to Sleep*, line 14.

18. I have learned, *in what state soever I am, therewith to be contented* . . .
> Burton II, p. 66. Part 2, Sec. 3, Mem. 6.

Who have not learnt to be content without her;
> First *Sonnet on Fame*, line 6.

19. Mine haven's found: Fortune and Hope, adieu!
Mock others now: for I have done with you.
> Burton II, p. 66. Part 2, Sec. 3, Mem. 6.

Make your best bow to her and bid adieu,
Then, if she likes it, she will follow you.
> First *Sonnet on Fame*, lines 13–14.

20. Helenas boule, the sole nectar of the Gods, or that true nephenthes, . . . which puts away care and grief.
> Burton II, p. 126. Part 2, Sec. 5, Mem. 1, Subs. 5.

That I might drink, and leave the world unseen,
> *Ode to a Nightingale*, line 19.

21. *Wine . . . brings gladness and cheerfulness of mind . . .* it makes an old wife dance, and such as are in misery, to forget evil and be merry.
> Burton II, p. 127. Part 2, Sec. 5, Mem. 1, Subs. 5

Dance, and Provencal song, and sunburnt mirth!

Fade far away, dissolve, and quite forget
> *Ode to a Nightingale*, lines 14 and 21.

22. Bacchus et afflictis requiem mortalibus affert,
> Burton II, p. 127. Part 2, Sec. 5, Mem. 1, Subs. 5.

Not charioted by Bacchus and his pards,

To thy high requiem become a sod.
> *Ode to a Nightingale*, lines 32 and 60.

23. Pleasant objects are infinite, whether they be such as have life, or be without life. Inanimate are countries, provinces, towers, towns, cities . . . The sun never saw a fairer city, *Thessala Tempe . . .*
> Burton II, p. 170. Part 3, Sec. 1, Mem. 2, Subs. 2.

In Tempe or the dales of Arcady?

What little town by river or sea shore,
> *Ode on a Grecian Urn*, lines 7 and 35.

24. No beauty leaves such an impression, strikes so deep, or links the souls of men closer than vertue. No painter, no graver, no carver can express vertues lustre . . . vertues lustre never fades, is ever fresh and green, *semper viva* to all succeeding ages.
> Burton II, p. 177. Part 3, Sec. 1, Mem. 2, Subs. 3.

Cold Pastoral!
When old age shall this generation waste,
Thou shalt remain, in midst of other woe
Than ours, a friend to man, to whom thou say'st,
Beauty is truth, truth beauty,—that is all
Ye know on earth, and all ye need to know.
> *Ode on a Grecian Urn*, lines 45–50.

25.   Hard is the doubt, and difficult to deem,
When all three kinds of love together meet,
And do dispart the heart with power extream,
> Burton II, p. 181. Part 3, Sec. 1, Mem. 3.

One morn before me were three figures seen,
> *Ode on Indolence*, line 1.

26. Whiteness in the lilly, red in the rose, purple in the violet, a lustre in all things without life, the cleer light of the moon, the bright beams of the sun, splendor of gold, purple, sparkling diamond, the excellent feature of the horse, the majesty of the lion, the colour of birds, peacocks tails, the silver scales of the fish, we behold with singular delight and admiration.

Burton II, p. 218. Part 3, Sec. 2, Mem. 2, Subs. 2.

> She was a gordian shape of dazzling hue,
> Vermilion-spotted, golden, green, and blue;
> Striped like a zebra, freckled like a pard,
> Eyed like a peacock, and all crimson barr'd;
> And full of silver moons, that, as she breathed,
> Dissolv'd or brighter shone, or interwreathed
> Their lustres with the gloomier tapestries——
> *Lamia*, Part I, lines 47–53.

27. a fine soft round pap gives an excellent grace
Quale decus tumidis Pario de marmore mammis!
and make a pleasant valley, *lacteum sinum*, between two chaulkie hills . . .

Burton II, p. 233. Part 3, Sec. 2, Mem. 2, Subs. 2.

> She fled into that valley they must pass
> Who go from Corinth out to Cenchreas,
> And rested at the foot of those wild hills,
> The rugged paps of little Perea's rills . . .
> *Lamia*, Part I, lines 173–76, 1st version.

28.　　 For the fair beauty of a virgin pure,
　　 Is sharper than a dart; and doth inure
　　 A deeper wound which pierceth to the heart . . .

Burton II, p. 237. Part 3, Sec. 2, Mem. 2, Subs. 2.

> A virgin purest lipp'd, yet in the lore
> Of love deep learned to the red heart's core:
> *Lamia*, Part I, lines 189–90.

29. We read, in the lives of the fathers, a story of a child that was brought up in the wilderness, from his infancy, by an old hermite: now come to mans estate, he saw by chance, two comely women wandring in the woods: he asked the old man what creatures they were: he told him fayries: after a while talking *obiter*, the hermite demanded of him, what was the pleasantest sight that ever he saw in his life? he readily replyed, the two fayries he spied in the wilderness. So that without doubt, there is some secret loadstone in a beautiful woman, a magnetique power, a natural inbred affection . . .

Burton II, p. 240. Part 3, Sec. 2, Mem. 2, Subs. 2.

Let the mad poets say whate'er they please
Of the sweets of Fairies, Peris, Goddesses,
There is not such a treat among them all,
Haunters of cavern, lake, and waterfall,
As a real woman . . .

Lamia, Part I, lines 328–32.

30. those curious needle-works, variety of colours, purest dyes, jewels, spangles, pendants, lawn, lace, tiffanies, fair and fine linnen . . .

Burton II, p. 242. Part 3, Sec. 2, Mem. 3, Subs. 3.

Sweeping into this presence, glisten'd o'er
With emptied caskets, and her train upheld
By ladies, habited in robes of lawn,
Sprinkled with golden crescents, others bright
In silks, with spangles shower'd . . .

Otho the Great, Act V, sc. v, lines 85–89.

31. Yet what is the event of all such matches, that are made for mony, goods, by deceit, or for burning lust . . . what follows? they are almost mad at first but 'tis a meer flash; as chaff and straw soon fired, burn vehemently for a while, yet out in a moment . . .

Burton II, p. 256. Part 3, Sec. 2, Mem. 3, Subs. 3.

Love in a hut, with water and a crust,
Is—Love, forgive us!—cinders, ashes, dust;
Love in a palace is perhaps at last
More grievous torment than a hermit's fast:—

Lamia, Part II, lines 1–4.

32. Like a summer fly or Sphines wings, or a rainbow of all colours . . .

Burton II, p. 299. Part 3, Sec. 2, Mem. 4, Subs. 1.

Every poet is full of such catalogues.

Burton II, p. 300, ibid.

There was an awful rainbow once in heaven:
We know her woof, her texture; she is given
In the dull catalogue of common things.
Philosophy will clip an angel's wings.

Lamia, Part II, lines 231–34.

33. Peter Abelhardus, that great scholler . . . as Heloissa writ to her sweet-heart Peter Abelhardus . . .

Burton II, pp. 311 and 317. Part 3, Sec. 2, Mem. 4, Subs. 1.

As I passed Colnaghi's window I saw a profil Portrait of Sands the destroyer of Kotzebue. His very look must interest every one in his favour. I suppose they have represented him in his college dress. He seems to me like a young Abelard——

Letter 156, pp. 407–408.

34. *And if it were possible to have a city or an army consist of lovers, such as love, or are beloved, they would be extraordinary valiant and wise in their government: modesty would detain them from doing amiss* . . . as Sir Blandimor and Paridel, those two brave faery knights, fought for the love of fair Florimel in presence——

Burton II, p. 333. Part 3, Sec. 2, Mem. 4, Subs. 1.

'twould please me more to scrape together a party of lovers, not to dinner—no to tea. The(re) would be no fighting as among Knights of Old.

Letter 156, p. 401.

35.   And then he did begin to prank himself,
        To pleate and combe his head, and beard to shave,
        And look his face ith' water as a glass . . .

Burton II, p. 336. Part 3, Sec. 2, Mem. 4, Subs. 1.

he must be in league with an excellent taylor, barber . . . have neat shooe-ties, points, garters, speak in print, walk in print . . .

Burton II, p. 337, ibid.

Whenever I find myself growing vapourish, I rouse myself, wash and put on a clean shirt brush my hair and clothes, tie my shoestrings neatly and in fact adonize as I were going out—then all clean and comfortable I sit down to write.

Letter 156, p. 399.

36.   First seas shall want their fish, the mountains shade,
        Woods singing birds, the winds murmur shall fade,
        Then my fair Amaryllis love allaid.

Burton II, p. 346. Part 3, Sec. 2, Mem. 5, Subs. 1.

There bad flowers have no scent, birds no sweet song,
And great unerring Nature once seems wrong.

To—— (October, 1819).

37.   Frustra blanditiae appulistis ad has,
        Frustra nequitiae venistis ad has,
        Frustra deliciae obsidebitis has,
        Frustra has illecebrae, et procacitates . . .

Burton II, p. 351. Part 3, Sec. 2, Mem. 6, Subs. 1.

Faded the flower and all its budded charms,
Faded the sight of beauty from my eyes,
Faded the shape of beauty from my arms,
Faded the voice, warmth, whiteness, paradise——
>   Sonnet: *"The day is gone"*, lines 5–8.

38.   For if thou dost not ply thy book,
            By candle-light to study bent,
            Imploy'd about some honest thing,
            Envy or love shall thee torment.
This kinde of divel is not cast out but by fasting and prayer,
>   Burton II, p. 352. Part 3, Sec. 2, Mem. 6, Subs. 1.

But, as I've read love's missal through to-day,
He'll let me sleep, seeing I fast and pray.
>   Sonnet: *"The day is gone"*, lines 13–14.

39. *bloud-letting above the rest*, which makes *amantes ne sint
amentes*, lovers come to themselves, and keep in their right mind . . .
>   Burton II, p. 355. Part 3, Sec. 2, Mem. 6, Subs. 1.

Physician Nature! let my spirit blood!
>   *Ode to Fanny*, line 1.

40. and as they must refrain from such meats formerly mentioned,
which cause venery, or provoke lust, so they must use an opposite
dyet.
>   Burton II, p. 353. Part 3, Sec. 2, Mem. 6, Subs. 1.

And all lascivious meats must be forsaken.
>   Burton II, p. 354, ibid.

I have left off animal food that my brains may never henceforth
be in a greater mist than is theirs by nature——
>   Letter 161.

APPENDIX B

DRYDEN AND *LAMIA*

1.   In Days of Old, when *Arthur* fill'd the Throne,
Whose Acts and Fame to Foreign Lands were blown,
The King of Elfs and little fairy Queen
Gamboll'd on Heaths, and danc'd on ev'ry Green;

The Wife of Bath Her Tale, lines 1–4.

Upon a time, before the faery broods
Drove Nymph and Satyr from the prosperous woods,
Before King Oberon's bright diadem,
Sceptre, and mantle, clasp'd with dewy gem,
Frighted away the Dryads and the Fauns
From rushes green, and brakes, and cowslip'd lawns,

Lamia, Part I, lines 1–6.

2.   In *Cupid's* school whoe'er would take Degree,
Must learn his Rudiments, by reading me.

The First Book of Ovid's Art of Love, lines 1–2.

As though in Cupid's college she had spent
Sweet days, a lovely graduate . . .

Lamia, Part I, lines 197–98.

3.   Or *Venus* Temple; where, on Annual Nights,
They mourn *Adonis* with *Assyrian* rites.

The First Book of Ovid's Art of Love, lines 80–81.

At Venus' temple porch, 'mid baskets heap'd
Of amorous herbs and flowers, newly reap'd
Late on that eve, as 'twas the night before
The Adonian feast;

Lamia, Part I, lines 317–20.

4.   In Spring's new Livery clad of White and Green,
Fresh Flow'rs in wide *Parterres*, and shady walks
between.

The Knight's Tale, Book I, lines 221–22.

Seem'd edged Parterres of white bedded snow,
Adorne'd along the sides with living flowers

Lamia, Part II, cancelled lines (Letter 149).

APPENDIX C

PARALLELS BETWEEN KEATS'S SCOTCH LETTERS AND HIS POEMS

1. KEATS'S DESCRIPTION OF LOCH LOMOND, LETTER 5 (Letter 78)

The Banks of the Clyde are extremely beautiful—the north End of Loch Lomond grand in excess—the entrance at the lower end to the narrow part at a little distance is precious good—the Evening was beautiful nothing could surpass our fortune in the weather—yet was I worldly enough to wish for a fleet of chivalry Barges with Trumpets and Banners just to die away before me into that blue place among the mountains—I must give you an outline as well as I can. Not B—the water was a fine Blue silverd and the Mountains a dark purple the Sun setting aslant behind them—meantime the head of Ben Lomond was covered with a rich Pink Cloud——

2. KEATS'S DESCRIPTION OF LOCH AWE, LETTER 5 (Letter 78)

The Approach to Loch Awe was very solemn towards nightfall—the first glance was a streak of water deep in the Bases of large black Mountains—We had come along a complete mountain road, where if one listened there was not a sound but that of Mountain Streams. We walked 20 Miles by the side of Loch Awe—every ten steps creating a new and beautiful picture—sometimes through little wood—there are two islands on the Lake each with a beautiful ruin—one of them rich in ivy—We are detained this morning by the rain. I will tell you exactly where we are. We are between Loch Craignish and the Sea just opposite Long Island. Yesterday our walk was of this description—the near Hills were not very lofty but many of their steeps beautifully wooded—the distant Mountains in the Hebrides very grand the Saltwater lakes coming up between Crags and Islands fulltided and scarcely ruffled—sometimes appearing as one large lake, sometimes as th(r)ee distinct ones in different directions—At one point we saw afar off a rocky opening into the main Sea—We have also seen an Eagle or two.

Trip'd in blue silver'd slippers to the gate
> *Extempore*, line 70.

Blue, freckle-pink, and budded Syrian (For Tyrian, i.e.
purple)
> *Ode to Psyche*, first version, line 14.

And every height, and every sullen depth,
Voiceless, or hoarse with loud tormented streams:
> *Hyperion*, Book II, lines 361–62.

Fledge the wild-ridged mountains, steep by steep;
> *Ode to Psyche*, line 55

The sedge has wither'd from the lake;
> *La Belle Dame Sans Merci*, line 3.

. . . .

3. KEATS'S DESCRIPTION OF IONA AND STAFFA, LETTER 6 (Letter 80)

But I will first mention Icolmkill—I know not whether you have heard much about this Island, I never did before I came nigh it. It is rich in the most interesting Antiqu(i)ties. Who would expect to find the ruins of a fine Cathedral Church, of Cloisters, Colleges, Monastaries and Nunneries in so remote an Island? The Beginning of these things was in the sixth Century under the superstition of a would-be Bishop-saint who landed from Ireland and chose the spot from its beauty—for at that time the now treeless place was covered with magnificent Woods. Columba in the Gaelic is Colm signifying Dove—Kill signifies Church and I is as good as Island—so I-colm-kill means the Island of Saint Columba's Church. Now this Saint Columba became the Dominic of the barbarian Christians of the north and was famed also far south—but more especially was reverenced by the Scots the Picts the Norwegians the Irish. In a course of years perhaps the I(s)land was considered the most holy ground of the north, and the old Kings of the afore mentioned nations chose it for their burial place. We were shown a spot in the Churchyard where they say 61 Kings are buried 48 Scotch from Fergus 2nd to Mackbeth 8 Irish 4 Norwegian and 1 french—they lie in rows compact—Then we were shown other matters of later date but still very ancient—many tombs of Highland Chieftains—their effigies in complete armour face upwards—black and moss covered—Abbots and Bishops of the Island always of one of the chief Clans. There were plenty Macleans and Macdonnels among these latter the famous Macdonel Lord of the Isles—There have been 300 crosses in the Island but the Presbyterians destroyed all but two, one of which is a very fine one and completely covered with a shaggy coarse Moss. The old schoolmaster an ignorant little man but reckoned very clever showed us these things—He is a Macklean and as much above 4 foot as he is under 4 foot 3 inches—he stops at one glass of wiskey unless you press a another and at the second unless you press a third. I am puzzled how to give you an idea of Staffa. It can only be represented by a first rate drawing—One may compare the surface of the Island to a roof—this roof is supported by grand pillars of basalt standing together as thick as honeycombs. The finest thing is Fingal's Cave—it is entirely a hollowing out of Basalt Pillars. Suppose now the Giants who rebelled against Jove had taken a whole mass of black Columns and bound them together like bunches of matches—and then with immense Axes had made a cavern in the body of these columns—of course the roof and floor must be composed of the broken ends of the Columns—such is fingal's cave except that the Sea has done the work of excavations and is continually dashing there—so that we walk along the sides of the Cave on the pillars which are left as if for convenient Stairs—the roof is arched somewhat gothic wise and the length of some of the entire side pillars is 50 feet—About the island you might seat an army of men each on a pillar. The length of the Cave is 120 feet and from its extremity the view into the sea through the large Arch at the entrance —the colour of the colum(n)s is a sort of black with a lurking gloom of purple ther(e)in—for solemnity and grandeur it far surpasses the finest Cathedrall—At the extremity of the Cave there is a small perforation into another cave, at which the waters meeting and buffetting each other there is sometimes produced a report as of a cannon heard as far as Iona which must be 12 miles—As we approached in the boat there was such a fine swell of the sea that the pillars appeared rising immediately out of the crystal—But it is impossible to describe it.

> Not Aladin magian
> Ever such a work began.
> Not the Wizard of the Dee
> Ever such (a) dream could see
> Not St John in Patmos isle
> In the passion of his toil
> When he saw the churches seven
> Golden-aisled built up in heaven
> Gazed at such a rugged wonder.
> As I stood its roofing under
> Lo! I saw one sleeping there
> On the marble cold and bare

While the surges washed his feet
And his garments white did beat
Drench'd about the sombre rocks,
On his neck his well-grown locks
Lifted dry above the Main
Were upon the curl again—
What is this and what art thou?
Whisper'd I and touched his brow.
What art thou and what is this?
Whisper'd I and strove to Kiss
The Spirit's hand to wake ~~him up~~ his eyes.
Up he started in a thrice.
I am Lycidas said he
Famed in funeral Minstrelsy.
This was architected thus
By the great Oceanus
Here his mighty waters play
Hollow Organs all the day
Here by turns his dolphins all
Finny palmers great and small
Come to pay devotion due—
Each a mouth of pea(r)ls must strew
~~Many a mortal comes to see~~
~~This cathedral of the S~~
Many a Mortal of these days
Dares to pass our sacred ways
Dares to touch audaciously
This Cathedral of the Sea—
I have been the Pontif priest
Where the Waters never rest
Where a fledgy seabird choir
Soars for ever—holy fire
I have hid from Mortal Man.
~~Old~~ Proteus is my Sacristan.
But the stupid eye of Mortal
Hath passed beyond the Rocky portal
So for ever will I leave
Such a taint and soon unweave
All the magic of the place—
Tis now free to stupid face
To cutters and to fashion boats
To cravats and to Petticoats.

The great Sea shall war it down
For its fame shall not be blown
At every farthing quadrille dance.
   So saying with a Spirits glance
He dived—

.   .   .   .

I saw pale kings and princes too,
Pale warriors, death-pale were they all;
La Belle Dame, lines 37–38.

I saw their starved lips in the gloam,
La Belle Dame, line 41.

what I had seen
Of grey Cathedrals, buttress'd walls, rent towers,
The superannuations of sunk realms,
Or Nature's Rocks toil'd hard in waves and winds,
The Fall of Hyperion, Canto I, lines 66–69.

like sullen waves
In the half-glutted hollows of reef-rocks,
Hyperion, Book II, lines 305–306.

'Hyperion, lo! his radiance is here!'
Hyperion, Book II, line 345.

It was Hyperion:—a granite peak
His bright feet touch'd,
Hyperion, Book II, lines 367–68.

Golden his hair of short Numidian curl,
Hyperion, Book II, line 371.

Yes, I will be thy priest, and build a fane
Ode to Psyche, line 50.

Far, far around shall those dark-cluster'd trees
Fledge the wild-ridged mountains steep by steep;
Ode to Psyche, lines 54–55.

APPENDIX D

LETTERS FROM ISABELLA JONES TO JOHN TAYLOR, WITH A NOTE ON MRS. JONES

(These letters were mentioned and one briefly quoted by Edmund Blunden, *Keats's Publisher*, pp. 96–98.)

1. My dear Sir,

   I most sincerely and selfishly hope that you are recovered from your late indisposition because I now claim your promise of assisting at my House Warming which takes place on Wednesday next—you shall have pretty women to look at—sensible men to talk with—the *coziest* corner in the room—a tass of real Farentosh[1] and last not least a hearty welcome from my dear Sir

   Yours very truly
Isabella Jones

   L.C.St 57
       Monday M . . .[2]
   Tea at 7 oclock

2. My dear Sir

   Will you favor me with your agreable society on friday evening next and persuade Mr. Reynolds to accompany you? I will not bribe you with a Bill of Fare as I did last year but will regard your accepting this invitation as a proof that you have not *entirely* forgotten

   Yours very truly
Isabella Jones

   57 L.C.St
       Monday E . . .[2]
   Tea at 7 oclock.

---

[1] i.e., Ferintosh, a well-known distillery of Scotch whisky.

[2] These may be the abbreviations for Morning and Evening. On the other hand, during the latter half of 1819, the rate-payer at 57 Lamb's Conduit Street was called Munday (Holborn Poor Rate Book). This would date these invitations late in 1819, after Taylor's indisposition that summer.

3. To John Taylor Esqr

My dear Sir
    I return the letters with many thanks for your kind
indulgence. I began to read them, with a heartfelt interest—
a favourable impression towards the author and with feelings
well calculated to fulfil your prediction—"that I should be
much affected"—What will you say when I confess that I am
greatly disappointed—that I *could* not shed a single tear—
and that I do not like Mr. S—.[1] I never saw so much
egotism and selfishness displayed under the mask of feeling
and friendship—I got through the first letter, pretty well; I
did not like his flood of tears[2] "en parenthese", as Mr.
Maturin[3] would say, or his liberal remark upon the Captain
of the Ship—[4] I took up the second, expecting to meet with
some account of the interesting Invalid without any interruption from the Lady's fits—[5] but no—the cloven foot,
appeared again—the eternal *I—I*—like Aaron's serpent
swallowed up all proper feeling and I threw the letter from
me, with the painful impression in my mind, that the fine
hearted creature we both admired—died in horror—no
kind hope to smooth his pillow—no philosophy—no religion
to support him! There follows a sentiment a la John Bunyan
about "Angels of goodness" and "dark wilderness"[6]—Where
was Mr. S— religion at this trying moment? Oh— he was like
the Pharisee in the Temple, thanking God for the *modicum*
he possessed! ! ! Instead of copying Raphael[7] I should advise

[1] Severn.

[2] "a plentiful shower of tears (which he did not see) has relieved me somewhat——" Severn to Haslam, Naples, November 2nd, 1820 (Rollins 77).

[3] Robert Charles Maturin (1782–1824), novelist and dramatist, author of
novels and tragedies of the Mrs. Radcliffe school, notably *Bertram*, produced
at Drury Lane in 1816, and the novel *Melmoth, The Wanderer*, published in
1820.

[4] "he is a good-natured man to his own injury—strange for a Captain."
Severn to Haslam (Rollins 77).

[5] "Miss Cotterell one of our Lady passengers." ibid.

[6] "this noble fellow lying on the bed—is dying in horror—no kind hope
smoothing down his suffering—no philosophy—no religion to support him . . .
but I pray that some kind of comfort may come to his lot. —that some angel
of goodness will lead him through this dark wilderness." Severn to Haslam,
Rome, January 15th, 1821 (Rollins 92).

[7] "a project—by which to copy (same size) Rapheles grand pictures in the
Vatican—the Sanctum Sanctorum of Painting—8 in number. —I think this
will save me at all events——" ibid.

his painting the Good Samaritan—My temper and patience
"broke down under the trial"[1] of the third letter, which I will
not comment on or you will think me the veriest shrew alive—
Of all the cants, in this canting world the cant of sentiment is
the most disgusting and I never saw better specimens than
these letters afford—they are extremely well got up and will
impose upon the most literate—but do let me flatter myself
that, *we* carry a test in the true feeling of *our* hearts, that
exposes all such hollow pretensions—*His* own letter to Mr.
B.[2]—with all its quaintness and harmless conceit is worth a
waggon load of Mr. Egotist's productions—When I have the
pleasure of seeing you—we will compare notes upon this
subject—my mind is always open to conviction and I have
been so often flattered by observing a coincidence of ideas
between us, and have so high an opinion of your judgment,
that I lose confidence in myself when I differ from you—I
have not forgotten the Knif(e) but must receive the "penny
fee" myself or the charm will be broken.[3]   I send you a
Banquet in a *classical jug* for your Mantle shelf—you will
require some sweets to qualify, the bitterness of this angry
letter—pray pardon me, I sat down to the task, with a mind
prepared to sympathise with all poor K—sufferings—and ones
best feelings are checked by an elaborate account of sweeping
rooms—making beds and blowing fires![4]   I feel a relapse

---

[1] "if I do break down it will be under this——" ibid.

[2] Brown. Keats to Brown, Rome, November 30th, 1820. "Yet I ride the
little horse,—and, at my worst, even in Quarantine, summoned up more puns,
in a sort of desperation, in one week than in any year of my life." This shows
that Isabella had seen one of Keats's most intimate letters, and knew about his
feelings towards Fanny Brawne.

[3] "It is, says Grose, unlucky to present a knife, scissors, razor or any sharp
or cutting instrument to one's Mistress or Friend, as they are apt to cut love
and friendship. To avoid the ill effects of this, a pin, a farthing, or some
trifling recompense must be taken in return." Brand's *Popular Antiquities*,
Book III. Brand has long been recognized as a source for the legend of
St. Agnes Eve. Her words echo the poem, stanza xxvi.

[4] "I light the fire, make his breakfast & sometimes am obliged to cook—
make his bed and even sweep the room. . . . What enrages me most is making
a fire. I blow—blow—for an hour—the smoke comes fuming out—my kettle
falls over on the burning sticks—no stove—Keats calling me to be with him—
the fire catching my hands & the door bell ringing——" Severn to Mrs.
Brawne, Rome, January 11th, 1821. (Rollins 89.)

taking placing (sic)—my ears tingle—my pen shakes—I shall be a *stiffened corpse*[1] if I do not conclude—
God bless you dear Mr. Taylor and make you as happy as I wish you. Remember me to Mr. Hessey Ever yours very truly Isabella Jones 14 April 1821

A Note on Mrs. Isabella Jones

What was Mrs. Isabella Jones's social status? Exhaustive enquiries have so far provided no complete answer; it is to be hoped that perhaps this book may provoke one. However, a great deal of information can be deduced from the company she kept. Mr. Edmund Blunden (*Keats's Publisher*, pp. 96–97) quotes a letter from Isabella Jones to John Taylor, which has since been lost, dated May 31st, 1819, from Tunbridge Wells. Mr. Blunden informs me from notes which he made at the time, that the letter was headed "Clifden House" (the present number 40 Mount Sion, Tunbridge Wells) and franked "J. O'Callaghan".

Since Members of Parliament had the privilege of franking letters, this is undoubtedly Colonel James O'Callaghan, M.P. (1748–1836), who is buried in Heighington Church, Co. Durham, together with his son Daniel (1771–1825). James O'Callaghan was member of Parliament for the notorious pocket-borough of Tregony in 1806 and 1807, and again in 1818 and 1820. He was unseated in the Election of 1812, and unsuccessfully petitioned the House of Commons. (*The Journal of the House of Commons*, Vol. 68, pp. 38–40.) He was a Whig in politics, and is described as "a connection, through Lord Lismore, of the pure Whig houses of Ponsonby and Cavendish". (W. P. Courtney—*The Parliamentary Representation of Cornwall to* 1832—p. 180, London 1889.)

Although her letter was franked by James O'Callaghan, Mrs. Jones's particular friend appears to have been a Mr. Donal O'Callaghan. Since Donal is the Irish form of Daniel, it is a reasonable conjecture that Donal was James's brother, as James's son was his namesake (see above).[2] Donal also was closely con-

---

[1] "our other passenger is a most consummate brute—she would see Miss Cotterell stiffened like a corpse. . . ." Severn to Haslam. (Rollins 77.) This is Isabella's parting shot in her many parodies of Severn in this letter.

[2] Donal may also be the Donough O'Callaghan (another form of the name), who matriculated at Oriel College, Oxford, in 1768, aged nineteen. If so, he would be one year younger than James, and both would be in or about their seventies at the time of their acquaintanceship with Mrs. Jones.

nected with the Whig party. In a long letter written to John Taylor in June, 1820, he claims to have had access to Shelburne, and to have been on friendly terms with Sir Philip Francis and his widow, all notable Whigs. The purpose of this letter was to order a book from Taylor for a young friend. He ends it by excusing himself for "this long trite Correspondence" and remarks "Let me take protection—under the gracious Mantle of Mrs. Jones—She may beg me off". The following correspondence shows the sequel.

Mr. Taylor
Bookseller
Fleet St.
    London   Hastings July 10 1820

Sir,

Having some time since troubled you—on a little matter But little worth your notice & perhaps out of your line, I presume—it has escaped your recollection as it well may for I have not heard, or received from you relative to it——

I now apologise to you for the trouble and expense of this letter, to request you will not send the Book or notice the order.

Should you even recollect about it

I have changed my mind on it—& have Designed another Memorial for the youth for whom I intended it—I am etc.

                Your very humble Servt.

                      Donal O'Callaghan

    There is not a Franker in this place, known to me.

LETTER WRITTEN ON OPPOSITE SHEET TO ABOVE: HESSEY TO TAYLOR

Mr Taylor
Messrs. Collett and Falkner
    Bath   London July 11 1820

My dear John,

Your Irish friend has written you another of his "Curse of Kehama" Letters, and as I guessed from whom it came I have opened it and replied to it as P annexed copy. Mrs. Jones was here a few days ago, and said she had heard from Mr. C.[1] who was surprised at not having any reply to his letter. I made her the same explanation & told her that in a few days the Book would be sent and that I should write to you to desire you to send him a few lines from Bath. As she said she was going to Hastings directly I thought this was quite enough & as the Book is only just come in I was prepared to send it off immediately with a letter when I recd. this combustible note. You will of course in common Politeness send him a few lines by the first Post and I trust you will approve of what I have said. If he wants the Book he will communicate with me I suppose—If not, it is of no consequence only we must not let the Irishman get the better of us in politeness. I suppose Mrs. Jones has not yet reached Hastings—or she would have explained the whole affair—I would not willingly have the old man offended as a friend of hers. I sent you by the hands of Mr. Norman Smith who is this day on his way to Bath, a packet of letters etc. We are all pretty well—Poor Tyson is extremely ill and past all Hope—his Friend has just been in here with much grief to tell me the sad news.

With kindest regards to all around you and believe me

Ever Yours
J. A. Hessey

It is evident therefore that Mrs. Jones was certainly on friendly, and possibly on intimate terms, with the Whig family of O'Callaghan. That she herself had Whig sympathies may be gathered from the fact that her room contained "a bronze statue of Buonaparte". Many people of Liberal sympathies still felt an affection for Napoleon at this time. It is possible that she was, in a minor way, one of the many Whig hostesses of the Regency period. On the other hand, she appears to have moved rather rapidly from one set of furnished apartments to another—34 Gloucester Street, Clifden House, Tunbridge Wells and 57 Lambs Conduit Street—and therefore seems to have been somewhat of a bird of passage.

[1] Hessey, not being familiar with Mr. O'Callaghan, misread his nearly illegible signature as "Callaghan".

APPENDIX E

KEATS'S COPY OF LEIGH HUNT'S
LITERARY POCKET BOOK FOR 1819

This copy is now in the Keats Museum, Hampstead. It is largely unmarked. The entries are in three sets of writing.

1. LEIGH HUNT. Proof corrections, made in ink, before he gave the book to Keats in December 1818. These include the names of various musicians and one dramatist (John Ford), entered in the diary-spaces on the anniversaries of their birthdays. Proof corrections are also made in the lists and poems at the end of the book. The fly-leaf is inscribed to Keats, also in Hunt's hand.

2. FANNY BRAWNE. Four entries, in ink, in an immature hand.

(*a*) Opposite the diary spaces for January 1st–7th, a version of Keats's lyric, *Hush, hush.*

(*b*) In the diary space for April 29th, the entry "Tommy's birthday, 1819".

(*c*) In the diary space for August 9th, the entry "Frances Brawne 1800".

(*d*) After the poems at the end of the book, the couplet
"N'avez-vous pas connu fur Monsieur Daube?
Q'une ardeur pour la dispute eveilla avant l'aube!"

The first two entries seem to date this hand early in 1819.

3. FANNY BRAWNE. Several groups of entries in a mature hand.

(*a*) In ink, opposite January 11th, a list of books, mostly taken from the printed list at the end of the Pocket Book.

(*b*) Opposite and in the diary spaces for October, November, and December, inside the diary space for January 4th, and in the diary spaces for August 9th and September 8th, pencilled entries which have been partly rubbed out. One of these, "for Saturday December 2nd" makes it clear that these entries were made in the last quarter of *1820*, as do other signs. December 5th, in the diary, is altered to December 3rd, to correspond with 1820 instead of 1819.

Of these entries, those opposite the diary spaces almost all refer to dressmaking work, "finished" or "unfinished". A typical entry is "Bind my lutestring body with scarlet"—Fanny Brawne's letters reveal that she had a black and red bodice. There is one list of books and prices, and the word "wages" occurs. There is a "Wanted" list, containing such entries as "Have my fan mended".

Three entries in the diary spaces are legible.

1. January 4th. "Written (*last* or *Keats*) twenty first of January." This refers to the poem opposite. See 2*a* above.

2. August 9th. "My birthday Frances Brawne."

3. September 8th. "Mr(?) Keats left Hampstead." This and the reading *last* (see above) are accounted for by the diary having been taken up again by Fanny Brawne and used in the autumn and winter of 1820. Keats actually left Hampstead on Wednesday September 13th, which was also the second Wednesday in September 1820, as September 8th had been the second Wednesday in September 1819.

APPENDIX F

KEATS IN CHICHESTER AND BEDHAMPTON

The houses in Chichester and Bedhampton, where Keats wrote *The Eve of St. Agnes*, are here identified positively for the first time from local documentary evidence. The house in Chichester, where Keats stayed with Mr. and Mrs. Charles Wentworth Dilke senior, is the present No. 11 Eastgate Square. The lease of No. 10 Eastgate Square for 1825, still extant in Chichester, speaks of the neighbouring No. 11 as formerly occupied by Mr. Dilke. Moreover, a chemist's prescription, now in the possession of Mr. Sidney Bastow of Chichester, gives Mrs. Dilke's address in 1814 as "Hornet Square", the old name for Eastgate Square.

The identification of the Old Mill House, Bedhampton, where Keats stayed with Mr. and Mrs. John Snook, has presented certain difficulties. Sir Sidney Colvin seemed to have had this house in mind when he described "the home of Dilke's brother-in-law, Mr. John Snook, a house standing on the shore at the inflow of a small tidal stream into Langstone Harbour." Other biographers, however, have described, and even published photographs of, quite a different house, much farther inland. The present occupiers of the Old Mill House, Captain and Mrs. B. R. Willett, have recently established from detailed examination of Bedhampton parish records not only that John Snook was the occupier of the Old Mill House at the time of Keats's visit, but also that the other house, to which the Snooks later moved, was in quite different hands.

The house gains additional interest from being the place where Keats spent his last night in England. I am very much indebted to Dr. J. R. MacGillivray for allowing me to use, as frontispiece to this book, a photograph of the Old Mill House, which he himself took on a recent visit.

BIBLIOGRAPHY

ADAMI, Marie. *Fanny Keats*, John Murray, 1937.

BESSBOROUGH, The Right Hon. the Earl of. "Stansted and Its Owners" in *The Sussex County Magazine*, Vol. 26, No. 8 (August, 1952).

BEYER, Werner W. *Keats and the Daemon King*, New York, O.U.P., 1947.

BLUNDEN, Edmund. *Keats's Publisher*, Jonathan Cape, 1936.

BRIGGS, H. E. "Keats, Robertson, and 'that most Hateful Land'." *Publications of the Modern Language Association* (of America), LIX (1944), pp. 184–199.
"Two notes on Hazlitt and Keats." *PMLA*, LIX (1944), pp. 596–598.

BURNE, A. H. *The Royal Artillery Mess, Woolwich*, W. H. Barrell, 1935.

BUSH, Douglas. "Notes on Keats's Reading," *PMLA*, L (1933), pp. 785–806.

BURTON, Robert. *The Anatomy of Melancholy*, 11th edition, 2 vols., 1813.

COLVIN, Sir Sidney. *John Keats*, Macmillan & Co. Ltd., 1920.

COURTNEY, W. P. *The Parliamentary Representation of Cornwall to 1832*, London, 1889.

DARBISHIRE, Helen. "Keats and Egypt" in *The Review of English Studies*, Vol. III, No. 9 (January, 1927).

DRYDEN, John. *Poems*, edited John Sargeaunt, O.U.P., 1925.

EDGCUMBE, Fred (editor). *Letters of Fanny Brawne to Fanny Keats*, O.U.P., 1936.

FINNEY, C. L. *The Evolution of Keats's Poetry*, 2 vols., Sir Humphrey Milford, 1936.

FORMAN, Maurice Buxton (editor). *The Letters of John Keats*, 4th edition, O.U.P., 1952.

GARROD, H. W. *Keats*, O.U.P., 1926.
The Profession of Poetry and Other Lectures, O.U.P., 1929.

HALE-WHITE, Sir James. *Keats as Doctor and Patient*, O.U.P., 1938.

Hampshire Telegraph and Sussex Chronicle (1819).

HEWLETT, Dorothy. *A Life of John Keats*, Hurst & Blackett, 2nd edition, 1949.

HOWE, P. P. *The Life of William Hazlitt*, New edition, Hamish Hamilton, 1947.

HUNT, Leigh. *Autobiography*, edited J. E. Morpurgo, 1949.

John Keats Memorial Volume, The Bodley Head, 1921.

Keats, The Poems of John, edited E. de Selincourt, Methuen & Co., 1936.

Keats, The Poems of John, edited H. W. Garrod, Clarendon Press, 1939.

Keats, Poems and Verses of John, edited and arranged in chronological order by J. Middleton Murry, 2nd edition, revised, Eyre & Spottiswoode, 1949.

LOVELL, Ernest J., Jr. "The Genesis of Keats's Ode to Autumn." *University of Texas Studies in English*, XXIX (1950), pp. 204–221.

LOWELL, Amy. *John Keats*, 2 vols., Jonathan Cape, 1925.

LOWES, J. L. "Moneta's Temple", *PMLA*, LI (1936), pp. 1098–1113.

MACGILLIVRAY, J. R. *John Keats: A Bibliography and Reference, 1816–1946*, London, O.U.P., 1949.

MARSH, George L. and WHITE, Newman I. "Keats and the Periodicals of his Time", *Modern Philology*, Vol. 32, pp. 37–53.

MURRY, J. Middleton. *Keats and Shakespeare*, O.U.P., 1925.
The Mystery of Keats, Peter Nevill, 1949.

RICHARDSON, Joanna. *Fanny Brawne*, Thames & Hudson, 1952.

RIDLEY, M. R. *Keats' Craftsmanship*, Clarendon Press, 1933.

ROBERTS, J. H. "The Significance of *Lamia*", *PMLA*, L (1935), pp. 550–561.

ROLLINS, H. E. *The Keats Circle. Letters and Papers, 1816–1878*, 2 vols., Harvard University Press, 1948, O.U.P., 1949.

SHARP, William. *Life and Letters of William Severn*, Sampson Low, 1892.

SKEAT, Walter W. (editor). *Chaucerian and other Pieces*, Oxford, 1897.

SPURGEON, Caroline F. E. *Keats's Shakespeare*, O.U.P., 1928.

STEELE, Mabel A. E. "The Woodhouse Transcripts of the Poems of Keats", *Harvard Library Bulletin*, Vol. III, No. 2.

STIRLING, A. M. W. *The Ways of Yesterday*, Thornton Butterworth Ltd., 1930.

TAYLOR, Tom (editor). *Autobiography and Memoirs of B. R. Haydon*, 2 vols., Peter Davies, 1926.

THORPE, C. P. "Keats and Hazlitt." *PMLA*, LXII (1947).

(UNDERHILL, Thomas). *Triennial Directory*, formerly Holden's Directory, 1817, 1818, 1819.

INDEX